C000178788

PETER GRANT
THE MAN WHO LED ZEPPELIN

PETER GRANT
THE MAN WHO LED ZEPPELIN

CHRIS WELCH

OMNIBUS PRESS
London/New York/Paris/Sydney/Copenhagen/Madrid/Tokyo

Jacket designed by Mike Warry
Picture research by Nikki Lloyd

ISBN: 0.7119.9195.2
Order No: OP48807

Exclusive Distributors:
Music Sales Limited,
8/9 Frith Street,
London W1D 3JB, UK.

Music Sales Corporation,
257 Park Avenue South,
New York, NY 10010, USA.

Macmillan Distribution Services,
53 Park West Drive,
Derrimut, Vic 3030,
Australia.

To the Music Trade only:
Music Sales Limited,
8/9 Frith Street,
London W1D 3JB, UK.

Typeset by Galleon Typesetting, Ipswich.
Printed in Great Britain by Cox & Wyman Ltd, Reading, Berks.

A catalogue record for this book is available from the British Library.

www.omnibuspress.com

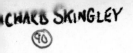

Contents

1

THE GODFATHER OF ROCK

"You're not throwing me in the f****** swimming pool . . ."
— Peter Grant

Peter Grant was the most charming, courteous and affable of men — until you slammed a car door on his foot, tried to throw him in a pool or attempted to rob or cheat his beloved Led Zeppelin. Then the wrath of Jehovah would be a welcome alternative to the splenetic fury of the 'Godfather of Rock'.

Peter Grant was a former South London wrestler who became one of the most powerful men in the music industry. The formidable figure of 'G' struck fear into the hearts of anyone foolish enough to try to rip off Led Zep or obstruct their inexorable rise to fame. 'G' was a towering, six-foot, 18-stone, moustachioed giant, a 20th century Genghis Khan of the rock world, who would brook no opposition. His favourite weapon was alarmingly abusive language delivered with machine-gun like precision that rendered argument futile. Coupled with his fearsomely powerful presence, which communicated the certain knowledge that should fighting erupt 'G' would win hands down, 'verbal violence' — as he termed it — won many a battle before it was actually fought.

Yet there was much more to Peter Grant than his semi-mythical status as the hardest of the 'hard men' in the band business. Adept at negotiation, policy making and strategy, he drove the world's most powerful and dynamic rock team to the top of their game with unrivalled skill and commitment. Grant understood better than anyone that a new phenomenon required special treatment. In the process of taking Led Zep to the top he laid down the ground rules that ensured that the ill-treated pop groups of the Sixties became the millionaire superstars of the Seventies and beyond. If Led Zeppelin were paid so well they were nicknamed 'Led Wallet' by awed rivals, then their tireless manager could take much of the credit. Such was his importance to Zeppelin, he became known as the 'fifth member'. It was an accolade he richly deserved.

Some saw his attitude as bloody-minded aggression. Others recognised he was single-handedly turning rock into a global business with massive rewards to match. Where once promoters demanded the lion's share of money from concert revenues, Grant ensured his artists received 90 per cent. Even as Led Zeppelin were stunning fans with screaming vocals, blistering guitar solos and dazzling light shows, Peter was hard at work behind the scenes, arguing with promoters and wading into bootleggers. He never missed a gig and he never missed a trick.

Unlike many managers, he was never tempted to interfere with the band's records or stage act. He left the music entirely in the hands of the musicians. When Led Zep were on the road, they became his family, surrogate sons to be protected and encouraged when times were tough. It was a caring attitude he had adopted right from the start of his career, when he looked after the rock'n'roll giants of an earlier epoch, Chuck Berry, Little Richard and Gene Vincent.

At the same time, the British band's huge success gave Grant the personal respect, status and power he had craved since he fought his way out of a tough childhood and tougher neighbourhood. Often his fits of temper seemed triggered by a sense of outrage that his personal space was being invaded or his hard won prestige eroded. Nothing angered him more than people 'taking liberties' or trying to muscle in on his territory. It was an attitude not always easy to comprehend, especially by those from comfortable, secure backgrounds where there was no need to shout, swear or raise a fist to make a way in life. In America especially, many were surprised at the way in which 'G' overturned their idea of the 'traditional Englishman'. Grant was no David Niven style gentleman nor another middle-class and slightly naïve Brian Epstein, waiting to be exploited and given the runaround. The tough talking Londoner, raised on a diet of street talk and cash, could take on the shady, the devious and the organised – and win.

When necessary, of course, Grant wouldn't bat an eyelid at demonstrating the kind of immense personal bravery necessary to ward off a threat. Indeed, he would take fiendish pleasure in offering his personal, physical protection to vulnerable young charges. When a group of sailors began mocking and jeering at Jeff Beck and Jimmy Page's long hair during a US trip by The Yardbirds, Peter stormed into action. He recalled later: "The three of us were flying down to Miami and I turned round and heard these blokes. One of them looked like a little tough, so I lifted him up under the arm and said, 'Okay, what's your problem Popeye?' And the other one ran."

If anyone ever needed reminding he'd say: "If I'm out at a concert and somebody is gonna do something to one of my artists, then I'll fucking tread on 'em, without thinking about it."

Yet like many supposed 'hard men', Peter retained a gentle streak, probably inherited from his mother. He was a man full of contrasts. At times pugnacious and abrasive, he could also be relaxed, polite, witty and stimulating company. He had a finely developed sense of humour and was surprisingly cultured in his tastes, displaying a genuine passion for antiques and works of art. Often dangerously overweight and improbably dressed in ill-fitting kaftans, baggy jeans and coonskin hats, he attracted the slim, the slight and the delicate. Both men and women found him a comforting, reassuring companion. It wouldn't take much, however, to tip the scales and the gently chuckling host would once again become the man with a face like thunder, erupting with cries of "What the fucking hell do you think you're fucking doing!"

Says journalist Michael Watts, who met and interviewed Peter on several occasions: "I think the interesting thing is you don't need to be a psychologist to see that for a man who was so overweight, having access to women and a certain kind of lifestyle through being the manager of what at one point was the most famous pop band in the world, must have been terrific. He was certainly the man who broke the mould of pop group management and did something different."

In later years, when Grant became a mellow family man, cherishing his own son and daughter and grandchildren, many were puzzled that such a friendly, relaxed individual could ever have been portrayed as a rock'n'roll monster. Certainly his 'gangster image', enhanced by his appearance in the movie *The Song Remains The Same*, had long since faded and was always something of an embellishment. He certainly delighted in telling anecdotes of his former exploits. "I did a lot of *that*," he'd say, prodding people in the chest with his finger and recalling how his wrestling techniques often came in useful when a point needed to be made.

But right to the end, there was always a glint of danger, a menace that would surface unexpectedly and put an end to any attempt to outsmart him. Some tried to dismiss the Peter Grant of his retirement years as 'a pussy cat' but even at his most relaxed and genial, when the danger signal flashed red, it was wise to take heed. The forces of impatience and aggression that drove him as a young man were ever present.

In an age when pop acts and bands are all too frequently entirely the product of auditions followed by intense promotion through TV and media, the creation of Led Zeppelin seems in retrospect like an even more remarkable achievement. How could they have become so *huge* when they had just one or two men behind them and a mountain to climb?

It wasn't even easy to convince the existing music industry of the Sixties that Led Zeppelin was something special, as Peter Grant quickly discovered to his chagrin and fury. Indeed, his early treatment by the media, including the radio and TV networks, more or less forced him into adopting an aggressive stance and isolationist policies. If no one would help his band, then he'd help himself, do the job his way, the only way he knew how.

A crucial moment in the early days of Zeppelin came when he invited a BBC TV crew to the Marquee Club in London to film the band in action for their regular rock show *The Old Grey Whistle Test*. The show was a sell-out. Hundreds of fans lined the streets, waiting in line to get in.

The BBC crew failed to turn up and never even apologised to Grant for letting him down. There and then he decided he wouldn't pander to the media or play by their rules. To the anguish and disbelief of his record company he promptly decided never to release a Led Zeppelin single in Britain, thus ensuring that Zep would never belittle themselves by appearing on *Top Of The Pops*. He would rely instead chiefly on the support of the fans who queued at the clubs – and bought the albums. As far as he was concerned Zep were and would remain a true 'underground' band.

This slightly eccentric, self-help attitude remained at the core of Zeppelin's line of attack for years, manifesting itself in the small number of staff Grant employed, the avoidance of lavishly furnished prestige offices, the playing down of 'official' corporate style PR and a reliance on direct contact with friends and supporters for press coverage. It also secured for Zeppelin a certain mystique which, buoyed up by Grant's firm belief in always leaving the fans wanting more, has somehow been sustained to this day.

When Led Zeppelin suddenly took off at the end of 1968, following their first visits to America and the release of their stunning début album, it was a time for bittersweet revenge. Yet Peter Grant never indulged in such tactics. He laughed and chuckled instead, and took great pleasure in seeing the looks on the faces of those who had scorned him. He knew himself how hard it was for any 'pop group' to make a name for itself, and understood the tough and cynical attitudes of the so-called music industry. He also recognised the blind incompetence that lay at the heart of many of its most important institutions – and he forgave them. After all, as Led Zeppelin was being showered with gold and platinum albums, he could afford to have the last laugh.

As he flew around the world on board private jets, sipping champagne and browsing through the pages of *Country Life* in search of property and antiques, he could reflect on the magnificently strange and fascinating paths his life had taken since the days when he was a lonely teenager, abandoned by a father he never knew, determined to rise above a life of poverty in the war-battered, crime-ridden London suburb that was home. There was a way out – to the glittering world of show business – via The Croydon Empire!

2

THE ROCK'N'ROLL YEARS

"He was a dreamer and he hustled."
– Mickie Most

Despite many attempts to unravel his past, a degree of mystery seems destined to forever surround the origins of one of the music industry's most powerful and controversial figures. What is certain is that Peter Grant, future manager of Led Zeppelin, was born on April 5, 1935, in South Norwood, a south London suburb. His mother, Dorothy Louise Grant, who on his birth certificate described herself as a private secretary, lived in Norhyrst Avenue, South Norwood. According to the birth certificate, Peter was born at an address in 'Birdhurst Road, U.D.' (sic). There is a Birdhurst Road in South Croydon, only three stations away on the railway line from Norwood Junction. However, there is also a Birdhurst Road in Wandsworth, not far from Battersea, where Peter grew up. No father's name is given on the certificate and as Peter took his mother's surname, this strongly suggests he was born illegitimate.

It is reasonable to assume, therefore, that Peter Grant was raised in what would nowadays respectfully be termed a 'single parent family', never knowing his father. While such circumstances are commonplace today, in the pre-war years and for at least two decades after, there was a stigma attached to illegitimacy which evoked the use of pejorative words and phrases intended to hurt and demean. "Peter was – to use the word – a bastard," says Richard Cole, his personal assistant for many years. "He didn't know who his father was and his mum brought him up. He was very close to his mum and he always took care of her. But he never spoke much about his childhood." From the secrecy that Peter adopted towards his early years, it was clear the subject was painful to him and one he was reluctant ever to discuss.

His son Warren – born February 23, 1966 – admits that little is known about Peter's upbringing, even within the fairly tight-knit circles of their small family. "He never talked about his father, although he adored his mum," he says. "I don't have many memories of my granny. Dorothy Louise died when I was quite young. There was a load of stuff that he kept very personal about his parents. After he died, a friend of my dad's gave me a lot of papers relating to the family background. I was told I should open the packet and have a look. But I didn't want to do that, because he had kept it so private all his life. So it went with him in the coffin. I thought it was best to keep it that way. It was a big envelope full of letters and bits and pieces. I just didn't want to open it. I know that his family were very poor. They were totally skint! He started from nothing and that made him hungry for success."

One close friend that Peter confided in to a certain extent was Mickie Most, with whom he would enjoy a fruitful business partnership in later years. Says Mickie: "Peter was half Jewish. He told me he was half Jewish and I think his mother was Jewish. Peter never talked much about his childhood. He was illegitimate which he didn't deny. He just didn't want to discuss it. He was very close to his mum, who had diabetes. She had a very serious condition and had to have her leg amputated. If you have diabetes badly you can go blind and lose limbs. It was terrible. I attended her funeral in Streatham with Peter in the Seventies."

Intriguingly, Peter's solid sounding surname 'Grant' is from the Latin *grandis*, which evolved into the 13th century Norman nickname, 'graund' or 'graunt' meaning large. It was usually given to 'a person of remarkable size' and while it can also mean 'elder' or 'senior', in most cases 'grante', as it became in Old English, simply meant 'tall'. It was highly appropriate, given Grant's formidable girth and dimensions, a condition increasingly evident from his late teens onwards. To what minuscule knowledge is known about Peter's father, it can safely be added that he, too, was probably very powerfully built.

There may not have been many Norman French 'Graunts' left living in South Norwood during the Thirties, but a hundred years earlier it was a happy hunting ground for roaming bands of gypsies. The area where Peter's mother lived was once the southern part of the Great North Wood of Surrey, which lay between Upper Norwood and Croydon. It was land owned by successive Archbishops of Canterbury and noted for its beauty. However, woodmen and charcoal burners destroyed the trees and over time the area became what has been chillingly described by historians as 'an immense wasteland inhabited by beggars'.

Once the miles of common land were enclosed and the railways built in the mid-19th century, the population increased and large numbers of suburban houses were built. Among the more celebrated inhabitants was Sir Arthur Conan Doyle, who lived at 12 Tennison Road, where he wrote the first of his famous Sherlock Holmes detective stories, including one entitled *The Adventure Of The Norwood Builder*.

Dorothy and Peter subsequently moved from Norwood to the inner city suburb of Battersea, just across the River Thames from fashionable Chelsea, where they lived in a two-up, two-down terraced house. Close to the southern banks of the river, Battersea (originally Bedric's Island) was once marshland and a Saxon settlement. By the middle of the 19th century the many acres of market gardens that made it such an attractive locale were engulfed with smoke belching factories, making candles, glucose, starch, gas and gloves. The final touches to this bleak urban landscape were made when the huge power station was opened in 1933 (and closed in 1983).

Peter's mother tried her best to adapt to her new home and took a secretarial job with the Church of England's Pension Board. Despite this touch of respectability, a twangy South London accent and tough attitude meant there seemed little chance that her son Peter would make it beyond the lower rungs of society. According to his teacher's somewhat despairing school report: "The boy will never make anything of his life." Indeed, so poor was his mother that for a period little Peter was placed in a children's home. Even his limited schooling was disrupted, this time by the outbreak of the Second World War in September 1939. With bombs raining down, London was no place for a child and four-year-old Peter was evacuated with thousands of others to the safety of the country. In his case, the entire school was relocated to Charterhouse, a famous public school not far from Godolming, deep in the wealthy stockbroker belt of the Surrey countryside.*

It was a far cry from the smoky streets of Battersea and Grant later talked of the way he was looked down upon by the public schoolboys he encountered. It's not surprising that he developed an early antipathy towards the pervasive effects of class-consciousness in society, not to

---

* Charterhouse later became the birthplace of another successful rock band, Genesis.

mention a withering attitude towards the upper-middle classes, especially those to whom fortune came without fortitude.

It certainly made him all the more determined to become a success, whatever his origins. As he said somewhat bitterly: "You can imagine. The scum had arrived from Battersea. They loathed us. World War Two was on and there was another war going on down there that nobody knew about. There used to be great battles and we'd beat them up."

After the war Peter returned to his mother in Battersea. Of his schooldays little is known, though it can be assumed that the world of academe held no attraction whatsoever. By his own account, he left school at the age of 13 and took a labouring job at a sheet metal factory a few miles away in Croydon. Peter lasted just five weeks in his one and only factory job. "I knew it just wasn't for me," he confessed later. "I had a bad, bad education. It was all mixed up with being evacuated during the war and my circumstances . . . not knowing my father."

Says his daughter Helen: "He never did anything at school. He was never an academic. But when his headmaster gave him that horrible report, it gave him an incentive. He thought: 'Right, sod you, I'm going to do something.'" Peter realised from an early age that if he were to achieve anything in life, he'd have to do it on his own terms, by the force of his personality and, if necessary, sheer physical strength. Fortunately, he was well endowed in that department, so much so that future employers probably assumed he was considerably older than he really was.

Attracted by the allure of show business, he took a more interesting job than sheet metal bashing, working as a stagehand at the Croydon Empire, a mecca for mass entertainment in south London. In 1948, before the arrival of television, variety and the cinema happily co-existed in the same premises. South London was full of superbly appointed cinemas with evocative names, Odeons, Rialtos and Gaumonts, where the magic of the silver screen offered a brief respite from the drudgery of post-war England. The Empire was situated at 94 North End, Croydon and opened as a music hall in 1906. It converted into a movie house in the Thirties, featuring a mixture of talkies, newsreels and the occasional 'live' variety act. There were so many cinemas in the locality that from 1938 onwards the Empire became a 'live' entertainment venue only.

When Peter Grant became an eager, 13-year-old stagehand, earning fifteen shillings a night, the Empire was owned by the Hyams Brothers. They had bought the theatre in 1946 and continued the policy of staging 'live' shows. In this rather oddly designed building, with its narrow street entrance leading to a grand foyer, young Peter caught his first glimpse of the stars of the day, albeit somewhat downmarket 'artistes' on variety bills. One of the last shows put on at the Empire, before it converted to the Eros Cinema in the early Fifties, was called *Soldiers In Skirts*. Skirts may well have been on Peter's mind as he excitedly swept up the stage, pulled back the curtains and ogled the actresses.

The Croydon Empire/Eros Cinema closed in May 1959 and was demolished to make way for a barren concrete shopping centre. However the closure of many such theatres did not deter the young stagehand from pursuing his dreams. It was an era of almost full employment and jobs were easy to come by for someone to whom work was second nature. Unemployment was never an option for Peter Grant and, eager for adventure and undaunted by his lack of education, he took a wide variety of casual jobs. They included working as a waiter at Frascati's restaurant in Soho and as a messenger for Reuters, the international news agency, in Fleet Street. He delivered the latest news photographs, taking wet prints on his arm to the various newspaper offices that lined the street that in those days was the heart of London's newspaper business.

In 1953, at the age of 18, Grant was called up to do his obligatory two years of National Service in the Army. Under the terms of the National Service Act of 1948, all of Britain's young men were called upon to undergo two years' military training. This was the first time that compulsory military service had been introduced in Britain outside of wartime, and its very existence contributed to the air of drabness and repression that pervaded the early Fifties.

It also evoked an atmosphere of authoritarianism in which young men of Peter's age and background were encouraged to believe that they should defer to their 'elders and betters'. Teenage years – that sublime interval between leaving school and adulthood – simply did not exist; whatever revolt may have been kindling in the soul was extinguished by the army.

This wholesale aura of oppression almost certainly supplied the launch-pad for the Teddy Boy phenomenon, which in the early-Fifties was beginning to emerge in working-class areas like Battersea and Clapham. In what history generally records as the first great youth cult of the 20th century, lads just out of the Army threw away their uniforms and 'demob suits' and, in a kind of homage to pre-war Edwardian fashions, began wearing drainpipe trousers and thigh-length drape jackets with velvet collars. Visitors to the Festival Of Britain Funfair in Battersea Park in 1951 were alarmed to see the first wave of Teddy Boys and their girlfriends rampaging around the grounds. In those days the Teds listened to big band jazz and bought the noisiest, brassiest records by Stan Kenton and Ted Heath. Later, when Bill Haley & The Comets hit the world with 'Rock Around The Clock' in 1956, they would switch their allegiance to rock'n'roll.

Peter Grant spent his late teenage years 'square bashing' and undergoing basic army training. Although some found National Service frightening or plain boring, Peter seems to have enjoyed his time in the army and progressed well in the RAOC (Royal Army Ordinance Corps). He was promoted to the rank of Corporal and placed in charge of the dining hall. He used his theatrical experience to work as a stage manager for shows put on by the NAAFI, the service organisation that provided tea, buns and entertainment for the troops. He later claimed it was 'a very cushy number'.

Many years later, when Peter was the rich and somewhat notorious manager of one of the world's great rock groups, he took a brief nostalgic trip back to his army barracks. He was driving through the Midlands with his assistant Richard Cole and Atlantic Records executive Phil Carson. Recalls Richard: "We were near Kettering and he drove us into his old barracks in his brand new Rolls-Royce convertible. The soldier on duty saluted us and opened the gates. We drove all around this army camp and Peter showed us the huts where he used to live."

His two years of National Service completed, Peter worked for a season in a holiday camp, an experience he would later succinctly describe as 'dreadful'. He was also employed briefly as entertainments manager at a hotel in Jersey. For a while he dreamed of becoming an actor, but instead found himself back in London's West End, working as a bouncer and doorman at the 2Is Coffee Bar at 59 Old Compton Street. This unpretentious café was soon to become the crucible of British skiffle and rock'n' roll, where Tommy Steele, the first UK post-Elvis pop star was discovered. Young Harry Webb & The Drifters also played there, before they became Cliff Richard & The Shadows.

Many of the key figures in the first wave of the British rock'n'roll music industry got their start at the 2Is. Andrew Oldham, who later managed The Rolling Stones, used to sweep the floor there and Lionel Bart, later Britain's most successful composer of hit musicals, painted murals on the basement wall. The waiter at the 2Is was Mickie Most, who went into partnership with Peter and became one of Britain's top pop record producers. The coffee bar itself became part of pop culture and during an outside broadcast in November 1957 was used as the setting for the pioneering BBC TV pop show *Six Five Special*. It was also celebrated in the witty and satirical movie *Expresso Bongo* (1958), starring Cliff Richard and Laurence Harvey.

Coffee houses had been established in London way back in the days of Samuel Pepys and remained popular well into the 20th century. But it was in 1948 that British coffee drinking was revolutionised by the arrival of the chromium-plated Gaggia espresso machine. The first Soho coffee bar equipped with a Gaggia was the Moka Bar in Frith Street, in 1953. Henceforth coffee bars provided an attractive meeting place for teenagers, excluded from the 'spit and sawdust' pubs at a time when publicans were very strict about the over-18 entry policy. The 2Is was opened in 1956 by three Iranian-born brothers who originally owned the premises and called it the 3Is. When one of the brothers left, it was renamed the 2Is. Business wasn't good and in April that year it was taken over by two Australian wrestlers, Paul Lincoln and Ray Hunter, who hoped to earn a steadier income from selling espresso than they could from wrestling. But they began losing money right from the start and matters were made worse when another coffee bar called Heaven And Hell opened right next door.

But change was in the air. In July 1956, during the annual Soho Fair, Wally Whyton, leader of The Vipers Skiffle Group, popped into the 2Is and asked if his group could play in the basement. The place was deserted and the desperate owners had nothing to lose, so they acquiesced, praying silently that 'live' music might bring in some customers. Their prayers were answered: the cellar bar was only 25 feet long and 16 feet wide, but soon it was packed with fans, jiving to The Vipers lively skiffle rhythms.

It wasn't long before teenagers were queuing around the block to get in. Many of them fainted in the heat, but copious cups of coffee brought them round to hear the stars of the future like Adam Faith, Tommy Hicks, Emile Ford, Vince Taylor, Wee Willie Harris and Terry Dene. They also heard Mickie Most, who sometimes leapt up from behind the counter to sing a few numbers.

On the door, struggling with the crush of teenagers desperate to get an earful of this liberating music, was Peter Grant. He later recalled his time at the history making Soho cellar: "I had known Mickie Most since 1957.

We used to work together at the 2Is. Mickie poured the coffee while I sold the tickets at the top of the stairs. You got a meal and ten shillings a night." He must have insisted that pay and conditions be improved because he later claimed: "We got paid a quid per night and the guy who owned the place, Tom Littlewood, took ten per cent of our salary, which left us with eighteen bob (shillings)."

As the year went by, Mickie Most would play an increasingly important role in Peter's life. Christened Michael Hayes, he was born in 1938, in Aldershot, Hampshire. He moved to Harrow in north London with his family and became friends with singer Terry Dene during the skiffle era. While Terry was becoming one of Britain's first pop idols, Mickie was still operating the coffee machine at the 2Is while his mate Peter worked the door.

Paul Lincoln, the manager of the tiny cellar, began to take an interest in Mickie's pal, the tough and confident giant from Battersea. Paul was still working as a wrestler and he decided the doorman at the 2Is was a perfect specimen for the professional wrestling game. Paul encouraged Peter to join him in a few bouts, to the delight of the punters. Weighing in at an estimated 23 stone, he was soon bouncing off the canvas, billed as 'His Highness Count Bruno Alassio Of Milan' or as 'Count Massimo'. Some recall him being dubbed 'The Masked Marauder', the fighter who would take on anybody in the audience who was daft enough to volunteer.

Wrestling was hugely popular in Britain at the time and television coverage made stars of the top wrestlers. Sporting authorities, unimpressed by the stagy nature of the 'grappling game', frowned upon it from on high, describing it as "a pseudo-sport, a form of entertainment in which performers do muscular feats, using body contact and stunts, patterned on the skills of wrestling". One rather pointed definition stated that: "For dramatic effect on the spectators, who believe they are observing a sports competition, the performance is likely to include expressions of anger, pain and helplessness."* Nevertheless, it filled the hour on TV on Saturday afternoons immediately before the football results, grabbing the attention of men just back from the pub who required undemanding entertainment to fill in the time before the pubs reopened.

Peter's wrestling experience would provide invaluable skills for his future career at the sharp end of the rock'n'roll business. Even so, he was

* Collier's Encyclopaedia.

rather anxious to forget those days, especially when he became a highly respected rock group manager. When his former exploits were revealed in a *Daily Mirror* article in 1971, it made him wary of giving interviews to newspapers. He later relented and would admit: "I was a wrestler for about 18 months when I needed some money." This did not stop tabloid journalists forever harking back to his past and calling him a 'giant', 'brute' and a 'devil' – often in the same paragraph. He was once described as 'looking like a bodyguard in a Turkish harem'. For his part, Peter would almost always refer to red-top tabloid newspapers as 'the rags'.

Mickie Most casts new light on the beginnings of Peter's wrestling career and explains: "We used to work together way back in the Fifties. We used to put up the wrestling rings for Dale Martin Promotions. Sometimes if a wrestler didn't show up for the first bout, Peter used to do a bit of wrestling. He was a big guy and if the other wrestler was a bit small, then it would be what they called a 'catch weight', which is an odd weight. They used to throw each other all over the ring for a few minutes as the opening act. It didn't happen a lot, but if Peter was available he'd have a go. I was a bit too skinny to have a go myself. They would have laughed if I'd come out in wrestling shorts. Peter was big even then, but in the early days he was in quite good condition. He wasn't heavy from overeating. He was well built. I never heard him being called 'Count Massimo', but Paul Lincoln was known as 'Doctor Death' and these Australian guys worked the circuit around England. I often went with them to their shows. I'd jump on a train down to Southend and go with them to the venue and help out. That was the basis of Peter's wrestling career. Peter was paid to put up the rings and take them down again. There'd be wrestling every Monday night at Wembley Town Hall and somebody had to put the ring up! I used to go to see wrestling there with Jet Harris. He loved it. When Peter butted someone with his stomach, that was just using a wrestling technique. Nobody ever got hurt. If they did get hurt it was an accident. It wasn't meant to happen. There was no physical damage because it was all showbiz. It's still big business in America, but nobody gets hurt."

Around the same period, Peter took on another job as a doorman, this time at Murray's Cabaret Club where he was the only man working amongst forty showgirls. "Being the doorman at Murray's was good fun too. I wasn't married then and what with me being the only man around and about forty girls on backstage, it was all right," he said, diplomatically.

Less appealing was his brief stint acting as a minder for the notorious slum landlord Peter Rachman. Mickie Most explains this as the sort of work which was a matter of expediency rather than a chosen way of life. "It was the Fifties. Nobody had any money and everybody needed it. He was a dreamer and he hustled."

Peter's overriding ambition was still to get away from this kind of rough stuff and find work as a movie actor. He told Malcolm Dome in 1989: "I wanted to be an actor, but I was never really good enough, although I did get quite a lot of work in the Fifties and early Sixties. I used to 'double' for Robert Morley, even though they had to pad me out quite a bit and I also put on a bald wig. I had hair back then!"

Peter acted as a 'double' for Anthony Quinn in *The Guns Of Navarone*, the hit war movie of 1961. He worked briefly in a mime act and also appeared in several episodes of *The Saint*, a TV series starring Roger Moore. He once popped up as a barman, with all of two lines to recite. Grant's children, Warren and Helen, would later fall about in hysterics whenever this episode was re-shown on TV. He also appeared in the popular BBC TV shows *Crackerjack* and *Dixon Of Dock Green*, and played a cowboy in *The Benny Hill Show*. In 1961 he had a small part as a Macedonian guard, clad in armour and make-up in *Cleopatra*, the movie starring Elizabeth Taylor and Richard Burton.

Cleopatra was made at Pinewood studios in England. However progress was slow as Liz Taylor was unable or unwilling to cope with the cold weather and kept walking off the set and returning to her hotel. This didn't bother the Macedonian guard in his rubber outfit. He was being paid £15 a day and enjoying the easy money, although getting up at 6 a.m. every morning was not to his taste. Eventually filming was transferred to Egypt, a more authentic location, where it was considerably warmer. All the scenes that featured Peter were scrapped, so he didn't appear in the final version, which in any case turned out to be an expensive flop. Peter also appeared as a sailor in *A Night To Remember* (1958), a better than average British version of the story of the sinking of *The Titanic*, starring Kenneth More. To Grant's vast amusement, it was filmed not in the iceberg-infested Atlantic but in the murky depths of the Ruislip Lido.

Although an acting career was attractive, there were few roles in the movies or on TV for an overweight south Londoner. In later, less restrictive times, he might have become a star of such people friendly soaps as BBC TV's *EastEnders*, or – more probably – as a villain in one of the

endless series of cop shows. Either way, it's unlikely he would ever have
progressed beyond the realms of a character actor, a sort of south London
Wilfred Hyde-White or even a George Cole who wouldn't bolt when
danger loomed.

Following his experience as a stagehand and bit part actor, Peter hit on a
more practical way to remain in show business. He invested in a couple of
minibuses and used them to transport variety acts around British US air
bases, where home-grown entertainment was in great demand. He often
drove The Shadows to gigs and even the popular comedians Mike &
Bernie Winters.

Recalls Warren Grant: "Dad started off doing minibus driving and
transporting artists around. He had already worked as a stagehand, pulling
the curtains, sweeping the floor and acting as a bouncer. It was all good
experience for him."

This is confirmed by Peter's friend, the former Dire Straits manager Ed
Bicknell: "He once told me the reason he got into the music business was
because he owned a minibus," he says.

Driving the minibus was to lead directly to Peter becoming a fully-
fledged tour manager. It thus became his exacting task to look after, cajole
and protect the wild and reckless American artists who visited Britain in
the wake of the rock'n'roll explosion. Bill Haley & The Comets and Elvis
Presley had caused a sensation with hit records like 'Rock Around The
Clock' and 'Heartbreak Hotel'. British youth was smitten with the new
music.

The fans might never be able to see Elvis Presley 'live' on stage, but at
least they could see Chuck Berry, Gene Vincent and Eddie Cochran. For
many, this exposure to the American stars of Fifties rock'n'roll would
spark a lifelong musical obsession. It certainly paved the way for a whole
generation of British artists, including The Beatles and The Rolling
Stones, who would emulate their heroes and in turn provide the raw talent
for the rock boom to come.

One of the biggest British pop promoters of the day was Don Arden.
Business colleagues and musicians knew Arden informally as 'the Al
Capone of Pop', a title which suited his hard man image. After acting as a
leading rock'n'roll impresario he went into management and handled such
groups as The Small Faces and ELO with considerable success. However
in the early Sixties he specialised in bringing in many of the American stars
and, together with agent Colin Berlin, put them on touring package

shows. A pugnacious businessman and former singer, Arden provided the prototype for Grant's own hard-nosed style. Not that a man who had survived National Service and professional wrestling needed much tutelage in streetwise tactics. However, as he later acknowledged: "In 1963 I got my first big break. That's when I began working for Don Arden, from whom I learnt a lot. He brought Bo Diddley over to Britain and I was his tour manager."

There's no doubt Grant took his cue from Arden, who showed him how a tough reputation could be almost as effective as the use of real force in dealing with people and situations. Don evidently regarded Peter as an apprentice, a useful man to have around, and taught him the ropes out on the road. Explains Arden: "If there was a cheque to be collected I had to make him aware that sometimes the promise of a cheque was broken. I gave him a list of people who were good, genuine promoters and a list of those who really weren't to be trusted. There was one thing Peter learned from me. If you don't like somebody, let 'em know from the first bell baby. And he did that pretty well."

Peter's background in such a wide variety of casual jobs had taught him about the flow of money, most especially the swift exchange of cash and the ways it can be subverted, delayed and – more importantly – grasped permanently. Peter Grant would always have a healthy respect for cash, the wad of notes at the end of the line that found its way into his back pocket, where it stayed. Adds Mickie Most: "He always made sure a contract was honoured . . . and he had a very good head for figures."

Don Arden hired Peter as tour manager for the cream of visiting American talent, including The Everly Brothers, Little Richard, Brian Hyland, Chuck Berry, Bo Diddley and Gene Vincent. The task of looking after them would provide a wealth of after dinner stories for Peter to relate with many a deep-throated chuckle. The late Gene Vincent was undoubtedly his most difficult customer. Compared to him, Led Zeppelin were like the Mormon Tabernacle Choir. Grant recalled later: "Gene was a bit of a loony. He used to drive cars at me."

The black leather clad singer from Norfolk, Virginia, USA was born Eugene Vincent Craddock on February 11, 1935 (just two months before Peter Grant). Gene was always a special hero to British rock'n'roll fans, with Teddy Boys flocking to see him for the manic intensity he displayed in *The Girl Can't Help It* (1957), the first Technicolor rock movie. When Gene Vincent & The Blue Caps performed their classic hit 'Be Bop A

Lula' there were screams of delight and riots in the cinemas.

When Vincent arrived in Britain in the flesh, he proved to be an anguished soul, whose life was ruled by pain. A former despatch rider in the US Navy, he had suffered severe injuries to his left leg in a motorcycle accident in 1955, which left him permanently disabled. The story goes that he'd had too much to drink one night and on returning to base, instead of stopping at the guardhouse gate, tried to ride under the barrier. The bike slid from underneath him and he smashed his leg. It was pinned back together, but he had to wear a calliper for the rest of his days. One of his greatest British fans was the late Ian Dury, who clearly empathised with Vincent's condition as well as his music and dark, brooding image.

Although Gene Vincent was deemed too working class and tough for American tastes, he became one of the biggest drawing artists in Europe and remained so until the advent of Beatlemania in 1964. He was prickly and prone to violent outbursts. Excessive drinking didn't help his temper, but he needed drink to dull the pain of his injury and overcome stage fright. Peter was not the first British tour manager to fall foul of the curly-haired, pinch-faced Vincent.

Hal Carter was tour manager on many early rock'n'roll package shows, working with Vincent and Eddie Cochran and later managing British singer Billy Fury. Although he enjoyed life on the road, Hal does not have particularly happy memories of his time with Vincent. It was Hal's job to look after Gene on behalf of promoter Larry Parnes and he travelled hundreds of miles with them by coach to the various draughty theatres where the stars were expected to perform.

In the early Sixties Britain lacked many of the comforts taken for granted in the USA. There was virtually no air conditioning, no central heating and no McDonalds style fast food restaurants. Credit cards were unknown, the black and white TV service was limited to two channels which closed down very early by American standards, shops shut at 5 p.m. and pubs and hotels were closed by 10.30 p.m. or 11 at weekends. Finding a bottle of Jack Daniels was a huge problem and there wasn't much either Peter Grant or Hal Carter could do to cheer up the miserable young American visitors. Hal remembers Eddie Cochran wailing: "Goddam – I'm never going to get home – I'm gonna freeze to death in this country!"

Carter describes Eddie as 'a lovely guy' but he confesses he didn't like Gene Vincent at all. Says Hal: "I never really liked him – he used to upset Eddie a lot on tour. Gene drove me crazy and made my life a misery a times. I was a young tour manager trying to make my way and he wouldn't listen to anything I said. Whatever you said – he'd disagree. In the end I thought he was a wicked, self-centred, selfish, evil man who treated his women very badly. I know this upsets his fans when I say this. Don't get me wrong – he was a great performer, but I had no time for him."

Hal gives an example of Gene's erratic behaviour that finally led him to walk out on the star. "He used to carry a knife called 'Henry'. It was a sharp, pointy switchblade. One day we were on a coach coming back from a gig in Ipswich. He was going crazy, shouting abuse at everyone. He went up to the young bass player with a group called The Beat Boys and sliced the front of his suit off with his knife. Just ripped it to shreds." Another member of the party was Hal's friend the late Henry Henroid, who pulled Vincent off the terrified kid. Carter was sitting next to singer Johnny Gentle, trying to ignore the scene.

"Just at that moment Johnny said something that made me laugh. Gene flew up the aisle of the coach and put his knife up against my throat and said: 'I'll teach you to laugh at me.' I said – 'Gene, we're not laughing at you, we're just having a conversation.' He then ripped my shirt with the knife. Well when we got to Dartford, the next big town before London, I said to the driver, 'Stop here at the lights, drop me off and take him (Vincent) to Marble Arch.' I jumped out, the coach drove off and I never saw him again. I'd had enough."

It was shortly after this episode that Peter Grant took over Hal's job as tour manager for the dreaded Vincent. Hal's advice to Peter was: "If Gene plays up grab him and put one on him." He was impressed when he learned later that if the singer was being difficult and wouldn't do a show, Grant would "grab him by the throat and push him on the stage".

On the other side of the coin, Peter was quite fearless in the lengths he went to save his artists from manic fans and – quite often – from themselves. On one occasion he was alleged to have disarmed Vincent when the singer went on a drunken rampage, waving a loaded gun in a house in Brighton. When he was in Italy he was said to have flattened no less than six Italian policemen, trying to protect Little Richard from harassment.

Journalist Keith Altham was a young writer on *Fabulous* magazine when he got to know Peter Grant. Keith has vivid memories of Grant in action, when he was still developing his firm but fair, no nonsense management style. "Peter was working as a tour manager for Gene Vincent when I first

25

met him," recalls Altham. "I remember going on a trip with him in 1963. Gene was always billed as 'Direct from America', although he had been living in England for three years. You got more kudos if you came from the States in those days. He was doing gigs up and down the country and Peter was charged with keeping him sober. That was quite a job in itself. Vincent had a hollowed out walking stick, which he filled up with vodka or whatever else he was drinking. Peter didn't know about this for ages, but as soon as he found out, he confiscated the stick. Yet Gene was still going on stage pissed and Peter couldn't understand it."

Grant locked Vincent in his dressing room for two hours before the performance. The tour manager alone had the key and nobody else was allowed in. "Then Vincent would stagger out of his dressing room and go on stage, pissed as a parrot! He had been bribing a member of the road crew to go out and get him a bottle of brandy. He had put a straw through the keyhole of the door, so he could drink the brandy, through the straw."

During the trip, Peter told Keith about all the problems he'd been having with the troubled rock legend. "We've got him in pretty good shape tonight, because we're doing a double header. We don't get the money unless, when the curtains open, he's physically there on stage."

This clause was written into the contract, obviously introduced after a series of 'no shows'. Meanwhile, Grant, Altham and the entourage arrived at a hall in Aylesbury, Buckinghamshire. Recalls Keith: "Gene was pretty good on the first show, which was early in the evening. He was travelling with his wife, who was also American. We got on the coach for a while between shows and as we got on board a fight broke out between Gene and his wife. Vincent got hold of her by the hair and was banging her head on the coach window. Peter heard the screaming and fighting and his 23 stone bulk came waddling down the centre of the aisle. He separated them both and said, '*What* are you doing? I'm trying to negotiate the fees with the promoter.' 'Oh, gee, sorry Peter . . .' He calmed them down and went back outside the coach to carry on talking to the promoter. Then the fight starts up again. But this time the roles are reversed and the wife has got hold of Vincent's hair and is bashing his head against the window. Peter comes down and separates them again and there's lots of crying and sobbing. Eventually we take off for the second concert."

Unfortunately the row had deeply traumatised Vincent. He found a bottle of vodka and downed about three-quarters of it without Grant knowing. He then decided he'd go down the coach to where Peter was sitting across two seats and inform him that he was unable to do the second performance. He only got about half way when he fell and trapped his good leg between an aluminium support pole and the seat.

Altham: "There was a scream of anguish and his leg started swelling up like a balloon. Peter got up and, rather like Hercules, bent the pole in half so Vincent could release his trapped leg. By this time he literally hadn't got a leg to stand on! One leg was in irons and the other was swollen up. So Peter had to find some way of getting him on stage for the next show. Gene's saying, 'I can't go on, my leg hurts!' We got to the gig and I went out front to see what would happen. The curtains were drawn and then the compère came out and said, 'Ladies and gentlemen, all the way from America, the king of rock'n'roll, Mr Gene Vincent!' "

The curtains opened to reveal Gene strapped to a microphone stand. Peter had rammed a tripod mike stand up the back of his jacket, which was holding him up! He gets as far as singing 'Bebop a–FUCK!' and he fell straight forward onto his face. He splatted his nose on the stage and there was blood everywhere. Two roadies came out and carried him off like a pig on a spit, completely unconscious. And Grant says to me: 'I've got the money Keith, because he was *there* when the curtains opened.' "

A few years later Keith bumped into Peter Grant again at *Ready, Steady, Go!*, the Friday pop show transmitted live from TV studios in Wembley. "He and Mickie Most were big pals. Mickie came into the dressing room and said to Peter: 'I've just got a brand new MG sports car. It's brilliant. You must come and have a look.' So we all went out to see the lovely new Red MG sports car. 'Very nice, Mickie.' He climbs in and fills the entire car. He's got the steering wheel in front of him and Mickie says: 'Well, what do you think Peter?' 'Very nice Mickie. How do I take it off?' "

Peter liked to recall his rock'n'roll touring days with a fondness mellowed by time. "I remember the sax player Tubby Hayes used to do all that farting and setting light to it. And when Gene Vincent did some Sunday concerts with Emile Ford (the popular West Indian singer), he used to paint Ku Klux Klan signs on Emile's dressing room door. We did a lot of bus tours. From The Everly Brothers to the support acts, we were all packed on the bus." The coaches used to leave from the side of the London Planetarium near Baker Street and they'd head north, to a land of cheesy digs, beans on toast and freezing cold dressing rooms.

The Everly Brothers in particular retained a fondness and respect for Peter that lasted for years. When they heard of Peter's death in the

Nineties, they were touring Britain at the time and, saddened, they dedicated a number in their set to the man they fondly remembered as 'the best road manager we ever had'.

Spicy it might have been, but it wasn't a lifestyle that Peter intended pursuing for long. He had a driving sense of ambition and deep-rooted desire to exploit every fresh opportunity. The Arden itinerary took them to Newcastle. One night, Bo Diddley's maraca player Jerome and Peter Grant went out to an after-show gig at a local blues club. When they saw a hot young band called the Alan Price Rhythm & Blues Combo in action, the visitors were impressed. Grant later claimed he immediately signed Alan's band to a contract and became their booking agent and co-manager with Mike Jeffrey. "They were rather successful after they changed their name to The Animals!"

They became one of the first British bands to emulate The Beatles' success in America, hitting number one there with 'House Of The Rising Sun' in 1964, two months after it had reached the top of the charts in the UK. The song was produced by Peter's pal, Mickie Most. Peter told *Melody Maker*'s Michael Watts in 1974: "At that time I was making a deal to bring over Chuck Berry and that was the blag, to get The Animals to sign with the agency. They wanted to do the Chuck Berry tour and they also wanted to record."

The Geordie blues fans hero worshipped Berry, but Peter Grant would confide in later years that the man who created 'Roll Over Beethoven' and 'Sweet Little Sixteen' could be "a pain in the arse". Nevertheless he knew The Animals would be impressed if he could arrange for them to work together. Recalled Eric Burdon: "We were all happy to find that Peter Grant had been appointed our tour manager. What a guy! He looked like he was ten feet wide and six feet tall, but he was very gently spoken and we all loved him."

Peter quickly established his credentials with The Animals when, displaying enormous bravery, he faced down a gunman threatening the band during an overnight stop in Arizona. He wasn't so gently spoken when Eric turned up late for a gig in England. Eric had driven to the venue alone in his brand new TR6 sports car. As the rest of the band glared at him, impatient to start the show, Peter Grant strode over and said icily: "Where the fuck d'yer think you've been?"

Eric explained he'd been driving to the gig. So what if he was a bit late. "I drove here as fast as I could."

"Well you fucking leave earlier next time, you cunt!"

Grant picked up Eric Burdon, the famous chart topping pop star, and threw him bodily, ten feet across the room. "I hit a wall, slid down and hit the floor. I was never late again. Peter got his point across. He was what I needed. He was what we needed."

The Animals were often brought down by the grim and dismal gigs they had to play, even during the time when their records were high in the charts. But one day their tour manager brought them good news. "Well, you guys will be pleased to know that Harold Davidson has got you the tour with Chuck Berry." The band regarded him as the greatest rock'n'-roll star of them all. Although famously grouchy and prone to bully his backing bands, Berry seemed to get on well with Burdon. He certainly appreciated the spontaneous waves of enthusiasm at his British shows. However he was never a man to confuse art with commerce, and laid down certain ground rules right from the start of his first UK tour in 1964. When he discovered that his fee was three shillings and eleven pennies short, there was hell to pay. "I ain't going on," said Berry, eyes narrowing. The crowd were yelling and drastic action was required to avert a riot. Mr Berry's driver and personal assistant for the duration of the tour found the nearest cigarette machine, smashed it open and extracted the small change. It was enough to placate the bill topper. Thanks to Peter Grant, Chuck Berry was ready to 'Roll Over Beethoven'.

On the last night of the tour, London's Teddy Boys went berserk and invaded the stage. But it was all good-natured and Chuck carried on playing. Grant and Arden stood nervously in the wings, wondering how much the damage to the theatre would cost. Eric Burdon watched Chuck duck walking with his guitar across the stage, shouting at Peter Grant, "Did you get the money yet?" Grant shook his head and shouted back, "No, we didn't." Berry moved back to the audience and sang one more encore. Then he duck walked across to Grant again and said, "Did we get the money yet?" This time Grant smiled and nodded his head. Chuck Berry unplugged his guitar and carried on duck walking, off the stage, down the stairs and into his waiting limo. Eric guessed he was probably in his hotel room having a cigarette while the audience were still yelling for more.

Burdon could see why Berry had become a hard man to deal with. Time served in prison had made him bitter and he didn't trust figures of authority, whether they were managers, promoters or agents. Eric once saw Peter Grant and Don Arden on their knees, peeling off one-pound notes and pushing them under Chuck's dressing room door. He had demanded payment up front before he would leave his room and start the performance. There were even rumours that a gunshot was heard in a London theatre auditorium during one such altercation, and the police were called.

When The Animals went to America they found themselves touring with Chuck Berry once again, while the old firm of Peter Grant, Don Arden and Mike Jeffrey were backstage, taking care of business. Eric Burdon would claim in his biography* that Peter had told him he had been to the States before. Intriguingly Grant claimed to have visited Gene Vincent when he was filming *The Girl Can't Help It* in Hollywood.

This would have meant Peter travelling to America during 1956, when he was still working at the 2Is. Given the pittance he was earning, it seems unlikely that he could have afforded such a trip. Mickie Most certainly doesn't remember him going to the States at this time. However, on early trips to the US, Peter handled Herman's Hermits as well as The Animals and gained plenty of useful knowledge about the US live music scene and record industry. He saw at first hand the gun-toting cops, the 'crazies' in the crowds who might attack long-haired pop stars and the racism and bigotry still prevalent in the South. Eric Burdon once witnessed him purple with rage, screaming abuse at Ku Klux Klan protesters handing out racist literature at a concert.

Back in London Don Arden began to sense that his assistant was getting the measure of the rock business and the huge potential of the American market for British bands. What he saw inspired him to make plans for the future. Said Arden: "He began to get involved in unnecessary politics. I could see he was drifting away from Don Arden Enterprises. Peter was very ambitious. I seem to remember his wife always urged him on. I remember one night we went out to dinner. My wife was wearing a diamond ring that cost $200,000 and his wife never got over that. She wouldn't let him be. She used to say, 'I want to wear jewellery like Don Arden's wife.' "

As well as working with Chuck Berry and Gene Vincent, Peter Grant also looked after Bo Diddley during the R&B pioneer's trips to England. The connection resulted in Peter getting The Rolling Stones their first

---

* *I Used To Be An Animal, But I'm All Right Now* (Faber & Faber 1986).

broadcast on BBC radio. The Beeb had already auditioned the Stones for *Saturday Club*, presented by Brian Matthew and had turned them down because they "weren't good enough". When Bo Diddley needed a band to back him on the show, Grant recommended the Stones should do the job.

"Brian Matthew agreed to it, but then I got a call from the producer of *Saturday Club* telling me that since the band had failed the audition, he felt it wasn't such a hot suggestion to use them. I replied, 'No Stones, no Bo Diddley!' They got the job and their first break on the radio." It was a kind of practice run for the sort of tactics he would employ managing his own artists. Many years later he saw himself described in an American music magazine as 'an ex-rock errand boy'. His laughter on reading this put-down was chilling. "Fucking great. Fantastic," he said impassively.

After his spell with The Animals, Grant worked for a while with The Nashville Teens, who in 1964 had a big hit with 'Tobacco Road', produced by Mickie Most. By now Peter felt ready to take the plunge and manage his own acts. He set up in business, sharing an office with Most at the Tottenham Court Road end of Oxford Street. Visitors would never forget the sight of the two go-getters facing each other across large desks, forever on the phone, doing deals, promoting bands and setting up hit records. It seemed like the engine room of Swinging Sixties London.

It had been six years since the Soho coffee bar and wrestling days. While Peter had been busy as a tour manager, Mickie Most had realised his own dreams of stardom and was already a wealthy man. He had formed the Most Brothers with Alex Murray back in 1958. The duo recorded for Decca and toured with Cliff Richard & The Shadows. Then, in 1959, Most put together Mickie Most & The Playboys and lived and worked in South Africa. He had eleven number one hits there by singing 'covers' of the latest American songs. Says Mickie: "I went to South Africa in the late Fifties. I had brought Gene Vincent out to South Africa with his manager Don Arden and we did a tour together. Don said, 'Just give me a ring when you come back to England.'"

It was during this period that Peter married his wife Gloria, a petite former ballet dancer, who he'd met in London. Says Mickie: "She was very nice Gloria. I had known her since 1962 when they first got married. I didn't go to the wedding because I was in South Africa. They had been married for a year when I did that first tour, which was in 1963."

Peter Grant's wife would remain in the shadows throughout their marriage, rarely attending public events and shying away from the kind of celebrity which her husband attracted. She concerned herself solely with the raising of their two children and maintaining the household. "I think they lived two separate lives," says film director Peter Clifton, one of few people ever to take a photograph of Gloria. "She just didn't want to be in the limelight at all."

At the time of his marriage to Gloria, Peter was still working for Don Arden. "He knew all the tricks in the book," says Most. "He was a master at promotions. He had this company called Anglo-American Artists in Curzon Street and he had the balls to bring over these people. I remember Peter Grant going to a prison in Arkansas, waiting outside the gates for Chuck Berry to be released. 'Wanna come to England to do a tour?' he said, as Berry walked free."

In 1962 Mickie Most returned to England, hoping to break into the beat group scene as a solo singer. But it was hard to gain acceptance, as there were so many R&B acts already pursuing The Beatles into the charts and the clubs.

"So I called Don Arden," continues Most. "He said: 'What are you doing?' 'Not a lot.' 'Well I'm just putting this tour together, do you want to go on it? There's the Everly Brothers, Little Richard, Jerry Lee Lewis, oh and we've got a group called The Rolling Stones.' So I did the tour and every time we were in hitting distance of London I drove home. I had a Porsche car that I'd shipped back from South Africa. I was already a millionaire at the age of 24. Mick Jagger said: 'Are you going back to town tonight?' I was married and had a place in London, so I didn't want to stay in a hotel if I could get back. I was opening the show and doing my 'Johnny B. Goode' Chuck Berry impersonation. The Stones were just doing their Bo Diddley impersonation, so we'd all be off stage in fifteen minutes. Then we jumped in the car and Mick, Keith and me drove back to London together."

It was during this UK tour that Mickie bumped into his old pal from the 2Is. "Peter Grant was the tour manager and he said: 'Ullo Mickie, how are you going?' We were like mates for the whole tour. Then after it finished we did another one with Duane Eddy and The Shirelles. Peter was brilliant as a tour manager and he really looked after you. If you needed a few bob he would give you a sub out of the programme money or something. He was great with artists and there were no bigger artists than the Little Richards of this world, not to mention Jerry Lee Lewis. He's not a stroll in the park, I can tell you! I toured with him and he was a bloody nightmare. You never knew when he was gonna smack you in the head for nothing. He was just a loony guy. He'd say to me, 'Hey, ya got some of that English money? Get me a cigar.' The next day he'd say, 'Mickie, ya got any more of that English money?'

" 'Jerry. You're top of the bill. You're getting thousands, I'm getting no pence, and I'm spending money buying you cigars. Go to the bank, change your dollars into pounds and get your own cigars.'

" 'Ah go on Mickie, get me a cigar.' And I'd give in and get him a cigar because you never knew if he was going to throw a piano at you. And Little Richard *never* had a clean shirt. So he'd decide to borrow my shirt with the cufflinks and halfway through his act he'd take his jacket off, then the cufflinks and throw them at the audience followed by the shirt. 'Oy, that's my shirt you're throwing!' Then his guitar player would turn up without a guitar, so he'd use mine every night and break all the bloody strings. Peter Grant saw all this and he was the only one who could take care of them.

"Although we had met in the Fifties we never actually did anything business-wise until the Sixties. I was telling Peter that the reason I came back from South Africa was that I wanted to go into the studio and produce artists. I could play and sing a bit but I wasn't that wonderful. It was on that tour, in fact, that we found The Animals. We were in New-castle and went to the Club A Go Go and on stage were The Animals. I loved the band and thought they were great. To get them to sign to me was difficult. They didn't know me from a bar of soap. But eventually they did, we went into the studio, cut 'House Of The Rising Sun' and the rest was history."

Most used all his experience and flair to achieve an astonishing success rate as a producer. He recorded some of the biggest pop acts of the Sixties. As well as The Animals, he produced Herman's Hermits, Donovan, Lulu and The Yardbirds. When he set up RAK Records he continued his success into the Seventies with a roster of artists that included Suzie Quatro and Hot Chocolate.

It seemed like Peter Grant was being left behind. Among the first acts he signed was a band called The Flintstones and the all-girl group She Trinity, originally from Canada. Unusually for a girl group in this era they played their own instruments but changing personnel weakened the band, although Beryl Marsden, formerly of Shotgun Express, was briefly a member. She Trinity signed to Columbia and released three singles, including a spirited cover of Bobby Fuller's 'I Fought The Law' retitled as 'He Fought The Law' but they were not a great success.

In the event, Peter Grant fared much better with a band whose music was poles apart from the blues or heavy rock. Unlikely as it may seem, The New Vaudeville Band – a pastiche Twenties act – would provide the unlikely stepping-stone for Peter's management aspirations. At least they had a smash hit record and their success ensured he went back to America in triumph. The band also served to introduce him to another important figure in his life, the equally hard-nosed and pugnacious Richard Cole. A former scaffolder from north London, Cole would become Grant's right-hand man in the excitement and battles to come. Peter had already come a long way from his humble beginnings in Battersea. Now he was about to embark on his greatest adventure.

Mickie Most: "At that time Peter was saying, 'I want to get into management myself.' So we formed a company called RAK Music Management. Peter and I were partners in this management company and it led to Led Zeppelin!"

3

STAIRWAY TO ZEPPELIN

"He was a big lump of jelly. You didn't look at him and think 'What a tough guy' – you thought 'What a big guy.'"

– Simon Napier-Bell

Under the stewardship of Peter Grant, The New Vaudeville Band hit the charts in 1966 with 'Winchester Cathedral'. A mock Twenties ditty, complete with megaphone vocals, the song was a long way from rock'n'roll and more of a novelty item, hardly the kind of thing to interest a budding entrepreneur in Grant's mould. Yet there were undercurrents of intrigue behind the scenes of this seemingly innocuous novelty outfit that might well have attracted Peter to them in the first place.

The New Vaudeville Band was the creation of London born songwriter and record producer Geoff Stephens. Session men had recorded the song and a touring band was hastily put together to exploit the hit. Peter was called in to knock them into shape. The record reached number four in the UK and, astonishingly for a novelty item steeped in nostalgia, it got to number one in America. The group enjoyed several more hits at home, including the chirpy 'Finchley Central' in 1967.

However, there was resentment from a rival outfit. The Bonzo Dog Doo Dah Band had been playing Twenties style comedy numbers since 1962. Their lead singer, Vivian Stanshall, was furious when the Bonzos' trumpet player, Bob Kerr, defected to help form the chart topping Vaudevillians.

Bob Kerr insists that he didn't quit the Bonzos to steal their act. He left because of arguments and was fed up with the band. "Vivian Stanshall had his own theory of why I left, because the New Vaudeville Band thing came up. But I left because I just couldn't take it any more. I really wanted to run my own band. A week later, a chap called Henry Harrison, a drummer friend of mine, phoned me up and said: 'Look, there's this record that is going in the charts called 'Winchester Cathedral'. I've got to get a band together and you're the only bloke I know who can help me.' Geoff Stephens, who wrote it, was a great mate of his. So I said, 'Oh, sounds good to me.'

"So we went up to meet Geoff, who'd recorded it all and Henry had got some other guys together – but they didn't look right. I suggested I could get some guys who could really fit in with that style of music. Three days later we were on *Top Of The Pops* doing it. I had the words strapped to the side of the Hammond organ so I'd remember how to sing it!"

Members of the *Top Of The Pops* orchestra had recorded 'Winchester Cathedral' with a secret vocalist (secret because he was signed to another label). Most of the subsequent Vaudeville Band songs were pre-recorded for them by session players. "There were rumours going around that Geoff Stephens had originally asked the Bonzos to do that record, but he never did. There was also this thing that Viv said we'd 'stolen his show', which was not true at all," says Bob. "He never saw the show, so he wouldn't know."

After doing *Top Of The Pops* and a couple of London gigs, Peter Grant took the New Vaudeville Band to America, where they appeared on the prestigious *Ed Sullivan Show*. The single had already been at number one, but as a result of their TV appearance, it went back to the top and sales exceeded seven million.

Americans just loved them. As the band's album went gold, Peter was on a tour of the States with Bob Kerr and his mates, playing cabaret in Las Vegas and sharing bills with The Beach Boys and The Mamas & The Papas. 'Winchester Cathedral' was even covered by Frank Sinatra and Dizzy Gillespie. It was all a far cry from the pubs of London. Said Peter: "They only had one hit song but I took them on tour to places like Las Vegas and Reno, Nevada, playing on the cabaret circuit. They weren't exactly a rock band, but it was a great experience."

Even in this apparently idyllic situation there were problems that could be solved only by the smack of firm management. The band wanted more money. Following disagreements with Grant over pay and conditions, Bob Kerr was fired.* Meanwhile Grant called in Richard Cole to take

---

* The recalcitrant trumpet player went back to England to form Bob Kerr's Whoopee Band, which lasted some 35 years, outliving both Led Zeppelin and their manager.

charge of American touring operations. Cole enjoyed his stint touring with the New Vaudevilles, the experience cementing his relationship with Grant and standing both men in good stead for future expeditions to the States.

Richard was a tough character from a tough district in north London. He had fought as a boxer and certainly knew how to 'handle his dukes'. His work as a scaffolder on construction sites ensured he had a vice-like grip of steel. "When I was a kid I did boxing so I picked stuff up from an early age," he says. "Also scaffolding is not an easy business. You develop very strong forearms and fingers to get a grip. It's very easy to shake people's hands and almost break their bones. Those scaffolding tubes weigh 90 pounds and you really have to hold them tight or you'd never lift them. You develop muscles that other people don't have. I could grab people by the throat and they couldn't move!"

Like Peter Grant, Cole wanted more out of life than labouring or fighting. He loved music and bands and, like most sharp young men of the Sixties, he was well into clothes. He even had plans to be a fashion designer and claims to have designed the shirts worn by John Lennon and Ringo Starr on the *Revolver* album cover. In the event, he found himself being drawn into the band business and eventually became one of rock's most respected tour managers.

His introduction to 'humping gear' for a living came when he was drinking in The Ship, a music biz pub in Soho's Wardour Street, just a few yards away from the Marquee Club. He bumped into Richard Green, a journalist from *Record Mirror*, fondly known as 'The Beast'.* Cole recalls the outcome of their meeting. "I was drinking with The Beast and I said, 'Do you know any bands who've got a record in the charts that might need a road manager?' He said, 'Why don't you try Unit 4 Plus 2?' He gave me a number and I went to see their manager John L. Barker and got the job. I was only with them for a couple of months. They were nice guys but they weren't really my type of people. They were such a straight bunch and I didn't get on with their personal manager, so I left."

Soon Richard had a reputation for being a tough 'road wrangler'. He

* It was a nickname bestowed on him in honour of Aleister Crowley, himself known as 'The Great Beast'. Richard Green was notorious for his heavy drinking and monosyllabic conversation, which consisted of intoning the word 'Accept' – meaning he'd accept a drink from anyone. He was once seen parading around London with a sign around his neck from a defective elevator, which read 'Out Of Order'.

worked with many London groups including Herbie Goins & The Night Timers, but deep inside he was looking for a job with a really successful hit band. One night he went to a party at The Moody Blues' house in Roehampton. The Who were there and one of their staff men, Mike Shaw, asked Richard if he wanted to 'roadie' for The Merseybeats who'd lately become managed by Kit Lambert, The Who's co-manager. Instead of taking up the offer, Richard went looning off on holiday in Spain where he enjoyed the sunshine, drank a lot and sat in on drums with a band he heard in a club. "After one number they threw me off. But there was a guitarist called Mick Wilshire. When I came back to London I called Mike Shaw and asked him if the job with The Merseys was still going. He said, 'No' but they had just fired The Who's road manager Cy Langston. Their van had got stolen outside Battersea Dogs Home and he got the bullet. So I joined The Who and was with them for about a year."

Caught up in the chaotic lifestyle of the Sixties, Richard lost his driving licence and fled again to the continent, this time to St Tropez in the South of France. He hung out with visiting musicians Long John Baldry and Elton John before returning to London where he found work with Freddie Mack & The Mac Sound. "He had so many musicians in the band he never even knew their names," says Cole. "He only knew them by the song they sang!" In the band was drummer B.J. Wilson, later with Procol Harum and at one time a contender to join Led Zeppelin. Richard went on to work with yet more bands, including The Young Rascals, over from America to tour the UK, and The Searchers. "They wanted to keep me, but I was coming out of The Ship again one night and bumped into Mick Wilshire, who was back from Spain and now in the New Vaudeville Band. 'We need somebody like you,' he said. 'The roadie we've got is no good at all! Why don't you come with us? We're going to America.' I was just 20 years old. Mick gave me Peter Grant's number. So I called Peter up and went to his office. He said to me: 'How much do you want?' So I said, 'I want £30 a week. Take it or leave it.' He kinda looked at me. Years later he told me that he thought: 'This is the guy for me. He isn't going to fuck around when he's getting the money off the promoters!' "

Richard remembers Peter's lair at RAK Management office at 155 Oxford Street. Grant sat at a large desk on one side of the room and Mickie Most sat at his desk on the other side. "I remember Peter wagging his finger at me and saying, 'If you ever fucking repeat anything you hear in this office, I'll cut your fucking ears off.' I said, 'If you are going to point

your fucking finger at me much longer I'm going to fucking bite it off!'
So, that's how I met Peter Grant."

The office that Mickie and Peter shared became legendary. The whole
building was full of music business companies and became known as the
British version of The Brill Building, the Manhattan office block, where
writers churned out streams of hit songs for music publishers and record
companies.

Of course being London, the RAK HQ wasn't quite as glamorous as its
New York counterpart. Recalls Mickie Most: "We used to be on the sixth
floor of the building in Oxford Street and sometimes the elevator wasn't
working because someone had left the bloody gate open. Peter would just
go all the way home again. He wouldn't walk up six flights of stairs. The
landlords were Millets, the camping gear store on the ground floor. They
were responsible for the heating of the building and sometimes they forgot
to put it on in the winter. I remember Peter going in there and grabbing
hold of the manager of Millets and saying, 'If you don't put that fucking
heating on I'll put *you* in the fucking boiler!' From then on we used to
have heat any time we wanted, even in the middle of the summer."

Another occupant of the building, who subsequently worked for Peter
Grant, was publicist and journalist Bill Harry. He handled the press for the
New Vaudeville Band and later became the first of Led Zeppelin's long
suffering PRs. Liverpool born, Bill Harry was an expert on The Beatles
and the entire Mersey scene. He had gone to school with, and befriended,
John Lennon and in July 1961 founded the magazine *Merseybeat*, one of
Britain's first ever fanzines and also one of the best. He moved to London
to work as a pop journalist and later became an independent PR with
clients that included The Hollies, The Kinks, Pink Floyd and Suzy
Quatro.

Bill had known Peter Grant when he was still a road manager for Gene
Vincent and working for Don Arden. "We met in Liverpool and had a
few drinks and got on quite well," he says. "He was a big man even then."
When Harry moved to London he began working for the Ellis Wright
Agency, run by two former university students, Terry Ellis and Chris
Wright. Before long these two budding entrepreneurs would merge their
names – Chris and Ellis – into Chrysalis.

"They had a small office in Regent Street and asked me to do publicity
for their acts like Ten Years After and Jethro Tull," says Bill Harry. "Then
they moved office into 155 Oxford Street. Every floor had a showbiz

company, which was quite unique. When Ellis-Wright decided to call themselves Chrysalis and move into Oxford Street, they asked me to rent an office there too. There were shops on the ground floor. Terry, Chris and me had a small office on the first floor. Island Music and Mike Berry, the publisher, occupied the next floor. On the top floor Peter Grant and Mickie Most shared their office. We were always going up there and chatting, so there was a lot of communication between the companies."

Bill Harry did PR for Chrysalis acts and the latest crop of blues bands, Chicken Shack, Savoy Brown and Free. When Peter spotted him bustling about the building he asked him to do PR for his acts as well. "Mickie and Peter had an open-plan office. It wasn't big by modern standards, but they seemed to get on really well, even though they were as different as chalk and cheese. They had their own separate businesses and Peter didn't even have his groups recorded by Mickie. Really, they were just sharing an office."

It was the era of pirate radio and Grant wasn't slow to pick up on the promotional potential of the offshore stations. On at least one occasion, Grant and Most's efforts to reach the pirates ended up in farce. Mickie: "I had a yacht and we used to sail out to Radio Caroline in the North Sea. We used to go out there to try and plug our records. There was him and I driving this bloody boat and what we knew about yachting was dangerous! We lost the anchor at Clacton. We dropped it overboard and it wasn't tied to the boat. The chain was going out and all of a sudden the whole lot went over the side. We didn't realise it was tidal and we tied up at the end of the pier and halfway through the night, we were hanging from the moorings because the water had disappeared!

"We were trying to get to Radio London and Radio Caroline I think, because they were stuck out there on some bloody sandbank off Clacton, or wherever. We eventually got out there on the boat and it was blowing a gale. I was trying to throw these records on board and they kept falling into the sea. We never got one of them onto the fucking boat! We had so much fun. I can't remember the artist we were promoting but whoever it was, his records are still at the bottom of the North Sea. If you wanna dive you'll find them because the old shellac never rots. They're still down there.

"I had just got the yacht and knew nothing about boats really, so how we got there and back beats me. Me and Peter just turned left when we got out of the Thames Estuary. It was highly dangerous. I didn't think about the sand banks and restricted areas. I just headed where I thought the pirate ships might be. They certainly weren't expecting us because there were no mobile phones in those days or telecommunications. The ships were illegal and you weren't supposed to communicate with them. Another thing was there was no alcohol allowed on board the pirate radio ships. We had all this booze on the yacht, but we thought we couldn't get them pissed. We'd get into trouble. One of the DJs was a guy called Tony Winsor. He was an Australian guy who had been around a long time and he was more interested in the Scotch we had on board, not the records. 'Throw the Scotch!' he'd shout. It was so funny. We had a big yacht with lots of cabins, but I told Peter to stay amidships because I didn't want him to tip us up! He'd be sitting there grumbling. 'What is there to eat? I'm fucking starving.' He was always hungry was Peter. I said, 'Don't worry, when we get to Southend, we'll have fish and chips.'"

Peter and Mickie never dared risk repeating their expedition to the pirate ships at sea but they did try boating up the Thames, with equally hilarious results. They were due to have lunch with a top producer at the BBC studios at Teddington Loch. "I said to Peter, let's go on the boat. So we had lunch with this guy and we said goodbye and the BBC guys were all waving at us out of the window, as we cast off. But we couldn't leave. The Thames had risen and we were locked in! I couldn't get under the bridge and so we had to go round and round in circles going 'Goodbye, goodbye!' We couldn't get under Hammersmith Bridge either and had to wait an hour for the tide to drop. We used to get into all sorts of trouble."

Peter once described his partnership with Most: "RAK Music Management was the name of the company, but names are not important in this business. People don't say, 'Let's get in touch with RAK,' they say, 'Let's go see Peter Grant.' It's the personal bit that matters. At one point just Mickie Most, myself and three girls worked in those offices and yet we had four LPs in the Top Twenty."

During his Oxford Street years, Peter also managed guitarist Jeff Beck and singer Terry Reid, and had a 'business interest' in Donovan. The working day could be hectic on the top floor with phones ringing constantly and a steady stream of visitors, some welcome, others not quite so welcome. Peter's explosive temper sometimes got the better of him. Usually calm, smiling and benign, he would suddenly become enraged at the incompetence – or worse – the discourtesy of others.

Mickie Most: "Peter on the phone was amazing. I remember he once had an offer for Led Zeppelin for a million dollars and he told them to 'fuck off'. He said, 'Listen, when you get some serious money together then we'll do it.' I said to him, 'What was all that about?' and he said, 'They're giving us a million dollars for that gig. Nah, it's not enough.' When he used to get really annoyed he'd kick the front of desk out. So if I came into the office in the morning and found the desk lying in pieces, I knew Peter had had a particularly good evening! The desk had this front panel and he would swear and kick the panel out."

Such antics undoubtedly amused and intrigued the parade of artists ascending the erratic lift to their office in search of work. One such visitor was the multi-talented John Baldwin of Sidcup. Better known as John Paul Jones, he was a classically trained musician, adept on the keyboards and bass, who could turn his hand to writing and arranging music. He was much in demand for sessions and did a lot of work for Mickie Most. Another visitor was a frail, curly haired young guitarist called Jimmy Page. Says Mickie: "Jimmy used to play on all the records I was making as a session musician and John Paul Jones used to be an arranger, bass player and keyboard player. They were both very talented musicians. John Paul Jones is a genius. I'm sure he's not as well appreciated as he should be, but he's a brilliant guy and he did some great stuff for me. He once told me that he took the name 'John Paul Jones' because it would look good on a cinema screen. His ambition then was to write music for the movies."

John Baldwin was born on January 3, 1946 in Sidcup, Kent. His father was a pianist and arranger for big bands and John was destined for a musical career from an early age. "I was a choirmaster at our local church at the age of 14. That's how I paid for my first bass guitar! I was at boarding school at Blackheath from the age of five because my parents were in a variety act, touring round the world. I spent three years at Eltham Green comprehensive school. But I didn't do very well with my exams, mainly because I was out playing in bands on American bases."

John's first band was called The Deltas with guitarist Pete Gage, who was later with Elkie Brooks in Vinegar Joe. "We played gigs all through our GCEs. I was asleep most of the time! That was my first serious band when I was 15. So I had a lot of experience. I used to play with my dad in a trio, playing weddings. We did waltzes and quicksteps and nobody knew what we were playing after a few drinks, so we'd play a bit of jazz. It was all useful stuff, which got used all through my session career and ever since. Keyboards were my first instrument, but my father was a really good pianist and I never felt I'd ever be anywhere near as good as him. So I took up the organ because it was different. I liked the way the notes sustained."

John had thought of going to the Royal College of Music but had to wait until he was 17. At the age of 16 higher education wasn't his main priority. He wanted to play pop music and earn some money. "So I stood on the corner of Archer Street in Soho every Monday for three months hoping for a gig. That was the place all musicians went looking for work. Eventually I met Jet Harris and asked him if he wanted a bass player. He said, 'Well I don't but see those people over there.' He was just forming a band as Jet & Tony, which I'd read about in the *Melody Maker*. That's why I was looking for him. But he'd got a bass player from the Jett Blacks, so I rehearsed with the Jett Blacks a couple of times."

John finally got called back to play with Jet & Tony when the group was number one with a number called 'Diamonds'. He toured with them for 18 months until they broke up. Recalls John: "The first time I met Peter Grant was in 1963 when I was still with Jet Harris and Tony Meehan. I went out on tour with their backing band, which included a tenor sax, baritone and another guitar. Jet played tuned down guitar and I played the bass. I was 17 years old and earning thirty pounds a week! I think we carried our own gear until we all chipped in a few quid to get a roadie. I ran into Peter when he was driving the van for Gene Vincent and we saw him in Wardour Street, outside The Flamingo Club. He was a big bloke but he seemed very friendly and a nice chap. I think you had to be – driving for Gene Vincent."

After the Jet & Tony experience, John began doing sessions for Decca records at the behest of Tony Meehan. He was earning good money in the studios, and between 1964 and 1968 recorded with a huge range of artists including Lulu, The Rolling Stones and Donovan. In April 1964 he released his own instrumental single 'A Foggy Day In Vietnam' without much success. However he began to make the switch from playing bass guitar on sessions to arranging the music. He did both jobs on Donovan's 'Sunshine Superman' and as a result came to the attention of the producer, Mickie Most.

Says John: "The next time I saw Peter Grant was when I was working for Mickie Most as his musical director. They had that huge forty-foot office at 155 Oxford Street. Mickie had a desk down one end and Peter had a desk at the other end. They used to face each other across this long room. So if you saw Mickie, you saw Peter. It was just a small bunch of people working there. They had an accountant and Irene the receptionist, who was wonderful. She more or less ran both of them! Peter was managing the New Vaudeville Band at the time and later The Yardbirds."

During 1967 the New Vaudeville Band took up much of Peter's time but he knew they were, at best, a novelty act, so he was anxious to expand his interests and look out for new projects. He was perhaps fortunate that The Yardbirds virtually fell into his lap while Mickie Most was producing their 1967 album *Mind Games*. John Paul Jones worked on several of the songs on the album at Mickie's behest. During these sessions John renewed his acquaintance with Jimmy Page, now a member of The Yardbirds, and a mutual admiration society was established between the two. Nothing came of it for now, though.

By 1967, the music business had changed drastically since Peter Grant cut his teeth as a tour manager with visiting American rock'n'roll stars. Most importantly, the emphasis had switched to promoting home-grown talent in the wake of the global success of The Beatles and The Rolling Stones.

After The Beatles' world-shattering 1964 US tour, British acts could now reasonably expect to conquer the American market, given a fair wind and a hit record. Such aspirations would have seemed like a pipe dream a decade earlier, when American product ruled the airwaves. The album market was also beginning to develop, and more serious – and talented – blues and rock bands were increasingly infiltrating the pop charts. Hippie favourites Cream, Jimi Hendrix and Pink Floyd were at the forefront of a social and musical revolution. Peter Grant was an Elvis Presley fan from way back, but he could relate to the kind of stuff young British bands were playing. He could certainly see their potential. The Animals had been a big hit in America, but hadn't personally made much money. Despite their cheesy image, the New Vaudeville Band had demonstrated to him the power of US radio play. Somehow there had to be a way of putting together a great looking band that played cutting edge rock and who could reap their just rewards.

The Yardbirds, he reasoned, might be the key to the puzzle. In view of their importance to Peter Grant's greatest enterprise, it is relevant to recap their exploits. First assembling in 1963, the original Yardbirds were dedicated to interpreting the blues riffs of their heroes, Chuck Berry, Bo Diddley and Muddy Waters. Hailing from the leafy suburb of Richmond in Surrey, these polite, good-looking young kids pioneered the R&B

revival in Britain, alongside the somewhat less well-mannered Rolling Stones and Pretty Things. Over the next four years the group was blessed with some extraordinarily talented lead guitarists, arguably the best of their generation. Eric Clapton, Jeff Beck and Jimmy Page all started their careers with The Yardbirds.

They were originally managed by the mercurial Giorgio Gomelsky, who in 1963 employed them to replace The Rolling Stones at Richmond's Crawdaddy Club. At this time the line-up included Keith Relf (vocals), Eric Clapton (guitar), Chris Dreja (guitar), Paul Samwell-Smith (bass) and Jim McCarty (drums). Boosted by 'Slowhand' Clapton's 'rave up' solos, the band quickly won a fanatical following. However Clapton was a blues purist and he grew increasingly unhappy with their deliberately commercial singles, particularly 'For Your Love', a Graham Gouldman song replete with harpsichord and bongo backing, and a choral chant that sounded as if it had been recorded by a congregation of monks.

In March 1965, as the record shot up the chart, Eric decided to quit, only to resurface in John Mayall's Bluesbreakers and then Cream. Chris Dreja, the band's rhythm guitarist still feels that The Yardbirds weren't entirely to blame for Clapton's shock departure. "It was 'Got To Hurry', the B-side of 'For Your Love' that got Eric the job with John Mayall. I often wonder what thoughts went through Eric's head when he left the group and 'For Your Love' did so well!"

Meanwhile the band had gigs to play and needed a new guitarist. First they approached Jimmy Page. Recalls Jim McCarty: "He'd seen us a few times and he knew our manager Giorgio Gomelsky, but he was too well established doing sessions to want to go out on the road." Jimmy recommended they try out his friend Jeff Beck, then leading his own band The Tridents. Chris Dreja recalls that when Jeff first joined the band he was regarded as a bit of an enigma. "We didn't know much about his background but although he wasn't very 'verbal' he used to talk through his guitar. It was the oddest thing. You'd be sitting in the van going to some dreadful place and Jeff would remain pretty quiet. Then he'd get his guitar out and he really came alive. Although it's hard for people to believe now, Eric wasn't a guitar virtuoso at that point. He was still learning licks and sometimes he wouldn't play lead guitar, he'd go and stand behind his amp."

Once Jeff Beck was established in The Yardbirds he clearly wanted to put his own stamp on the music. Says Chris: "He worked from emotions and although he was pretty good with us, if something got up his nose he just blew up, stormed out, walked off and smashed his guitar. He had a control problem!"

Beck developed his unique sound on The Yardbirds' albums and singles like 'Heart Full Of Soul', 'Evil Hearted You' and 'Shapes Of Things' during 1966. Says Chris: "Jeff was probably the best thing that happened to the band because during his era the music was outstanding. He's such a lovely guy and such a talented, original guitarist."

Despite the band's successful second wind with Jeff Beck at the helm, the endless touring, particularly in America, began to take its toll. Their blond-haired lead singer Keith Relf began to drink heavily, which badly affected his performances on stage. Dreja: "As Keith was very fragile, both health wise and mentally, the drink started to get on top of him. There were pressures on him that we didn't know about, but it was hard for him to compete with the lead guitarist and front a band. So he started to get seriously out of order at times."

On one occasion, The Yardbirds were booked to play at the Cambridge May Ball, where the drinks were plentiful and the upper crust set were more interested in partying than listening to music. Keith Relf got completely out of his head and began abusing the audience during their set. Jimmy Page had gone along to see the gig and found the whole thing most amusing. But bass player Paul Samwell-Smith was extremely embarrassed.

Chris recalled the scene: "They do treat you very well in terms of food and drink and you do go on very late at night. Keith had a real skinful and by the time we got to play the set all he could do was blow raspberries. He'd forgotten where he was and what he was doing. He literally had to be tied to the mike stand, and of course it was in front of the Establishment crowd which really got up Paul's nose, to be let down in this way. This was the last straw for Paul. He announced he didn't want to continue. Ironically Jimmy Page was at the gig and he loved it. He thought this is great – this is rock'n'roll!"

The next day Keith rang everybody to apologise and to reveal that he had broken two fingers in his right hand trying out karate chops. He had been 'wound up' by Allan Clarke of The Hollies and tried to break some plastic trays with his bare hands. The next time the band saw him he had his hand in a sling. Sometimes Keith got so drunk at gigs the band used to pack him in the back of the van with all the gear. They'd dump him outside his house with his harmonicas and bottle of whiskey.

Chris: "There were demons going on in his head one can work out now. The band was becoming more guitar oriented and he was never a great singer. He was a brilliant harmonica player, but PA systems weren't as sophisticated as they are now. So things got to him. The thing was Jimmy was there and when Paul pulled out Jimmy was so keen to play in the band he came in on bass. He decided he wanted a bit of life on the road."

Jimmy Page played his first date with The Yardbirds at The Marquee after just a couple of hour's rehearsal and stayed with the band for two years. Page's first Yardbirds tour came in September 1966, supporting Ike & Tina Turner and The Rolling Stones. Next came the States, by which time Jimmy had stopped playing bass and started playing lead guitar alongside Jeff Beck. They were pals – but on stage they could be deadly rivals.

Recalls Chris: "They were very different personalities – Jeff and Jimmy. There was this slightly out of control egomaniac and this guy who had spent years doing sessions for Burt Bacharach. Jimmy was so professional and very fresh, as he hadn't been on the road. He was a very astute guy too and knew the business. We were just naïve really. Jimmy knew exactly where he was going. Very disciplined, very controlled.

"Jimmy was a doctor's son from Epsom and had a very similar background to us. But he had a certain shrewdness that most people in rock'n' roll didn't have. He was also a very adaptable guitar player. As a businessman he had quite a tough edge to him because he'd spent a lot of time around producers and had probably picked up all the vibes."

Indeed, by the time he became a Yardbird Jimmy Page was among the most experienced pop musicians in Britain – even though he was largely unknown outside the music industry itself. Born James Patrick Page on January 9, 1944 at Heston, Middlesex, he grew up in Epsom, the home of the Derby in genteel, Tory-voting Surrey, a world away from the swamp-infested American south where the blues took root. Like John Paul Jones, he sang in a choir and seemed precociously gifted as a musician. He took up guitar from the age of 13, had a few lessons but was essentially self-taught, and remembers having his guitar confiscated at school when he tried practising during classes. He was turned on to rock'n'roll in 1959 when he heard Elvis Presley's hit 'Baby, Let's Play House'. Thereafter he devoted almost all of his spare time to perfecting Scotty Moore's solos on Elvis's early Sun recordings. After leaving school he joined Neil Christian & The Crusaders, who had seen him playing in a local dance hall, and by the age of 15 Jimmy's reputation as a skilled Chuck Berry style R&B player was starting to spread, albeit within musicians' circles only. Around this time he befriended Jeff Beck. "He looked like a shrimp who was as thin as a pipe cleaner," said Beck. "He used to play fiery, fast stuff. The trouble was, no one was listening."

Heavy touring, late nights and comfortless berths took their toll on Jimmy, who was just out of school, and he suffered a bout of glandular fever. So, after two years gigging with The Crusaders, Jimmy quit and went to Art College for 18 months, although he often took time out to jam with his friend Jeff Beck. As the R&B boom took off he visited all the clubs and sat in with bands, and in late 1962 was invited to play on his first session by producer Mike Leander. Intriguingly, the session yielded 'Diamonds' the number one hit by Jet Harris & Tony Meehan. Sensing that this was where his future lay, Jimmy studied music more closely and embarked on a career as one of London's most in-demand young session guitarists. He played on hundreds of records over the next few years, working with everyone from Burt Bacharach to Johnny Dankworth. He also played on records by The Who, The Kinks and Them. Jimmy even released his own solo single called 'She Just Satisfies' in 1965. That same year he did some work for Immediate Records' boss Andrew Oldham and produced some blues tracks with Eric Clapton. By 1966 he was ready to quit the studios and go back on the road. The Yardbirds seemed like the ideal setting.

By this time manager Giorgio Gomelsky had dropped out of the picture, to be succeeded by Simon Napier-Bell, who had formerly managed Marc Bolan and John's Children. Says Chris Dreja: "We never made any money with Giorgio. He admitted that he was very loose with money. We didn't really make a lot more with Simon Napier-Bell. Now Jimmy Page knew this guy Peter Grant from way back, having done lots of sessions for Mickie Most. Apparently Jimmy had gone up to Grant saying we were a world famous band, we'd done all these tours, had all these hits and he was only getting twenty quid a week. So Peter started to go on the road with us and partially manage us. Simon Napier-Bell spoke to Grant and said: 'Well, the boys are all right but there is one troublemaker,' meaning Jimmy Page."

Jimmy himself laughed when he heard this description. "Too right!" he said, emphasising the way the band toured endlessly for little financial reward.

Chris Dreja: "Simon Napier-Bell did get us one publishing advance, which was the first real money we had ever seen. He had film connections and through that we appeared in the film *Blow Up* which probably was good for us."

In the movie Jeff Beck smashed up his guitar, Pete Townshend style, while the band played 'Train Kept A Rollin'' renamed for the movie as 'Stroll On'. It was one of the best moments in the ambitious 1966 cult film, directed by Michelangelo Antonioni and starring David Hemmings, but despite this coup The Yardbirds were still not satisfied with their management. Napier-Bell admits there were difficulties after he took over from Giorgio Gomelsky: "I was finding them very troublesome, especially recording them. Mickie Most then suggested that he should record them, which I thought was outrageous. On the other hand, he'd had success with The Animals and had some credibility. I didn't think he was right for The Yardbirds, but they didn't seem to mind. I think they'd probably had enough of me. So I agreed that he should record them. I think he'd had it in mind for quite a long time. I went to see him at his office in Oxford Street, next to the Academy Cinema and above the original Marquee club. Peter Grant sat at his big desk, right opposite Mickie. They both knew Jimmy Page very well because Mickie had used Jimmy on all the Herman's Hermits sessions."

Napier-Bell says he found Jimmy quite difficult to handle and confirms they didn't hit it off. "I think Jimmy thought I was an inexperienced young manager and that he knew more than I did. He was probably right! In fact I never even had a management contract with Jimmy Page. I said that he could join the group, but I would just manage them."

Simon could see the internal pressures that were gradually tearing The Yardbirds apart. "The problem was when Jimmy played lead, Jeff was no longer the star solo hero and neither enjoyed the situation very much. When they played the same lines in stereo, Jimmy was just playing Jeff's line and both felt unfulfilled. They began to fall out and halfway through a tour of America it collapsed badly. Jeff went off in a bad mood and Jimmy and The Yardbirds just finished the tour without him. Peter Grant always amused me because he had such a dry sense of humour. I told him that The Yardbirds were a bloody nuisance and he said, 'Oh, I could deal with them, I'd just hang them out the first floor window.' I'd laugh because it was exactly what he might do!

"I never felt intimidated by him but he was very wobbly. He was a big lump of jelly. You didn't look at him and think 'What a tough guy', you thought 'What a big guy'. On the other hand, when it comes to being a wrestler, being big counts for a lot. You wouldn't want him to roll on you. But he was always fun and he said, 'Oh I'd deal with Jimmy, no problem.' So I said, 'Well why don't you manage the buggers?' He said, 'All right,' and I said I'd manage Jeff Beck, because I liked him a lot. The Yardbirds were all nice people really, but they weren't getting on very well and I wasn't into conflicts. I didn't really understand that's what groups are all about. I thought they were all supposed to be nice! So he took on The Yardbirds and occasionally I'd meet up with him for a chat and find out how they were doing."

Recalled Peter Grant: "I had known Jimmy Page for some while when I took on The Yardbirds. He'd done loads of session work over the years and had become involved with the band only just before I was approached to take over their management. What happened was that Simon Napier-Bell wanted to offload the band, because he was keen to become a film producer. So I took them, along with Jeff Beck."

Whenever Simon spoke to Peter, his successor took pains to explain his philosophy for managing a group and plotting their career strategy, a key tenet of which was not issuing singles. Clearly the failure of all recent Yardbirds' singles had shown that releasing them might no longer be the best option for an underground rock band. "He did that at a very early stage," says Simon. "The funny thing was – with Mickie Most – chart success with singles was *all-important*. Yet Peter thought that if you put a single out you were competing to get into the chart and if you don't get into the chart, you are then a failure. If you don't put a single out – you can't be a failure!

"Maybe working with Mickie had made him think about this, because charts ruled Mickie Most's life, or perhaps Jimmy Page had given him the idea. Either way, he and Jimmy worked very well together. Peter always thanked me for giving him Jimmy Page and earning him £200 million! He spent a lot of time travelling with Jimmy and The Yardbirds. In fact he spent his whole time with them and in effect they became the prototype Led Zeppelin. It was funny how well Jimmy and Peter got on because Jimmy was a very softly spoken, gentle guy and Peter was from a very different background and education."

Simon didn't think The Yardbirds saw Peter as their father figure. "They weren't looking for fathers, they just recognised what talents he had and he did well for them. It was a relationship that suited everyone very well. Meanwhile, I took over Jeff Beck and in those days I used to think that simple talent won out. He was and is the greatest blues guitarist ever, I think. Eric Clapton almost wrecked himself trying to play the blues, while Jeff just drank a cup of tea and played better anyway!"

With The Yardbirds behind him, Jeff Beck put together his own group with Rod Stewart on vocals, Ronnie Wood on bass guitar, Nicky Hopkins on piano and Mickey Waller on drums. On paper it was a dream ticket, but in reality it was riddled with tensions. "What I hadn't allowed for was that Jeff didn't really rehearse his first group properly," says Napier-Bell. "He formed the group with Rod Stewart and Ronnie Wood and I thought they couldn't go wrong. They opened up for The Small Faces on tour at the Astoria in Finsbury Park and it all went wrong. Rod came on stage with his flies undone and the curtain fell on top of the guitarist and then somebody from The Small Faces pulled the plugs out, so the power went off. It was a dismal concert and I couldn't snap my fingers and come up with a solution. The real problem was they hadn't rehearsed. The trouble was, I was the same age as them and felt too intimidated by them to tell them what to do. I couldn't say, 'You lazy cunts!' like Peter Grant would have done. I just sidled out of the whole management thing for a few years and came back again in the Eighties with Wham! and found I could do it this time."

Despite his association with Grant, Napier-Bell didn't take any cues from his style of management. "I didn't really take any tips from Peter. All managers are completely individual and there was nothing that Peter did which would have worked for me. I admired Andrew Oldham and Kit Lambert enormously, but I couldn't have managed artists in the same way. I wouldn't say that Peter wasn't a tiny bit villainous. He just wasn't villainous with me!"

The giant from Battersea proved his worth as the reconstituted Yardbirds set off for America one more time. One of his first decisions was to bring back Richard Cole as his assistant. Recalls Cole: "I had worked for him for a year with The New Vaudeville Band during 1967. Once again I lost my driving licence, so basically I was out of work. Then Tony Stratton-Smith gave me a job. He knew I couldn't drive but I had an international permit and I did his band The Creation. We did a three-week tour of Germany and Holland with Ronnie Wood on guitar, Kenny Pickett singing and Kim Gardner on bass. After that tour I flew over to

America and got a job with Vanilla Fudge. Then I found out The Yardbirds were coming to America, so I wrote Peter a letter and said I'd love to be their tour manager. So from then on I worked for Peter Grant from the beginning of 1967 until 1980. In 1968 I worked for him with The Yardbirds, Jeff Beck, Rod Stewart, the New Vaudeville Band and Terry Reid."

The Grant management empire was expanding, but the biggest and best was yet to come. In the event it was all thanks to his association with The Yardbirds. Says Chris Dreja emphatically: "The best manager we ever had was Peter Grant. Giorgio was very creative but hopeless with money. Peter would almost die for his artists. We were booked to do a State Fair in Canada one winter and we were travelling in a Greyhound coach. We hit terrible weather and we were many hours late. There were lorries jackknifed on the highway and you couldn't get through. Of course the State Fair, like so many venues, was Mafia run and we'd arrived late and virtually missed the first performance. These two Mafioso guys with veins popping in their necks were going to kill us. Peter was sitting in the back of the bus and they pulled guns. They actually pulled a pistol on him. I'll never forget this but he got up and he barrelled them away with his stomach.

"He said: 'You're gonna do WOT?' And they were so taken aback that someone had the nerve to do this, they just ended up laughing. It broke the ice, but it was quite something to take a pistol in your stomach."

Thanks to the assiduous attentions of their gutsy minder, The Yardbirds finally began to make money out of their gruelling tours. But they were becoming exhausted. The young musicians who had set out with dreams of recreating the authentic blues found life had now become a dreary pop music treadmill, without even a supply of new hits to boost their confidence. They were increasingly confused over their musical identity. Many of the original Yardbirds team had gone. Jeff Beck would be next to quit.

Chris: "Unfortunately for us, by the time Peter Grant came on the scene we were going downhill and we were knackered. There was no break in that four-year period. It was one of the reasons Paul left. There was no time to do an album. If we had taken a year off and regrouped, the band would have sustained a lot longer. But there were so many gigs to perform."

Jim McCarty: "It stopped being fun a long time before we broke up. We were travelling huge distances in the States and we didn't have limousines or private aircraft."

It was a bad time for a British band to be on the road in America. The country was still stuck in the Vietnam War, and anti-war protesters used rock gigs as platforms to stage demonstrations, turning concerts into battles between police and hippies. Elsewhere conflicts erupted over civil rights for black Americans. "There was a lot of bad vibes and a lot of rioting going on," says McCarty. "We once drove to California in a couple of station wagons from Virginia and we inadvertently drove into Los Angeles via Watts right in the middle of a riot. Houses were burning, there were tanks on the streets and we were lucky to get out alive. All that takes its toll, because we were constantly in the front line. We were put on some crazy tours by Simon Napier-Bell like the Dick Clark tour. We were travelling huge distances to do two gigs a night and that was the tour when Jeff walked out. In fact he didn't do it. The only person who pulled through that show was Jimmy Page, because he was still fresh. But that's when we sacked Simon Napier-Bell and went with Peter."

Jim: "Jeff Beck became unreliable, especially in America. When Jeff kept letting us down, Chris went on bass and Jimmy played lead. The Dick Clark tour was really heavy, hard work, playing two towns a night. Jeff did a couple of nights then he blew his top and smashed his Les Paul up in the dressing rooms. So he went back to England and we finished the tour with Jimmy on lead. Originally it was Jeff's idea to bring Jimmy into the group, but I think they had a few differences. They would try and outdo each other's solos and it put Jeff under quite a bit of strain. It was exciting but it was bloody loud! They used to do 'Over, Under, Sideways, Down' as a stereo dual guitar riff. I remember we did a tour with the Stones and they got quite worried. We finished the band, with Jimmy as our lead guitarist, around 1968. We did a string of pretty dire singles, which were Mickie Most's ideas, but we did some good gigs."

Chris: "I liked Jimmy's energy and he was so professional. Obviously the ideas and material and arrangements were undoubtedly moving towards Led Zeppelin, but it was fresh enough to keep my interest."

As well as the singles and album Mickie Most produced there was also a live Yardbirds album from the Anderson Theatre, against which Jimmy Page later injuncted to ensure its withdrawal. The band was already playing a version of a song Jimmy played called 'Dazed And Confused', but it seemed he'd have preferred to earmark this for a future project. As it turned out the Most-produced album *Little Games* was released only in America and British fans began to assume the group had dissolved. Indeed, the group spent most of early 1967, its final months, touring the US, Australia and the Far East.

Despite Peter Grant's best efforts, The Yardbirds were crumbling "Jimmy had already seen Led Zeppelin coming towards him," says Chris Dreja. "Everybody had their own different agendas, and at the end of the day, we didn't make it work for ourselves."

The group played its last date at Luton Technical College in July 1968. Relf and McCarty went off to form new group Renaissance, while Dreja hoped to stick around with Page to form the next version of the band, which they intended to call The New Yardbirds. In the end Dreja decided to quit music entirely and become a photographer. Oddly enough, many years later, when Peter Grant reminisced about the end of The Yardbirds, he could not remember the band playing their alleged last date in England.

"As I recall, we never played a gig after that American tour, so in reality it fell apart in America. Jim McCarty wasn't in the best of health and we had to use a session man. We had a club date in the States for $5,000. That was a lot of money. Jimmy wanted to do it and so did Chris, but the others didn't. There was a big row in a Holiday Inn. So I drafted out a letter giving Jimmy the rights to the name, which they all signed. I don't remember them doing a gig in Luton, but distinctly remember driving Jimmy around Shaftesbury Avenue near the Savile Theatre after the split. We were in a traffic jam and I said to Jimmy, 'What are you going to do. Do you want to go back to sessions or what?' And he said, 'Well I've got some ideas.' He didn't mention anybody. So I said, 'What about a producer?' He said, 'I'd like to do that too, if you can get a deal.' He seemed keen to form a new band, so I thought, great, let's do it. We took the name New Yardbirds to get some gigs."

As a first step to promote the new band, Peter went to see his old journalist pal Keith Altham of *NME*, who politely turned down the opportunity for an interview with Jimmy Page. The Yardbirds, old or new, weren't big news in 1968. "It was something he always regretted," said Peter.

It is generally assumed that after Chris Dreja dropped out, Page immediately thought of John Paul Jones as his first choice recruit for the new band. However, John says that he first heard that Page was forming a band when he read about it in *Disc* magazine. "My wife Mo read the story and she told me to give Page a call. I wasn't doing much for Mickie Most at that time but I was always going up to his office with Peter. There was lots of banter flying around and it was always a fun place to go.

"Now how did I get in touch with Page? I didn't have his number, so I probably asked Peter about it and he must have spoken to Jimmy, who must have said, 'Yes.'"

Peter and Jimmy had found their bass and keyboard player. Now there was the matter of finding a singer and drummer. They clearly wanted the sort of powerful performers who could wipe the floor with the competition. One contender for the job of vocalist with The New Yardbirds was Terry Reid, whom Peter was already managing. "But he had a dreadful father who I had to deal with," recalled Peter. "Jimmy was keen on Steve Marriott too but he wasn't approached. I knew Jimmy was really keen on Terry Reid and one day we came out of Oxford Street and bumped into Terry. It was at that point he told us he didn't want to do it and suggested Robert Plant instead."

Peter, Jimmy and Chris Dreja went up to Birmingham to find Robert, who was then singing with a group called Hobbstweedle. At first they couldn't find the lad Reid had enthused about. Said Peter: "This big guy with a University of Toronto sweatshirt appeared to let us in backstage and I remember Jimmy saying, 'Crikey, they've got a big roadie!' He came back and he turned out to be Robert Plant! Jimmy loved Robert straight away."

Various names were bandied about as a possible drummer, including Barrie 'B.J.' Wilson, the heavyweight from Procol Harum, and Aynsley Dunbar, another alumni of John Mayall's Bluesbreakers who had also worked with Jeff Beck. "We definitely approached Aynsley Dunbar," says Dreja. "I knew him well and he was a great drummer – but he went off to Frank Zappa's band."

While Jimmy debated who to have on drums, Peter went to America with The Jeff Beck Group. It gave him an opportunity to observe how young, principally male audiences, many of whom were strung out on 'downer' drugs like Qaaludes, lapped up the loud, frenzied, blues-rock music that the group offered. He also couldn't help but notice that for all their musical invention, Beck's group was desperately unstable. With ten years' experience of the music industry behind him, a clear head on his broad shoulders and an ambition that matched his physical strength, Peter Grant was in a unique position to take advantage of the change from pop to rock. He must have seen it coming. With Jimmy Page delivering the music and Peter providing the kind of management muscle hitherto lacking in British pop, they were unstoppable.

Back in the UK in the meantime, singer Robert Plant had recommended to Page his old Birmingham mate John Bonham, whom he described as the loudest and heaviest drummer in the country. Jimmy went to the Marquee to see him play with American singer Tim Rose.

Jimmy was so impressed he called Peter Grant in San Francisco. "I saw a drummer last night and this guy plays so good and so loud we must get him," he told his manager. "He plays so loud promoters won't re-book him!"

Peter was with Jeff Beck when he got the message that Jimmy had called. He was astonished. Jimmy's parsimony was a source of much mirth within Yardbirds' circles. "Jimmy Page? Making an outgoing phone call to America? I knew something important had happened," said Peter.*

The problem was that John Bonham, whose financial circumstances were fairly dismal, didn't have a working telephone. Grant came back to London and sent what in the end amounted to 30 telegrams to try to get Bonham to join the band. John, a former bricklayer and builder's son from Redditch, was convinced that his gig with Tim Rose was much more viable than an unlikely future with an outfit called The New Yardbirds. I sounded like The New Vaudeville Band. He was convinced it was a cabaret act, until Robert told him, "Look mate, you've gotta join this band!"

Eventually Bonham was dragged down to London and the four musicians finally met up to play for the first time, in a tiny, hot and cramped rehearsal room in Gerrard Street. As soon as they played together they realised there was a magical chemistry at work. They seemed very well suited to each other, although the unpredictable and bombastic drummer was prone to great outbursts of panic.

Recalled Peter: "They had been rehearsing at the weekend and Bonham came to see me on the Monday and said: 'Mr Grant, I might have dropped a clanger. I was meant to go to the Isle of Wight to play with Chris Farlowe this week.' I said, 'Why didn't you tell me?' He was supposed to be working for Rik Gunnell, a heavy-duty promoter.

"And he says, 'I've already had the 40 quid last week as I needed the cash.' So I said I'd phone Rik and sort him out. Rik told me to forget it and we left it at that. Both him and Robert were a bit naïve in those early days."

---

* Peter once quipped, "If you want to bump off Jimmy Page, all you have to do is throw tuppence in front of a London bus."

Rumours were rife on the London music scene that Page and Grant were going to poach many 'name' musicians and even turn The New Yardbirds into a five-piece band. Steve Winwood was among those mentioned. "The only time we talked about a five piece as I recall was after the first couple of tours," said Grant later. "There was talk of adding a keyboard player and I can remember that Keith Emerson was mentioned. And there was also a thing that Brian Lane, the manager of Yes, was paranoid that we were going to nick Chris Squire as a bass player and move Jonesy to keyboards. But that was never a serious proposition."

Oddly enough Peter Grant never went to the band's first rehearsal in Gerrard Street. "No, I wasn't there. The first time I saw them play was in Scandinavia. I remember standing on the side of the stage and being amazed. Bonzo was only on £50 a week and he came back afterwards and offered to drive the van for another £30!"

John 'Bonzo' Bonham, Jimmy Page, Robert Plant and John Paul Jones, would soon be earning much more than £50 a week, once Peter Grant got into his stride. But if the new boys thought they would be pampered prima donnas, they were in for a shock. John Bonham was the first to receive a Grant tongue-lashing.

When John started to play in his usual busy and boisterous fashion, Jimmy Page told him, "You're going to have to keep it a bit more simple than that." Bonzo bashed on regardless and Jimmy was annoyed.

Peter Grant came over to Bonham. "Do you like the job in the band?" he asked coldly.

"Well – yeah," said Bonham.

"Well do as this man says – or *fuck off*," said Grant menacingly, adding for good measure: "Fucking behave yourself Bonham, or you'll disappear – *through different doors*."

The *modus operandi* of the man who led Zeppelin had been established at the outset.

4

A WHOLE LOTTA PETER

"In Peter's day, you put the money in the Hammond organ and you made a dash for the border."

– Ed Bicknell

Peter Grant and Jimmy Page spent the summer of 1968 plotting their strategy for the concept born out of The Yardbirds that became Led Zeppelin. It was a combination of skill, timing and an indefinable chemistry that resulted in the triumph of their enterprise.

While the manager was crucially important to the band's commercial activities, it was the artistry of Page, Plant, Jones and Bonham that ensured that *what* they played mattered and had relevance. This was no mere Machiavellian ploy and exercise in pop exploitation. Led Zeppelin undoubtedly played a crucial part in the vast outpouring of creative youth culture that made the late Sixties so special. Dozens of bands, singers and songwriters blossomed in the wake of The Beatles and The Rolling Stones' achievements earlier in the decade. Yet somehow the band devised by Jimmy Page and backed to the hilt by Peter Grant captured the mood and expressed the energy of the times with all-conquering gusto.

This was the band that eventually produced such songs and arrangements as 'Kashmir', 'The Song Remains The Same', 'Black Dog', 'Trampled Underfoot', 'Achilles Last Stand' and, of course, the pantheon of Zeppelin standards, 'Communication Breakdown', 'Dazed And Confused' and 'Stairway To Heaven', songs that ensured the band's place in history. As radio stations played their records around the clock, the albums sold in millions and the band toured for months on end, it seemed as if Grant's merry men had *become* the rock industry. But it was a hard struggle to get Zeppelin off the ground.

There can be no question that Peter Grant loved Led Zeppelin. As the only child of a single parent, strong relationships were especially important to him. He was married to his wife Gloria and they cherished their two children, Warren and Helen, but there was no doubt that Grant treated his band as if they were an extension of the family, surrogate sons perhaps, to be indulged and disciplined, as required. He certainly spent more time with them than anybody else during the first exciting years of the band's existence. Peter rarely missed a gig, was always there when they needed guidance or protection, and was out battling for them in the wider world of the music industry and media.

Yet there was nothing overtly sentimental about his attitude. Led Zeppelin presented a challenge to his pride; to see if he could make this dynamic new outfit the commercial success they deserved to be. It was his crusade. He had the utmost faith in Jimmy Page and now he brought into play all his accumulated experience, all that streetwise acumen and reserves of pent-up aggression and energy. The reigning moguls of the music business were about to face the deadliest combination since Elvis Presley and Colonel Tom Parker. They would scorn Grant at their peril.

The birth pangs of Led Zeppelin were strangely convoluted, but favoured by fortune. Even before the break-up of The Yardbirds and that casual in-car conversation between Page and Grant, there had been a succession of intriguing omens. During the period when Beck and Page worked together in The Yardbirds, Jimmy wrote and produced a tune called 'Beck's Bolero' which appeared on the B-side of Jeff's hit single 'Hi Ho Silver Lining', a track produced by Mickie Most. A star-studded line up was assembled for the recording session that included Beck and Page on guitars, Nicky Hopkins on piano, John Paul Jones on bass and, moonlighting from his regular band The Who, Keith Moon on drums.

Recalled Grant: "It was a jam session really, but it went terrifically well. We ended up using it as the B-side of the single and it also appeared on the *Truth* (Columbia) album." This was Jeff Beck's solo début, featuring Rod Stewart and Ronnie Wood, which appeared in August 1968, some six months before the first Led Zeppelin album was released in March 1969. It was later suggested that Zeppelin had in some way plagiarised the style of this Beck album. Indeed, some recall that when Jeff heard the first Zeppelin album, "He was incandescent."

The charge of ripping off Beck was something that Peter Grant always vehemently denied. "That was rubbish. I produced *Truth* mainly because

Mickie Most wasn't available and Zeppelin definitely didn't rip it off.*
The only point of contact on the two albums was a cover version of 'You
Shook Me' done by both acts. When *Truth* was finished I sent Jimmy a
white label copy, because I assumed he'd want to hear what Jeff had
done. Some time later Jimmy asked me why I hadn't told him that Jeff
had done 'You Shook Me'. This was after *Led Zeppelin 1* had been
recorded. I told him about the white label . . . and he hadn't even heard
it. *Truth* was the only album I ever produced. I wasn't a musician and
didn't profess to know much about music. My main contribution to
Zeppelin was marketing and dealing with the business."

In the wake of the 'Beck's Bolero' session but before he'd recruited
Jones, Plant and Bonham, Jimmy had considered the idea of leading a
regular group featuring himself, Beck, Moon and ace session pianist
Nicky Hopkins. Keith Moon suggested they bring in his Who colleague
John Entwistle to play bass instead of John Paul Jones. All these machina-
tions were kept highly secret at the time, as Pete Townshend, The
Who's *de facto* leader and principal songwriter, would not have relished
the idea of losing his star drummer and bassist. There was much discussion about bringing in Steve Winwood as their vocalist, but he was too
wrapped up in Traffic. Steve Marriott of The Small Faces was also
approached, and according to Jimmy: "He seemed full of glee about it.
Then a message came through from the business side of Marriott, which
said: 'How would you like to play guitar with broken fingers? You will
be if you don't stay away from Stevie.' After that the idea just fell apart.
Instead of being more positive about it and looking for another singer,
we just let it slip. Then The Who began a tour and The Yardbirds began
a tour and that was it."

In discussing this putative supergroup, Keith Moon had joked that it
would go down "like a lead balloon". John Entwistle agreed, but said it
would be "more like a Lead Zeppelin". It was a name that would hang in
the air, slowly sinking into the subconscious of their lead guitarist and his
manager. A year or so later, when Jimmy finally put his own band
together, he would have preferred to use the more original name but
The New Yardbirds had to be used, for contractual reasons. Recalled
Grant: "It was Keith who coined the name, although he meant it as
'Lead Zeppelin'. The phrase just stuck in my mind. I played around with

---

* Whatever Grant said, Mickie Most insists today that he produced *Truth*.

it and changed the spelling to 'Led' because otherwise it might sound like 'lead [as in] you up the garden path'. I suggested it to Jimmy and he said that's great and he went for it. So I decided to call the band Led Zeppelin."

Jimmy later said that the name wasn't really that important and he might as well have called the band 'The Vegetables' or 'The Potatoes' for all he cared! Early rehearsals brought together Page, Robert Plant, John Paul Jones, and John Bonham musically armed and ready for the first time, although there had been various meetings at Jimmy's boathouse on the Thames at Pangebourne. John Paul remembers their first jam resulted in instant musical chemistry, although it wasn't easy to find a tune they could all play.

"We went to a small room in Lisle Street, Soho for the first rehearsal. We set the amps up and not being a rock'n'roll fan at the time, I knew nothing. And so Jimmy said, 'Well do you know 'Train Kept A Rollin'' by The Yardbirds?' I said, 'No,' and so he said, 'Well it's a 12-bar with a riff on G'. That was the first thing we ever played. It gelled immediately. And Jimmy is still playing it today!"

In September 1968 The New Yardbirds set off on their début tour of Scandinavia. Accompanied by Grant, the newly constituted quartet unleashed a mighty assault on the unsuspecting Danes and Swedes. All they had to do now was convince a sceptical British public and record industry. Their name seemed to be the biggest problem. Sadly 'The Yardbirds' no longer held any cachet. It was an era when fresh pop sensations were occurring daily, and the old group had been away so long they were almost forgotten. As a result Peter found to his chagrin that nobody wanted to book his boys and nobody wanted to sign them to a record label.

Recalled Grant bitterly: "Pye Records laughed me out of their office. I went to see their boss Louis Benjamin and asked for an advance. The figure was £17,500. He just said: 'You've got to be joking.'" He also talked to Mo Ostin at Warner Bros, who at least knew Jimmy from his session work, but was again shown the door.

Even if record executives didn't know Jimmy Page from Yellow Pages, he was highly regarded by the most hip musicians on the scene. Jimmy's reputation would, to a large extent, be their salvation. Grant: "Jimmy and I were walking down Sixth Avenue in New York while we were on tour with The Yardbirds. This limo screeches to a halt, backs up and out gets

Burt Bacharach, wearing a white tuxedo with a beautiful woman in the back seat. He greets Jimmy enthusiastically, because he remembered him from all those sessions he'd done in London. All the important guys in the US biz knew about Jimmy Page. It was funny that when I first signed The Yardbirds, Simon Napier-Bell told me to get rid of Jimmy Page because he would be 'a problem'. When I spoke to Jimmy about that he told me about all the trouble they were having, not getting paid for months of work. I would soon change all that."

As soon as The New Yardbirds returned from their 10-date Scandinavian tour they went hotfoot into Olympic Studios in Barnes to record their début album, together with the aid of engineer Glyn Johns. The studio by the river in south west London was rapidly becoming the studio of choice among rock's cognoscenti.

It was taped in just 30 hours and cost just £1,782, including the artwork for the cover. It was an historic piece of work that would have far-reaching consequences for the future of rock music. And yet Jimmy, Robert, John Paul and 'Bonzo' Bonham had already participated in an earlier recording session together, before they made the Led Zeppelin album.

They laid down the backing tracks for a P.J. Proby album called *Three Week Hero* and in the process the hot young band practically blew the singer away, notably on a track called 'Jim's Blues'. The record was eventually released on Liberty in 1969 and became a collector's item. John Paul Jones explained how this came about: "I still had some commitments for recording sessions. There was a guy I knew (Steve Rowland) who was producing *Three Week Hero* for P.J. Proby. I was committed to do all the arrangements and as we were talking about rehearsing I thought it would be a handy source of income for the band for us all to be on the record. I had to book a band anyway, so I thought I'd book everyone I knew. We had Robert on tambourine! That was the first thing we ever did. Everybody thinks we did 'Hurdy Gurdy Man' with Donovan and he seems to remember it differently. But I booked the band and it was myself, Alan Parker and Clem Cattini. Jimmy Page knows he wasn't on that Donovan session.

"We had begun rehearsing out at Page's place in Pangebourne, basically to fulfil those Scandinavian dates that The Yardbirds had left over. We'd rehearsed for that tour and the first album was pretty much a recording of the first show, which was why it had so many 'covers' on it. That's all we had ready to play at that time, but the sound and the performance was fantastic. It was old style recording. We just sat there in Olympic with a few screens to cover the amps up and it was a big 'live' room, so everything leaked into everything else, which was part of the sound. We did it in about 15 hours with another 15 for mixing, so it was 30 hours in all to make *Led Zeppelin*."

John Paul remains fascinated by the primitive way the first album was produced. One of their ideas was to put John Bonham's drums on a wooden riser, to give them a bigger sound. "I'm sure there is one point where the vocal 'bleeds' off one track into another. You could never erase anything properly.

"Robert did some guide vocals in the studio and we couldn't get rid of them, so we turned them into an effect. That sort of thing happened all the time. I remember there was a Hammond organ in the studio, which I used and I wrote the riff to 'Good Times Bad Times'. Peter didn't interfere at all. He had no say about the music. We always thought he deserved to be called 'executive producer' of the albums, because he'd cleared a space for us to do what we liked. He dealt with the record companies and trusted us implicitly with the music. That was one of his great strengths, I always thought. There was no pressure to change anything and his only comment was, 'That sounds great.'"

The artistic freedom that Grant gave his musicians was unique in management terms. John Paul: "That was one of the joys of being in that band. You could do anything you liked. That was our only formula – 'Do anything you like.' That was why (a) it worked and (b) it was so pleasurable. We knew that as long as we kept on doing things that pleased us, we knew it would work. That's why we kept on experimenting and why all the Zeppelin albums have a different feel. We got away with it, every time. If something took our fancy we'd have a go. We all listened to different kinds of music – all the time."

As well as being endowed with a sense of freedom the new band felt secure in having Peter Grant as their manager. "It was nice to know that everything was taken care of. In return for him staying out of our stuff, we stayed out of his stuff. If he said, 'I think you should do this,' we said, 'Fine, let's do it.' We allowed ourselves to be guided by him and we trusted his decisions and he was always right. 'Don't release a single,' he said. 'Okay, sounds odd, but if you say so, we won't.' We left that and the whole touring strategy to him. His idea was to be everywhere – and then nowhere. Just at the point where everyone was going to get fed up with seeing us, we were gone! He was just right, all the time."

In the beginning, though, Led Zeppelin needed to be everywhere all of the time, and Peter had to grit his teeth, swallow his pride and fight the apathy of the local music business. He knew he had a superb album in the can, a great band raring to go and the support of 'underground' blues and rock fans. All he needed was help and encouragement from bookers and A&R men. One eyewitness to the sight and sound of Peter Grant in action during this crucial period was a student from Hull University, who booked the bands for college dances, happened to be in town and met Peter at his office. The booker was Ed Bicknell.

Bicknell, who would go on to become the manager of Dire Straits, would one day become a close friend of his hero, the man who led Zeppelin. But in October 1968, Ed was just an enthusiastic student booker with a fascination for the workings of the music business. During his second college year he had become the secretary of the entertainments committee and he ran all Hull University's entertainments, including a jazz club and Saturday night dances.

"During that period what became known as progressive rock got underway," recalls Bicknell. "One of the first bands I booked was The Moody Blues for £100. It was standard in those days that every band played two 45-minute sets. I would put the set times up in the dressing room. I went in and John Lodge came up to me and said, 'We don't play two 45-minute sets, we do a concert. The audience will have to sit down.' And this was a Saturday night in a student union bar. Between the time I'd booked them and the time they came to Hull, they had got rid of Denny Laine, Justin and John Lodge had joined the group and they had recorded *The Days Of Future Past* and they were going to do a concert based on the album. That was the first time we had a band that weren't playing for dancing. And to my astonishment 900 students sat down on the floor of the refectory and The Moody Blues played a concert that lasted for an hour and a half. Subsequently we had Pink Floyd and The Who and these were all bands you couldn't dance to."

Bicknell made regular visits to London to meet booking agents and in the autumn of 1968 went to the Chrysalis Agency at 155 Oxford Street, where Peter Grant also had his office. "I was in the agency that was run by Kenny Bell and Richard Cowley and this huge figure shuffled into the booking department. I immediately recognised him as Peter Grant. He said, 'Hello young man. The New Yardbirds are playing at the Marquee tonight. Why don't you come down and see them?' He was trying to get the agents to come and see them too. And they were saying things like, 'Oh, fuck off Peter, we don't want to come and see your dodgy band.' "

Grant didn't give up. "Peter kept saying, 'You should come and see them because Jeff Beck is going to sit in,' " continues Bicknell. "This was the carrot! This was the band that hadn't quite metamorphosed into Led Zeppelin. Peter had done some sleight of hand whereby the name Yardbirds had been transferred from Relf, McCarty and Dreja into the willing hands of Jimmy Page. It was like a magician's trick whereby somehow Jimmy ended up owning the name. They were playing the contracted gigs and tidying up."

On October 15, 1968, the band hitherto known as The New Yardbirds played its first UK shows as Led Zeppelin at Surrey University. There was still some confusion over the name. Three days later, on October 18, the band made their début at the Marquee, at 90 Wardour Street, in central London, but they were billed once again as 'The New Yardbirds'. The manager of the club, John C. Gee, recalls Grant getting very excited about the gig. "He told me this was going to be a fantastic new group. He really had a lot of faith in them," says Gee. "But the group was very loud. I thought they were overpoweringly loud for the size of the Marquee. Anyway, the lads received an enthusiastic, but not overwhelming response from the audience."

Ed Bicknell: "Peter couldn't get anybody from the agency to go and see them. I was in London on my own so I went down to the Marquee and was astonished to see a queue right down Wardour Street and into Old Compton Street. There must have been 300 people standing in line. So I joined the end of the queue and eventually got in to see this gig. My memory was they didn't play many songs.

"Jimmy was banging away with the violin bow, so I guess they did 'Dazed And Confused' and they did a rock'n'roll medley at the end with some Little Richard and Elvis Presley numbers. On the strength of that I booked them to come up to Hull on a double bill with Jethro Tull, who were the headliners. Jethro Tull got £400 and that was big money. They played in the Mecca ballroom in Hull, as it was too expensive to put them on in the Student Union hall. I still have the contract for the New Yardbirds for £100 and I showed it to Peter years later. Peter had crossed out 'New Yardbirds' and written 'Lead Zeppelin' and signed it Peter

Grant. And then they cancelled. They didn't do the gig. They went to America instead."

It didn't matter to Ed because Jethro Tull had a hit album with *This Was* that week, the ballroom was packed and the student promoter did very well on the night. "We actually made money and usually we lost money! But I kept the Zeppelin contract with 'Lead' on it, which was how it was originally spelt. Peter told me years later that he was concerned that in America they would pronounce it 'Le-e-ed Zeppelin'. He knocked out the 'a' and rang Pagey up to say, 'I've done it "L-E-D".' That's how the name metamorphosed into that spelling. But what most interested me was that he couldn't get these hard-bitten agents to go and see his band! But he would have been philosophical about that."

While Peter was trying to enthuse the bookers, he also had another go at the music press. Keith Altham of the *New Musical Express* had turned down the chance of an interview with Jimmy Page, but at least he went along to see a show. He shared John Gee's opinion about their volume levels.

Keith: "When Led Zeppelin first started Peter invited me to the Elephant & Castle to see his band playing one of their first gigs. So I went along and they played about three numbers and they were deafening. Zeppelin was always loud, but in a tiny pub they were overpowering. I lasted the first few numbers and my ears were ringing. I couldn't stand it anymore, so I left. The following morning I got a call from Peter saying: 'Well, what did you think of my band?' So I said, 'To be honest with you Peter, I thought they were far too loud. They're brilliant musicians but they sound like four guys put together to make a band. It's all improvised rock without any structure. I can't see it myself.'

"Well of course every time I saw him after that it was: 'Well my band's doing quite well, despite what you thought of them.' By which time they had become the biggest band in the world. 'Still too loud for you Keith?' But I was never a Led Zeppelin fan. All those long guitar and drum solos used to bore me to death. I used to think, 'For fuck's sake, get to the song.' It was all too self-indulgent. 'Look how clever I am.'"

The band played their last 'New Yardbirds' date at Liverpool University on October 19, 1968. Three weeks later, on November 9, Led Zeppelin finally made their London début under their new name with a gig at the Middle Earth Club, which was then held at the Roundhouse, Chalk Farm. They earned the princely sum of £150 and got a standing ovation.

There were six more UK dates lined up, mostly pubs and clubs like The Richmond Athletics Club (November 29), another Marquee show (December 10) and the Fishmongers Arms, Wood Green (20).

When Zeppelin played at Exeter City Hall for £125 on December 19, their manager was en route to America, clutching the tapes for the first Led Zeppelin album, together with the completed artwork and some 'live' recordings from gigs. His plan was to secure a worldwide deal for Led Zeppelin. His old pal Mickie Most was watching all this frenzied activity with considerable interest.

"The deal was as simple as this. We financed the first album and Jimmy said he'd like to produce it, but as he'd never produced an album before, I would help out if he got lost and it wasn't going right. But that never happened at all. As soon as he got into the studio he did a brilliant job. I remember he came back with the first acetates. There were no cassettes in those days.

"I was up in the office at 155 Oxford Street when I heard the first tracks they had done and they were brilliant. We started making the album and then Atlantic heard what was going on. Peter had got hold of Ahmet Ertegun and he flew over and listened. We had the Jeff Beck albums on the charts in America – *Truth* and *Beckola* which were like forerunners to Led Zeppelin. *Truth* was a great album – which I made! Then I made the *Beckola* album, but Jimmy produced the first Led Zeppelin album, which I thought was brilliant. Then Peter went to Atlantic, they gave him a deal and the rest is history."

Mickie's recollection of events is slightly at odds with Peter's, but the crucial fact is that Grant caused a major upset amongst the moguls of the New York record industry. As The Yardbirds with Jimmy Page had been signed to Epic, part of Columbia, it was assumed that Jimmy's new band would re-sign with them. Columbia executive Dick Asher said later: "We at Columbia felt that Epic had done a really good job in promoting The Yardbirds. We thought we had done well by Jimmy Page. When we heard that The Yardbirds had split up and Jimmy had formed Led Zeppelin, we naturally assumed that the rights to Page would go automatically to Columbia, the other three being subject to mutual agreement. So Grant and Steve Weiss (Zeppelin's attorney), arrived in Clive Davis' office (President of Columbia) and we all sat down. It was Clive's first meeting with Peter Grant and we talked and talked about all sorts of things. It just went on and on but there was no mention of Led Zeppelin. Finally Clive said,

'Well, aren't we going to talk about Jimmy Page?' Grant replied, 'Oh no, we've already signed the Zeppelin to Atlantic.' "

It was explained that Page had never been signed as an individual to Columbia, only as part of The Yardbirds group. At this point Clive Davis went berserk. It turned out The Yardbirds had been one of his favourite projects. Said Dick Asher: "We were all stunned, especially after all we had done for the group."

Peter had been leading them on. It was the kind of scenario he relished. Behind their backs he'd signed a five-year contract with Atlantic Records, having negotiated a $200,000 advance with label bosses Ahmet Ertegun and Jerry Wexler. Grant wanted to sign with Atlantic because, he said, "They had a fantastic reputation and, of course, Cream had been on the label. The Ertegun brothers and Jerry Wexler owned the company and we shook on a deal. That's how it was back then. Ahmet was the finest record man of all time, and every time we negotiated he just said, 'Peter, shake on it,' and you knew it was done."

It was announced in the press that this was the highest advance ever paid to a new group. Quite whose decision it was to release this statement is not known, but if it was Peter's, then it must stand as a rare lapse of judgement since it led directly to charges that Led Zeppelin was a 'hype'. In the climate of the times, when hippies denounced 'breadheads' as the antithesis of everything the underground stood for, Led Zeppelin became tarred in the press as mercenaries, at least in America where *Rolling Stone* magazine, staffed by these very same idealists, was the epitome of cool. It was further claimed that the record company had never even seen the band, another questionable statement in view of prevailing trends. Surely, it was alleged, if a record label has signed a band it hadn't even seen, then there was the sniff of something resembling subterfuge, or 'hype' in the parlance of the times.

None of this reasoning took into account Led Zeppelin's unquestioned abilities as musicians. The tapes Ahmet Ertegun had heard were all he needed, together with the recommendation of many respected music biz figures. Dusty Springfield was among those who told Atlantic they should sign these upcoming English boys, as Peter Grant fondly remembered. "The story is that she was down at Jerry Wexler's house and he told her about this new group that was in the offing with Jimmy Page and John Paul Jones. She said she'd worked with Jonesy on arrangements and such like, and Jerry was knocked out."

Wexler wanted to sign the band purely on Dusty's recommendation and the fact that Jimmy was in the group. Said Peter: "We signed largely on the strength of Jimmy's name. At the time the deal was agreed in principle, there was no band. It was just Jimmy Page. Ahmet Ertegun and Jerry Wexler really believed in his talent. They said to me, 'You've got the deal. Just make sure the band is okay.' When we did eventually play Atlantic the album, I recall them saying they wanted to remix it. Jimmy said, 'What are they talking about?' But I said it's just politics. Tom Dowd was there and Jimmy foxed him with a few technical questions. That was an early battle we won."

At the same time Peter set up the Atlantic deal, he also established his own production and publishing companies, thus ensuring that the group took control over all the creative aspects of their business. Explained Peter: "We didn't sign direct to the label, we had a production company called Superhype. The title came from Jimmy, who was aware of the hype surrounding us at the time. So I did a tongue-in-cheek number and called it Superhype Music Inc. We sold off the publishing company some years later. The whole deal with Atlantic gave us various clauses that we were able to use in our favour." Not least, they could veto any publicity pictures of the band, which a nervous young advertising executive soon discovered.

When Andrew Sheehan, from *Melody Maker*'s advertising department, went to see Grant at his London office about booking an ad, he took with him a transparency of the band. Peter grasped the expensive 'tranny' between two fingers, took out a cigarette lighter and set fire to it. He then produced another one from his drawer and said, "*This* is the picture you're going to use."

The Grant revolution had begun.

Despite his severity with record companies and the media, Grant was quite relaxed about his business deals with Zeppelin. Says John Paul Jones: "Peter never had a contract with us. That was a very strange thing. In fact when Atlantic eventually found out, they nearly went mad. They said, 'You can't be serious.' But we just had a gentlemen's agreement. Much like I have with my record company now. We were signed to Atlantic, but we weren't signed to Peter. We never had a management contract. He got the normal management fees and royalties from the records as executive producer."

Mickie Most: "I never remember seeing a management agreement between Peter and Zeppelin. Peter and I were in business together and we never had a piece of paper either. We never had any serious problems. Peter would say, 'Well there's the management commission' and that was it. He used to do his thing and I did mine. There were never any fisticuffs."

John Paul Jones thought the arrangements with their manager were, "All pretty above board and as a result it was a really happy band. We could never believe how other bands got on. They never spoke to each other and travelled in separate cars. Why did they play together if it was that bad? Everybody thought *we* were the Prima Donnas, yet there was hardly an ounce of attitude in the whole band. Page and I had seen it all before. We just didn't want to make the obvious mistakes."

Col. Tom Parker once said, "I'm Elvis Presley's manager, because Elvis says I am." The same was true of Peter Grant and Led Zeppelin. Says Ed Bicknell: "Peter's first principle of management stated that it was him and the act – versus everybody else. The general philosophy in the Sixties was that the artist was at the very bottom of the economic totem pole. It was the unstated position of the record company and the publishers and the managers of the day.

"Peter didn't have a degree from a university, like so many of the managers who followed. His approach was instinctive and he'd be the first to say he made a few mistakes. But management is about flying by the seat of your pants.

"The most important thing for Peter was to believe in the act he was working with and he was absolutely dedicated to those artists. Peter absolutely believed in Jimmy and right up to the end of his life, they still spoke almost every week. It's important to remember that the music scene was much smaller than it is now and all the acts were interweaving and crossing. It was all the same people moving around in different bands. Peter was fascinated by the way I did management with Dire Straits. He observed my methods in complete disbelief and his conclusion was the way we had to operate in the Nineties was really boring – and he was dead right about that.

"He had no knowledge of law. I had a huge knowledge of law, which I picked up. He had no knowledge of the minutiae of record contracts. Peter's thing was to be with the band on the road, which was the bit that was the most fun. Nowadays, in every country you have to pay tax. In Peter's day, you put the money in the Hammond organ and you made a dash for the border. You can't do that any more. Now we have computerised ticketing. In those days you could get a bag of cash. It was a cash driven thing. I'm pretty sure that a certain amount of the financing for their operation came out of shoeboxes. 'Led Zeppelin shoe box money' was quite famous. Even The Beatles got paid in brown bags. Nowadays that's virtually impossible. Everything has to be very straight, which is also very tedious. But it means you don't get a bang on the door in the middle of the night from the Inland Revenue.

"This wasn't particularly a Zeppelin thing. It was the way bands operated in the UK and America in those days. He also made a conscious decision to go after the American market. Nowadays people wouldn't do that, because America is less interested in British music than at any point since The Beatles. They don't give a flying fuck! The idea that bands like Oasis are big in America is rubbish. If all the members of Oasis were on fire and they ran down Fifth Avenue, nobody would piss on them. With very few exceptions, there is no interest in British music. But in those days what influenced Peter's decision was that Led Zeppelin was essentially playing music that was derivative of American blues.

"There was also an underground scene developing, promoted by people like Bill Graham who had venues like The Fillmore and the Boston Tea Party where bands like Zep could play.

"The underground in Britain basically consisted of the college circuit, run by people like me, Mother's Club in Birmingham and the Marquee in London. There were few opportunities for bands like them to play and even less opportunity to get on the radio. So Peter made a pragmatic decision. He went where the action was. The funny thing about the deal with Atlantic was that he signed them to everywhere in the world, except for the UK. That's when he went to Pye Records in London and he was bemused that even Pye turned them down. In the end he basically gave the band to Atlantic in the UK and threw it in as part of the deal."

Immediately after Christmas 1968, Led Zeppelin was due to go to America to play for the first time. Peter Grant knew all too well that the future of the band depended on how well they performed in the States. He observed later: "Before we got the album out, we couldn't get work in Britain. It seemed to be a laugh to people that we were getting the group together. I don't want to name the people who put us down and thought we were wasting our time, but there were plenty of them."

The opportunity arose for Atlantic's latest signing to support Vanilla

Fudge and MC5. It meant travelling over Christmas and playing their first US show on December 26, 1968, in Denver, Colorado. Peter was nervous about asking the boys to give up their holiday but in the event they all jumped at the chance. Uncharacteristically, especially in view of the role that America would play in the Led Zeppelin saga, Peter Grant actually missed the group's first date on American soil: "I had to tell them to fly out on December 24 and I caught up with them at the Fillmore West. Robert Plant said that if we didn't make it there, then there was no hope, because The Yardbirds had a good following at the Fillmore."

A couple of days later, on December 28 they played at the Boston Tea Party, blowing the other bands off stage with a famously blistering set. Said John Paul Jones: "We played for hours. We did old Beatles numbers, Chuck Berry, anything. It was the greatest night. We knew we had definitely done it by then."

The American dates continued into January 1969, this first American tour having been arranged by Premier Talent, the major rock music booking agency run out of New York by Frank Barsalona. From his days with The Animals, The Yardbirds and the tour with Jeff Beck, Grant already knew which were the best cities to play. He also decided to concentrate on the West Coast, where rock and underground music were strongest. At the Fillmore West in San Francisco, they supported Country Joe & The Fish, an amiable bunch of anarchists whose 'Fish Cheer', a tirade against conscription and the Vietnam war, was very popular – but hardly a band with the firepower of Led Zeppelin. Somewhat predictably, American headliners were becoming wary about going on after these British lads. Meanwhile, their sets were getting longer and longer.

The Californian reaction to the band was overwhelming. To Grant's immense satisfaction, young American fans cheered and whooped with an enthusiasm that was a million miles away from the drab indifference of the folk at Wood Green's Fishmongers Arms. The knock-on effects were immediate. Recalled Peter: "The first album went on the charts at 98 just by FM radio play. The impact was incredible. I didn't expect it to happen so quickly but I just knew it would happen eventually because of the thrill of the music. Right from the first time I saw them play as a band in Copenhagen, I thought they were just wonderful. I wasn't so much concerned with the commercial success; it was the creative part that impressed me. I wanted to be part of it and made my mind up there and then that I would do everything for the band I possibly could. I was 100 per cent devoted to that band and there was no room for time wasters. In fact the music stood up so well we didn't need a publicist."

On February 1 the band played at Bill Graham's Fillmore East in New York City and Zeppelin found they could win over the East Coast fans as well. Heavy bands like Iron Butterfly ran for cover once they heard the thunder of Zeppelin in action. Said Peter: "Bill Graham really liked The Yardbirds and so I had a good relationship with Bill, which sadly deteriorated at the end. So Bill got us on at the Fillmore with Iron Butterfly. I knew a girl who worked with the band and she tipped me the wink that they had signed the contract for the show without knowing it was us they were up against. Sure enough, the kids were still shouting, 'Zeppelin, Zeppelin!' as Iron Butterfly walked on after our set. One up to us."

There was more joy to come. That same month the band's album shot higher up the *Billboard* charts, finally peaking at number 10 in May. The *NME*'s US correspondent June Harris wired the news to London: "The biggest happening of the 1969 heavy rock scene is Led Zeppelin! The reaction to the group's first tour here has not only been incredible, it's been nothing short of sensational."

Zeppelin were forging ahead. Nevertheless, the former members of the 'old' Yardbirds didn't harbour any bitterness over the success of the 'new' Yardbirds. Says Chris Dreja: "I remember in New York some years later, Peter Grant ringing me up and asking me to come and see the boys at Madison Square Garden. I went there in a time warp, having experienced Yardbirds gigs with dreadful PAs and equipment problems. I went to meet Zeppelin in their dressing room and they were charming, because they realised they owed us a helluva debt. Then they went up the concrete ramp to perform and I remember them going into 'Whole Lotta Love', and the whole building shook. I went out on the stage and heard the band blasting through some huge PA system to an audience of thousands and I was just astounded at the magnitude of it all. In two years the whole scene had changed. We never had those sophisticated, powerful PAs to interpret that music. It happened all of a sudden in 1969. I realised we had missed out, but it was all irrelevant because this was where it had progressed to."

Chris didn't think the original Yardbirds could have competed psychologically with Led Zeppelin, who seemed born to a life on the road. "I think everybody in our old band was a pretty sensitive, complex person. We were all a bit stiff upper lipped. We didn't even revel in our fame. We were terribly low key. We shied away from being stars."

Their successors were now well on the way to superstardom. Except back home in England, where Led Zeppelin were *still* playing pub venues like Klooks Kleek, Hampstead, and the Toby Jug, Tolworth. Peter Grant still had a whole lotta work to do.

5

"HELLO. IT'S PETER GRANT CALLING"

"[When] he was laying down the law to people, they would be visibly shaking.
People were actually terrified of him. He had this immense power to project strength.
I always found he was like a cuddly bear."

– Bill Harry

Peter Grant rolled his sleeves up over his bulging biceps, lit another cigarette and lifted the telephone. Strange how these days he always seemed to
be able to get through to whomsoever he wanted to speak. The mammoth
task that would reap both himself and Led Zeppelin undreamt of fame and
riches was meat and gravy to him, just the sort of challenge he revelled in,
and once Led Zeppelin had established a toehold in America there was no
stopping them. As word got back to Britain, promoters and agents at home
woke up to the presence of a rock'n'roll behemoth on their doorstep.
Peter was now in the enviable position of being able to say, "I told you
so."

During the early months of the band's success there was a rapid trans-
formation from studied apathy to frenzied hero worship. Yet it was untrue
that this was simply the result of 'media hype' or Grant's power to intimidate. The fans were the true arbiters of taste. They were buying the tickets
and queuing round the block at small English clubs like Hampstead's
Klooks Kleek long before critics or the industry were aware of the band's
existence.

Indeed, Zeppelin ran into a rather sniffy response from the rock estab-
lishment, especially in America, where an anti-Zep vibe lasted for years.
Rolling Stone was still describing Zeppelin as a "heavy metal beast" and a
"one-man band" dominated by Jimmy Page as late as 1977 and even called
John Paul Jones and John Bonham "the clumsiest rhythm section in rock".
It may have been hard to hear the acoustic numbers above the firecrackers,

or to appreciate Bonham's influence on the future of rock drumming from the back row of a packed stadium, but the broad range of Zeppelin's music and their understanding of dynamics should have been obvious from their albums alone.

This negative attitude towards Zeppelin fuelled Peter Grant's anger and mistrust of the media, presaging the edgy relationship that would exist for years. Peter once chased the British *NME* journalist Chris Hutchins around the Fairfield Halls, Croydon. Fellow scribe Keith Altham remembers the scene. "He had said something to upset Peter and he pursued him over the stalls. Chris was jumping them like hurdles, but Peter kept putting his foot on the rows of seats and they went down like dominoes." Peter's sense of humour often came to the rescue in such situations, and he was hostile only towards those press that he perceived as cynical or ignorant.

Indeed, he was quite happy for his charges to do occasional interviews and even took journalists on tour to see the fanatical response the band was getting from audiences all over Europe and the States. Despite his own often voiced protestations that he "didn't need a PR", he did employ his old mate Bill Harry from the New Oxford Street office to take care of the deluge of press enquiries. But he was never going to kowtow to "the papers". Journalists might well quake in their boots when their phones rang and those familiar nasal tones began to vibrate the earpiece. "Peter Grant here, now what the bloody 'ell do you mean by that write-up . . ." Usually he would resort to sarcasm rather than threats. When a gushing lady from the prestigious *Hollywood Reporter* said, "I must call you at the hotel tomorrow to get some interesting facts," he told her, "Ring me at midday and I'll tell you something really boring." As far as Peter was concerned "being boring" was almost as great a sin as trying to rip off his band. Peter recalled that the lady journalist "swept out of the reception in a great long dress".

Zeppelin concentrated their early touring in America, ably assisted by Frank Barsalona at Premier Talent, an arrangement that played a significant part in the band's success. After their early dates with Vanilla Fudge Zeppelin went on to the Fillmore West in San Francisco, where they supported Country Joe & The Fish. This was the night when Robert Plant introduced the group at the beginning of 'How Many More Times' and someone in the audience shouted, "And who are you?" Plant and Page enthralled fans by spinning out their erotic 'call and response' blues routines. Indeed the reaction to Robert's howling vocals and Jimmy's wailing guitar was so frenzied that audiences joined in the caterwauling and the Fillmore concerts began to resemble nights in the jungle or feeding time at the zoo. Many Zeppelin fans claimed these were their most exciting shows – ever. There were many such highlights during the band's first full year on the road.

The workload was punishing. They packed in four US and three UK tours as well as trips to Europe, and Peter Grant was at every one, prowling around backstage, sorting out problems, overseeing the road crew and checking the gate money. "He was a roadie at heart," says writer Johnny Rogan, the author of *Starmakers And Svengalis*, the authoritative book on British rock management. "Some managers sit behind desks, dealing with paperwork and pay others to be on the road with their bands. Grant wasn't like that. He loved the road."

In addition to the many live shows, Led Zeppelin recorded sessions for radio and TV and were filmed for an all-star movie called *Supershow,* shot on March 25, 1969, at a studio in Staines, Middlesex, alongside such diverse artists as Roland Kirk, Stephen Stills and Buddy Guy. The completed movie was denied a cinema showing by short-sighted distributors, who actually walked out of a preview. Rare colour footage of Zeppelin's almost frantic performance on the show is now regularly shown on the cable TV channel VH1.

In October, Zeppelin flew to Paris to record a TV show where they were invited to a party by French record boss Eddie Barclay. Grant was uneasy about both these projects, which he thought were more trouble than they were worth, particularly the *Supershow*.

Grant: "That was down to a mate of Jimmy's who buttonholed us into doing that. I wasn't that keen. I didn't even go down to the filming. As for the French TV – that was another difficult one. They never knew how to get the sound right in a TV studio. The thing I most remembered about France was the Eddie Barclay party when we didn't play because we couldn't get the gear in the place. Jimmy only wanted to go so he could meet Brigitte Bardot. Anyway we didn't play live but all the papers gave us great reviews next day, presuming we had. That was a laugh."

Much of Grant's mistrust of TV as a medium was based on what he perceived as the failings of television in-house producers and sound engineers. A British ITV producer approached him about making a 'special' featuring the band. "We already had two hit albums," recalled Peter. "I didn't really want to do his show anyway. If I had I wouldn't have done it when he ended the conversation with: 'It sounds like a lot of demands from your side. Tell me, have Led Zeppelin got their own backing group?' "

During that hectic year they also appeared at various festivals including the Newport Jazz Festival, on July 6, 1969, when thousands of Zep fans blocked all roads to the site and almost caused their appearance to be cancelled by the police. It is an event recalled with dread by the band's hapless British PR who found himself trapped in the mayhem.

Bill Harry: "Cor, the problems I had there. Oh my God! The band was fine but it was everything that went on around them. My job basically as a PR was to keep the press away. Peter wasn't interested in the band doing interviews. I'd present him with a list of requests from magazines and he'd say, 'No, no, no.' He might let some of the underground magazines talk to them like *Friendz*. He wasn't even interested in having them on TV. He wanted to make them superstars that nobody could get near, rather like movie stars today. But in those days pop stars would do anything for publicity. Peter just wasn't interested. He'd say 'no' to everything. Yet it wasn't really so hard for me, because I was hired to speak to the press and act like a filter."

Bill was advised that the press could come to gigs, of course, and review the shows and they might even grab a chat with one of the band, but official interviews were supposedly 'out'. However, this wasn't really the situation as each case was taken on its merits and there was no block on coverage by prestige publications that could advance the cause of the band's career and image. In fact a young lady reporter from *Life* magazine had been sent on assignment to cover the band's second US tour, which had begun in New York in April, 1969. She had travelled with them to Chicago and Detroit and seen at first hand the kind of pressure the band was under from groupies, fans and the sometimes hostile 'real world' of snooty hotel guests, cab drivers and belligerent passers by. She had felt great sympathy for Led Zeppelin and believed she had a good relationship with them, until she was attacked and had her dress ripped when she called by to wish them farewell at the Fillmore East, New York, on the last night of the tour (May 31). Peter Grant came to the rescue as she 'fought them off'. She later wrote an insightful account of the tour, but added a damning postscript, expressing bitterness and anger at her treatment. "If you walk inside the cages of the zoo you get to see the animals close up, stroke the captive pelts and mingle with the energy behind the mystique.

You also get to smell the shit first hand."

This was not the kind of press coverage the management and record company had in mind when they discreetly co-ordinated publicity campaigns for the supposedly 'underground' act that never gave interviews. However, their PR Bill Harry dutifully arrived in New York in July 1969, perhaps unaware of events on the previous tour, but unlikely to have been surprised. He based himself at Loews Midtown Motor Inn, where he also acted as PR for Jethro Tull and Ten Years After. "A lot of things went on in the hotels with all the British bands that I can't reveal, even now, because they were so outrageous," he says.

When Led Zeppelin was booked to play Newport, Bill was supposed to go there and wait for the band to arrive. He was booked into a hotel on Rhode Island. As all the expenses were to be paid by Zeppelin, he didn't have much cash with him. The hotel was full of jazz artists and celebrities and Bill and his wife Virginia were impressed by the glamour of the surroundings. If they felt uneasy about the escalating hotel bill, they were reassured by the knowledge that Peter Grant was on his way and would take care of the tab. Then it was announced on the radio that Led Zeppelin's appearance at the festival had been cancelled as the authorities were alarmed at the dangerous situation the band were creating. Tens of thousands of rock fans were descending on the festival site and were blocking the roads. The group had been asked not to appear. Bill and Virginia thought they were stranded, unable to pay the hotel bill or even get back home to England. "We didn't have any contact numbers and didn't know where Zeppelin were in America. We were sweating! Then I got a phone call from Peter who said, 'Everything's fine, we're coming.'"

Bill Harry then went on radio to say to all the fans, "Yes, Led Zeppelin *are* coming to Newport, don't worry."

The show turned out to be one of the most memorable of an already memorable summer. Zep put on a stunning performance, despite all the pre-gig hassles. They played 'The Train Kept A Rollin'', 'I Can't Quit You', 'Dazed And Confused' and 'You Shook Me'. Beset by PA problems, Robert Plant had to sing without a microphone for much of the time and the band were reduced to playing 'Communication Breakdown' as an instrumental. Even so, Robert screamed his famed 'Ooh-Ah' duet with Jimmy's guitar on 'How Many More Times', to the delight of fans.

One member of the audience was less than delighted when he found he had been robbed. Bill Harry: "I was very silly because I'd put all the money I had into my wallet. Then I suddenly found it was gone. I'd been pickpocketed. I went to see the police and they weren't interested. Peter sorted everything out and got me back to New York and we travelled around the States with Zeppelin for a while and went to the Spectrum at Philadelphia, which was also the scene of much mayhem. It was a hairy time.

"I do remember a party at a posh Newport hotel after the show. All the jazz greats like Buddy Rich were sitting around and we had a table, knocking back the lagers. Then Bonzo and Richard Cole got up on the table and started dancing and all the 'jazz greats' left the room. So Richard went to the fridge and took out all the cans of lager and loaded them up in a sack. 'Let's go back to Bonzo's room.' He was dragging this sack like Santa Claus. Then we stopped and looked out in the car park. We could see a bare arse moving up and down. And it was one of the group with a girl in a car. We went up to the room and a detective followed us because we had a couple of girls with us. Richard slipped him a few dollars and he vanished. So we went into the room and one of the boys went to say something to one of the girls and he was sick all over her."

The party was over and everyone hastily withdrew to their own rooms.

When Led Zeppelin was in town it was party night, every night. Even their manager began to be drawn into the fun, although he had his work cut out dealing with police, security guards, promoters, roadies, bootleggers, scalpers, groupies and hangers-on. A relaxed drink with the band locked in the safety of the hotel rooms was a luxury, while outside screaming girls were climbing up the walls in desperation to befriend their satin clad, bare chested idols.

It all became a blur as night after night the group played themselves into a state of exhaustion at convention centres, sports arenas, clubs and theatres across America. In October they played at Carnegie Hall in New York, the home of classical and jazz music. The previous year they were an underground band. Now they were hailed as the pop and rock sensation of the age. Everyone wanted to grab a piece of the action. Where once Grant had begged people to come to see his boys, now he had to fight them off. He also had to reassure and motivate the highly strung, exhausted musicians as they faced the temptations of an unreal existence.

First there was the nightly adrenalin rush of the show; the screaming hero-worship that accompanied their every move. Then came the downside: threats, abuse and jealousy. When the band played at the Grande

Ballroom, a converted mattress warehouse in Detroit, Robert Plant went out for a walk in the street, hoping to do some shopping. As he crossed the street a motorist skidded to a halt, drew up beside him and spat in his face. Robert was appalled. Such incidents shattered his confidence. He couldn't help but wonder whether he was up to the job, or whether his role as vocalist was properly appreciated – by the fans or the group themselves.

When tempers frayed there were even disputes between him and his old mate John Bonham. Jimmy Page was often ill and Bonham became terribly homesick. Yet Grant had to keep the juggernaut on the road. There was too much at stake to let it all go under. He became a man under siege. It was hardly surprising he lost his cool under pressure.

When his young son Warren was old enough to be taken on tour with the band, he had a child's eye view of father in action. "He always looked after the crew as well as the band, including the lighting and sound engineers. But I saw him steam into people a few times," says Warren. "If anyone messed the band around, he'd give them a right bollocking or prod them with his finger. He was always doing that! It was something he learnt to do as a wrestler. He'd occasionally give people a slap. There was some sort of way of cupping your hands, so it would sound really bad, but it didn't actually do very much! There were advantages in being that size. He was over six foot three as well as being overweight, so he was quite an imposing figure. The only times he'd really lose his temper was if someone was trying to rip off the band. Anything to do with bootlegging T-shirts or records would upset him. If he found out something hadn't been done right, then he'd deal with it himself. Most managers would send somebody else to sort out a problem. He would wade in and sort it out himself straight away. He wouldn't use other people to do his dirty work."

Parts of America still resembled the Wild West, with criminal elements involved in various aspects of the music business. Grant, with his south London underworld connections, understood the art of bluff. On more than one occasion he found himself facing down recalcitrant US concert promoters who were reluctant to hand over the cash after a concert. One time Peter was collecting a modest thousand dollars in cash which had been left lying in front of him in a pile on a table. It was like a dare – to see if he'd try to take the money from the promoter, who wanted to keep it.

Grant: "I said, 'I've come for the thousand dollars you owe me' and the guy said, 'You're not getting it.' So I said, 'You ain't leaving this caravan pal until you give me the money.' He pulled a gun on me and I said, 'I don't care what you've got. You're going to pay me that thousand dollars.' He then said, 'I'm gonna shoot you.' I said, 'I very much doubt if you are going to shoot me for a thousand dollars. Don't be so fucking cheap.'" Grant picked up the money in both hands and walked out without turning back.

He was no stranger to such situations. As a former minder, bouncer and 'bag man' he'd often been called on to confront heavies or provide a degree of intimidation himself. According to the memories of some former security men, Grant had a history of using strong-arm tactics as far back as the Fifties. During such moments a dark shadow would pass over his face and he became an angry, dangerous and vengeful man. He may have been feted as a new captain of the music industry, but there were plenty who had reason to fear and dislike him. He had his rivals too, and there were those who felt that his power was purely down to the success of his band. There was the unspoken feeling that he only had to make one slip and they would be down on him, ready to usurp his position. This lingering, silent threat led to a heightened sense of mistrust which escalated over the years into a form of paranoia. Like most manipulative people, he could be suspicious and hostile, assuming that everyone around him was 'on the make'. Then it was his job to be alert, to second-guess people's motives. Doubtless there were times when his suspicions were entirely justified, but on other occasions it seemed that Peter Grant was unnecessarily obsessed with maintaining his grip on power.

As a result he appeared to many outsiders as a coarse, harsh tongued and threatening man, at odds with a music scene wherein youthful performers and an increasing number of switched-on promoters had eagerly adopted the high-flown idealism of the hippie era. For 'bootlegging' read 'freedom'. Although Led Zeppelin had superseded such bands as Love and The Jimi Hendrix Experience, it was still the era of 'free concerts', love, peace and communal living. Quite how Peter reconciled this attitude and lifestyle with his own deeply protective and basic materialist instincts was something of a mystery. But at least he made an attempt to fit in. He exchanged his old shirts and ties for a caftan and beads. He made an unlikely hippie, but he felt comfortable about the loins as he waded into those promoters still grumbling about his *modus operandi*.

Many of his predecessors had experienced difficulties trying to promote their acts in America. Their gentlemanly behaviour simply didn't wash. An oft-cited example of mismanagement is Brian Epstein's problems with

The Beatles, specifically his inexperience with regard to merchandising which led him to virtually give away valuable rights in this area. The Beatles' merchandising fiasco preyed on Epstein's already fragile psyche, inspired numerous lawsuits and cost him and the group untold millions of dollars. Though Grant took little interest in subsidiary merchandising, he was quick to pounce if he discovered anyone selling unauthorised Led Zeppelin T-shirts or photographs. This being the era before merchandising became such a money-spinner for top acts, for most of their career there was no such thing as 'authorised' Led Zep T-shirts, other than those given away free by their record company. Grant was also keen to remind commentators that he had seen how the US market worked during his tours with The Animals and The Yardbirds, and fully understood the ground rules. Unlike Epstein, he wasn't about to be conned by sharp American businessmen who saw Led Zeppelin only as a cash cow.

Chris Dreja of The Yardbirds was one of those British artists who appreciated that Peter was on their side and at the same time, fully cognisant of American business practice. "A lot of managers didn't discuss money with their artists, not necessarily because they were ripping them off but they themselves were very naïve," he says. "They didn't understand how the Americans worked and they didn't know about transportation costs or withholding taxes in different States. Peter had learned all about that before he began to manage Zeppelin. He was a streetwise, sharp cookie."

Mickie Most understood the kind of problems Grant faced in America and the need to be on guard. "I don't think he was involved with gangsters," says Most today. "He was a sweetheart really. All that stuff about being a muscle man and beating people up . . . it was all nonsense really. It was more bravado. I only ever had one argument with him and that was in the days of The Animals and it almost came to fisticuffs. We laughed about it afterwards. 'What are we doing?' In those days I admit we did use a bit of old-fashioned scare tactics. But nobody had any guns. It was handbags at ten paces really. You had to use scare tactics sometimes because there weren't the rules around there are today to protect artists. They used to get ripped off terribly. Record companies are notorious for being thieves. They never paid you too much. It was always too little. They are dishonest! Not *all* record companies of course, but I can't think of too many that are not. The bigger they are the worse they are."

Most points out that today's artists are now responsible for their recording costs, but they never own the tapes. "So they pay for them, but they don't own them. Think about it. 'You've just paid for that car. But you don't own it. Do you like that?' Of course you wouldn't like it. Not only that, the artist has to pick up fifty per cent of the bill for promotion. So they pay for the recording costs, the video and any promotional costs, which could be up to a million dollars, especially in America where you have to give the radio stations money to play the records. So you sell three million albums – but you're still in trouble. Peter wouldn't allow that to happen. He'd say: 'We made the records and we paid for 'em. We want paying from record one.' And that's what happened."

Most is at pains to point out that the way Peter managed Led Zeppelin was at odds with the way many current pop groups are exploited. "The record companies today deduct everything. They send a car for you? They deduct it. They send someone to take you to *Top Of The Pops*? It's being deducted. Can't you get to a TV studio on your own? You need someone to take you? It's ridiculous! Go on a bus. 'Oh no, I've gotta have a limo to take me and I've got to have a make-up artist, a dresser and a stylist.' You mean to say you can't dress yourself? Who takes you to the toilet these days? Grow up!' "

Although some dubious record company practices still exist, Mickie Most insists that Grant made a difference; certainly to the way bands continue to earn income from their all-important live performances. "Peter changed the industry. He could dictate. He really was the 90/10 guy. Before that it was 60/40. He said, '90/10, take it or leave it.' 'Waal we've gotta promote the show . . .' 'Promote it? You don't have to promote Led Zeppelin. Just take an advert in the *Jewish Chronicle*. Face it; you didn't have to put up any posters for Led Zeppelin. Just announce on the radio that they're playing at Madison Square and an hour later there won't be a ticket to be had. So what is the "promoting" about? You're gonna get ten per cent for just turning up.'

"So he turned it from 60/40 to 90/10. Peter didn't care really. He cared about what he was doing, but he didn't care about how he did it! He didn't have any great conscience about anything. If he had to be aggressive and tough he would. The Americans are the toughest business people in the world. We are pansies compared to them. But he stood up to them because he had product. He said, 'I want the best for my band.' The Americans had never met anyone like him before. I remember him talking to Bill Graham, who had the biggest venues in rock. He'd say to him, 'It's 90/10 or you don't fucking get Led Zeppelin.' I'd be sitting there listening to the conversation and the phone would ring again. I'd hear Bill Graham say, 'How about 80/20?'

" 'What, are you deaf? It's 90/10'. He'd put the phone down. Then Bill would phone back. 'Okay, you've gotta deal.' Then it became normal practice. Everyone now does that. Peter Grant started it. If you've gotta band you are trying to break, you give 'em 50/50. The promoter has got to try and fill the venue with people who don't really wanna come. That's promoting. So they deserve every penny. But when you just have to whisper 'Led Zeppelin' and it's sold out in an hour, well you don't need to promote. Even at 10%, if they took a million dollars at the box office, they've got a hundred thousand bucks for doing absolutely nothing! All they have to do is announce on the local radio that Led Zeppelin will be playing at the Cow Palace on May 14. An hour later, every ticket is sold.

"Did Peter need to act tough? Well every now and then some guy would come up with a gun and wanna shoot him. 'So fucking shoot me then. Go on!' He used to front them out. Peter Grant was good at that. 'Go on. Shoot me. If you're not gonna shoot me, put the fucking thing away.' That happened quite often. I remember being backstage and a guy pulled a gun on us and we started to laugh. It's laughable really, like playing cowboys and Indians. But the people who did all this stuff, we knew wouldn't really shoot us. But the ones who really would do it, wouldn't get an argument. Fortunately the guys who were into promoting rock concerts – they weren't gangsters. Record companies? Strike a hard deal but don't fuck around with them. Some of them are connected."

Most can recall that many record companies in America had their origins in the jukebox business, which began in the Forties. "The Mob ran the jukeboxes," he says. "They'd go into a place and say, 'You don't want a jukebox? You're having one.' They'd put them in all the cafés and bars and then they'd say, 'We're putting in all these juke boxes, why don't we own the records as well?' So they started record companies and that's why they are all so gangster-ish.

"When I first went to America in the early Sixties, the heads of the record companies were all tough guys like Morris Levy who owned Roulette Records. He was one of the first people I went to see in New York with my three records. I went to see all the record companies and couldn't get a deal with any of them. I went to Philadelphia and Los Angeles and I couldn't get them released. They weren't interested.

"Eventually I got them released and they all went to number one. So that shows you what they knew. The records were by The Animals, The Nashville Teens* and Herman's Hermits. They were the three records I took to America in 1964. I wasn't asking for any big money. 'Just put 'em out!' They couldn't see it at all. I wasn't impressed because I realised they didn't know. The Beatles were only just breaking, they weren't up to speed. I was just surprised they didn't know.

"In Peter's case, even as the manager of a big rock group, there are area you don't go wandering down. It's a difficult thing and you don't need it. There are some serious people in the music business, especially now in rap music. That's a whole new phase. Now they really kill each other. You wouldn't want to fuck around with them. At least, I wouldn't! There's money in music and where there's money there's crime."

In planning his battle front strategy, Grant wasn't a one-man army. He had his able-bodied assistant Richard Cole who had now been joined by another likely lad, Clive Coulson. He could certainly rely on Richard to sort out difficult people and situations on his behalf. After working with Grant on The New Vaudeville Band and The New Yardbirds, Cole was back in the fold just in time for Zeppelin's early tours of America, but even he was daunted by the job in hand. The logistics were alarming and the pressures enormous. The band had to be ready to cover vast distances in short spaces of time. You didn't miss a gig because that would have meant having to apologise – and Peter Grant was never one for saying sorry.

Road crews had to be marshalled; equipment set up and taken down and shipped out each night. He had to ensure the band's security and travel arrangements and get everyone from gig to hotel and on to the next city. He was rough and tough but everyone agreed, Richard was the man for the job. And he took pride in his work on behalf of 'G' – his ultimate boss.

"Peter had a master plan and he did a lot of smart things," says Cole. "Zeppelin was moving so fast I had to come up with ideas for him and virtually design how touring was done. That's when we decided to hire a private jet and base ourselves in one city, stay in one hotel and just fly in and out. We were the first British band to bring our own gear to America. Most people used to rent and you never got what you wanted. When our bands started using Marshall equipment, Marshall hadn't even

* 'Tobacco Road', The Nashville Teens only *Billboard* Top 40 entry, actually only reached number 14.

rrived in America. So we brought in everything ourselves."

As well as blitzing the States with gigs, the band understood the impor-
ance of US radio. "In those days it was primarily AM radio and FM had
nly just come out," says Cole. "So they could play the *whole* of Zep's first
lbum on FM. That's why Peter didn't want to release singles, so people
vould have to buy the album. We did one or two television shows, but
ecause the sound was so bad, we would never do anymore TV shows
fter that. Peter said if you wanted to see the boys, you had to go to a
oncert. He had a lot of shrewd ideas, believe me."

Bill Harry confirms the view of Grant as a mover and shaker in the bur-
eoning rock business. "Promoters had always ripped off artists for years.
'eter changed all that. He had the vision. Just as The Beatles changed the
ace of pop music, so Led Zeppelin made many innovations. Peter really
ooked after the band and made sure they weren't fiddled or screwed. He
vent out of his way to get the highest percentage from the gate and he was
tough negotiator."

During the first year of heavy US touring Led Zeppelin's fees continued
o rise dramatically. When they first played at the Kinetic Playground in
Chicago on February 7 and 8, 1969, they earned $7,500. When they
eturned to the same venue on May 23/24 of the same year they were
etting $12,500 a night. Jimmy Page enthused about his manager's negoti-
ting skills in a 1969 interview. "The new system is to put groups on a per-
entage of the gate money and we drew $37,000 from one amazing gig in
os Angeles."

By the middle of 1969, less than a year after Led Zeppelin were formed,
Grant knew he could guarantee to sell out any venue, and so he was able
o impose his 'take it or leave it' deal for the promoters. After Zeppelin got
0 per cent of the gross, the promoter was left to pay his expenses and take
profit out of the remaining ten per cent.

Peter rationalised the new arrangements: "The days of the promoter
iving a few quid to the group against the money taken on the door are
one. Managers, agents and promoters ran the business when the funny
hing is it's the groups who bring the people in. I thought the musicians
hould be the people who get the wages. We take the risks. We pay the rent
f the hall, we pay the local supporting groups and we pay the promoter to
et it up for us. That's the way big names are made these days. Not by the
ress, but by people seeing them and making up their own minds."

Grant's much vaunted philosophy and his attitude towards management

policy was, he claimed, based on 'handshakes and trust' rather than highl
detailed contracts. He saw Zeppelin as a kind of personal crusade. As h
once explained: "A manager needs real enthusiasm; belief in the band, thei
music and the people. You can't just think, 'This is great, I can make }
amount of money.'" Whatever his behaviour in situations that called fo
strong-arm tactics, he saw himself as a man of principle in a sea of sharks.

Observed Ahmet Ertegun: "Peter put his artists on a pedestal. Thei
word, their wish, their music, that was the most important thing in hi
life."

Grant: "In the old days everybody thought the artist worked for th
manager. In America they'd say: 'Oh, so and so owns those people.' You
don't *own* artists. They hire you and give you a percentage of their mone
to do your very best for them."

Matching his policy of obtaining the best deals was his determination t
avoid old-fashioned methods of promotion. Refusing to allow Zeppelin'
Atlantic Records to release singles could be compared – in the current er
– to refusing to co-operate with MTV; in other words commercia
suicide. Explained Peter: "The reason we decided not to put singles ou
was because of that trip you had to go through. It was also such an E
Greaso job! You had to go and wine and dine all these people and all tha
crap and they weren't even keen on anything that didn't sound poppy.
think Led Zeppelin failed their audition.

"As long as the people wanted to see you, you were all right, and that'
the way it should be. If musicians are talented, why should they have to d
a grease job on the media?"

In October 1969 Led Zeppelin's second album was released with advanc
orders of over 400,000. The fact that it was called simply *Led Zeppelin II*
and not some clever title, further reflected Grant's basic approach t
everything surrounding the band. It leapt straight to number two in th
UK album charts and before long was topping the LP charts in both th
US and UK.

The first album had already gone gold and both eventually achieve
platinum status. The following month Peter appeared to have bowed t
commercial pressure when the album's standout track 'Whole Lotta Love
was released as a single by Atlantic, albeit only in the States. It was a
edited version, cut by two minutes to make it suitable for US radio play. I
got to number four in the *Billboard* chart in January 1970.

It would have been logical to put the single out in England but Peter and the band had other ideas, enforcing their 'no singles' policy, at least at home, where they had more control over Atlantic. Phil Carson was in charge of the London office and had already made plans to release 'Whole Lotta Love' in the UK. Then he got a phone call from Peter Grant. *" 'Ere Phil, it's Peter here. What the bloody 'ell do you think you're doing . . .'*

Speaking to Carson with a directness that left no room for discussion, Grant emphasised that 'no way' did they want a single out. He advised Carson to check with Ahmet Ertegun in New York. The agreement with Atlantic stipulated he had the right to say whether singles could be released or not. Those singles that had already been pressed had to be swiftly recalled and destroyed.

Recalled Peter Grant years later: "That was down to Phil Carson. He came to the office and told me he had pressed five hundred copies and they had been shipped to Manchester. I said, 'Look – we don't do singles.' He was a bit pushy in those days. I said, 'Have you told Ahmet?' He promptly called him and there were red faces all round. Our contract clearly stated we had the last say on such decisions."

A press release was put out stating that Zeppelin would be recording a 'special single' instead of releasing 'Whole Lotta Love'. "It was just a cover-up," admitted Grant later. "We never ever went in just to record a single. That was the golden rule. No singles. I could never understand why he only pressed five hundred. I mean, thanks for your confidence in us, Phil!"

Grant's stubborn attitude towards singles was matched by his approach towards Zeppelin film footage. He was adamant that many of the films made of the band during their early years would never be shown. If he or the band was unhappy with the quality, they stayed in the can. One such event was the Royal Albert Hall concert on January 9, 1970, which was filmed for posterity but never reached the screen. Explained Grant: "We filmed that and some of the Bath Festival. The wrong speed film was used and it came out too dark. So that was no use."

As well as battling record executives, Peter was still taking on those promoters who didn't fully acquiesce to the idea of giving up such a large percentage of the take. One man, who thought he could pull a fast one over Zeppelin's formidable manager, was quickly disabused of this idea.

Peter: "We had to watch the promoters. I remember we caught one guy fiddling on a date we did with Jethro Tull. I went out front to see what the crowds were like. The box office was on a corner. This guy was taking five dollars from the fans in the queue and selling them tickets [so as to avoid using the box office]. So I took my rings off, joined the line and as it came to my turn I shouted 'Gotcha!' and took him back to the dressing room and had him empty his pockets and took every last dime and nickel from him. He didn't do it again.

"We went to the States a lot that year [1969] and we did loads of festivals. We had a falling out with Blood Sweat & Tears. They wouldn't come off. So I stood on the steps and nobody got through until they cleared off. I recall another row with Chicago Transit Authority or whatever they were called. I used to say to our boys on these big bills: 'Tear the place apart, take the roof off. I don't want to see you afterwards unless you succeed.' That normally got the required response."

Says Bill Harry: "Peter had this image and people said he was ferocious and terrible, but throughout all the years I knew him he was always very polite and thoughtful. He made sure there were no problems and he was a complete gentleman. He was good company and always smiling. And yet when we went to gigs like the Royal Albert Hall and he was laying down the law to people, they would be visibly shaking. People were actually terrified of him. He had this immense power to project strength. I always found he was like a cuddly bear. But theatre managers and staff were in awe of him when he went marching backstage. He would come in and demand things and if they weren't done properly he'd soon let them know. In the States he always insisted that the promoters gave the band the best rooms and the best food. He would stand no nonsense.

"But it didn't always work out, even for Peter. I remember we were booked into the best hotel in Amsterdam and they were appalled at Led Zeppelin's hair and clothes. They refused to allow them into the hotel. So we had to go to another one out of town. Same reaction. Peter had to talk them into letting us stay. Zeppelin were allowed in but only if they wouldn't eat their meals in the restaurant. Everything had to be served in the rooms."

As they sat incarcerated in their hotel room John Bonham began getting very frustrated. Bill: "People don't realise how very tedious it can be sitting around waiting for hours and hours in recording studios, concerts, airport lounges and hotel rooms, waiting for some action to start. Sitting all day in a hotel, the band felt like prisoners. You can feel the stress building up. They wanted to tear their hair out."

The room was equipped with a large radio set for guests and Bonham began playing with it, trying to get an English station so he could listen to some news or music. He switched the channels around and he couldn't get what he wanted. "In the end he kicked the whole thing to smithereens," says Bill. So began the first steps on the road to a policy of complete hotel destruction.

By the end of 1969 Grant's poll-winning band were showered with gold albums. Sales of $5,000,000 worth of records in the US alone, coupled with the high royalty deal that Peter had negotiated from Atlantic, enabled them to buy country homes and estates. Peter himself, who by now had moved his family from Norwood to Shepherds Bush, began looking at property on an upmarket estate in Purley, south of Croydon.

At the start of 1970 the group began a short British tour, which included the Royal Albert Hall show. During February and March they toured Europe and played at the Montreux Jazz Festival. A fifth North American tour began in March, which included 27 dates and grossed $800,000. The group now had ten roadies in tow and during the Southern States stretch of the trip, they had to employ eight bodyguards to protect them from gun toting rednecks.

And after a rare trip to Reykjavik, the capital of Iceland, on June 22, they flew back to England to play a blockbusting show in front of 200,000 fans at the Bath Festival at Shepton Mallet, Somerset, for local promoter Freddie Bannister. It was a show that would long remain in the memories of fans and all those associated with the band. Grant was absolutely determined his boys would blow all the other groups off stage and he took pains to ensure they had the optimum conditions amidst the competitive atmosphere. It was considered so important that Zeppelin had turned down offers to play at Boston and Yale, US gigs worth $200,000.

For British fans the Bath Festival was the first opportunity to see Led Zeppelin playing a full-length set at an outdoor show. It was also the first time many local music business folk got an eyeful of their manager, who seemed to have taken over control of the festival from the promoter, at least during the hours immediately before, during and after his act was playing.

Grant planned his campaign carefully. "I went down to the site unbeknown to Freddie Bannister and found out from the Meteorological Office what time the sun was setting. It was going down right behind the stage. By going on at sunset I was able to bring the stage lights up a bit at a time. And it was vital we went on stage at the right time. That's why I made sure the previous band Flock, or whoever they were, got off on time."

Among those who witnessed the traumatic scenes at the side of the stage was an open-mouthed young reporter from *Melody Maker*. Chris Charlesworth, soon to become the paper's news editor and later its American correspondent, would come to enjoy privileged access to the band and travel extensively with them across America. But his first taste of Zeppelinmania took place deep in the heart of the Somerset countryside.

Says Charlesworth: "The first time I met Peter Grant was at the Bath Festival in 1970. I was hanging about backstage and there was an incident. The band were due on stage on Sunday night at 8 p.m. which Grant correctly assumed was the time when the sun would be going down behind them and would make a nice setting on stage. The trouble was the previous group were overrunning. They were the American band Flock, led by a violinist called Jerry Goodman. When they came to the end of a song at about 8 p.m. they still had more songs to go – and an encore. So Grant led his team of roadies onto the stage and he started unplugging their equipment. 'Hey, we haven't finished yet man,' said Flock's crew. 'Oh yes you fuckin' have,' shouted Peter. There was a stand-off between the two sides but Flock's roadies took one look at Led Zep's gang, led by Grant and Richard Cole, and decided there was no way they were gonna fight these guys. So Zeppelin came on a few minutes after 8 p.m. just as the sun was setting.

"Whenever Zeppelin did a show, Peter was in charge, not the promoter. As the manager of the headlining act, he just took control. The attitude was – his band were attracting 200,000 people to the festival – if it wasn't for him the show wouldn't happen."

As it turned out Peter Grant didn't have too much to worry about, even if his tactics at manhandling Flock off stage seemed more than a tad unfriendly to these American visitors. Grant: "We hadn't got anything to lose as we'd already been paid £20,000 upfront! Bath was a turning point in terms of recognition for us. It was a great day. I remember Jonesy arriving by helicopter with Julie Felix and his wife Mo and we had to get the Hells Angels to help us get them on site. I'd made a contact with the American Hells Angels in Cleveland with The Yardbirds, so we had no bother with them."

The band was accorded five encores by the massive festival audience and the music press acclaimed their triumph. The following month the band went to Germany for a tour where they broke all attendance records, including the show where 11,000 fans packed into the Frankfurt Festhalle.

Peter Grant and Jimmy Page took time out from the mayhem to visit the town's flea market, where they looked out for items of antique furniture and art nouveau. Away from the gigs, the groupies and the parties, the band and their manager were often quiet, contemplative and far more concerned with domestic matters at home. If they had broken up in 1970 they would still have been able to look back on a remarkable success story and remained happy, healthy and sane. But they had another decade to go and much more music to make. Given their workload during these early years, it was a miracle they ever had time to produce music of such quality.

In August they started their sixth US tour, which ended in September with two shows at New York's Madison Square Garden, which grossed over $100,000 each. By the autumn they had released the relatively low-key *Led Zeppelin III* with advance orders of 700,000 in the US alone. They were winning magazine popularity polls and being showered with awards, some even from HM Government who were pleased at the unexpected windfalls of tax revenue from these high earners and their contribution to the balance of payments.

Said Peter: "They wanted to give us the Queen's Award for Industry and I turned it down. That was too Establishment for Led Zeppelin." However the band accepted their gold records, presented on behalf of the record industry by Mr Anthony Grant, Parliamentary Secretary to Trade & Industry. "We had a string quartet come down for the presentation and we told the press they played on the album!" said Peter, who never missed an opportunity to wind someone up for laughs.

When work began on Led Zeppelin's fourth album in London at the beginning of 1971, Peter decided that in a belated attempt to combat his weight problem he would spend time on a health farm. It had got to the point where he had to book two seats for himself on every aircraft. There were problems with broken toilet bowls and chairs and quite apart from these personal embarrassments, he was aware that being so overweight could only have a detrimental effect on his heart. His heavy smoking, over-eating and unhealthy diet coupled with constant stress and all the travelling through different time zones contributed to a potentially-life threatening condition.

It was all very well looking like a man mountain with a reputation to match, but his bulk was a sensitive subject and a self-perpetuating source of anxiety. It did not do his temper much good to be the object of ridicule, real or imagined, from passers-by. It is said that when the two young recruits from Birmingham first came to London to join the band, John Bonham asked Robert loudly, "Who's that great big fat bloke?" Replied the stick-thin singer, "Sssh mate – that's our manager."

On one of their early American tours, the road crew spotted a gigantic pair of trousers on a pole above a clothing store shop, displayed as a kind of crude advertisement. The crew went in and offered to buy the trousers for cash. When they presented the enormous pants to their boss he took it in good part and joked that although they were a little too big for him, he might grow into them by the end of the tour.

Grant took a less amiable attitude when a cartoon published in *Melody Maker* portrayed him as a whale. It was drawn by Gibbard, a political cartoonist briefly employed, and probably briefed, by editor Ray Coleman. The cartoon was supposed to depict a rumour in the music business that Peter was poised to take over the management of Emerson, Lake & Palmer alongside Zeppelin, and featured a truly enormous whale, its face resembling Grant, complete with luxurious moustache. Inside its vast stomach was a pair of rafts floating on water, one of them holding Led Zeppelin, the other ELP. Out of the whale's blowhole gushed dozens of £5 notes. "Peter called up Ray Coleman and indicated his displeasure," recalls Chris Charlesworth, then *MM*'s news editor. "He wasn't just mad about the whale but because the story wasn't true. He was angry that Led Zep might have thought he was deserting them, which he'd never have done. Ray was a bit shaken by the call. Gibbard didn't stay on the paper long after that."

Often Peter would be irritable and uncomfortable, suffering from back trouble exacerbated by his condition. He would fly off the handle, even when proffered compliments or gifts that were well meant but open to misinterpretation. He once let slip that he was partial to raspberries, his favourite dessert fruit. When a well-wisher sent him a large box of raspberries, he went ballistic; convinced it was some kind of piss-take. He didn't want anybody's flattery, sympathy or patronage.

Away from the grind of constant touring, negotiating deals and handling his artistes, his own family life provided an escape route to stability and normality. He doted on his son Warren and did his best to be a supportive father. Warren was growing up in a hectic household where telephones rang constantly and strange hairy people turned up at the door clutching guitar cases. Yet he regarded the band business as a normal adjunct to everyday life.

As a child Warren was more interested in football than rock'n'roll but he couldn't help but notice how his father's success meant the family was able to move up in the world. Warren: "I can remember when I was a wee lad I asked my dad for a football kit and he got me an Arsenal outfit, so I have followed them ever since. I was born in South Norwood and then we went to live in Shepherds Bush for a few years. When Dad started getting successful we went to a posh estate in Purley. Ronnie Corbett the comedian lived opposite us. From there we moved to Horselunges near Eastbourne. We worked our way down the A22!"

Richard Cole suggests that Zeppelin's need to start buying property was not just a personal whim or wild extravagance. Big spending was usually the result of sound advice from accountants. "When they finally made a lot of money they had to get rid of it, for tax reasons, so that's why they bought the big houses and cars. In 1971 Peter bought a house in Purley, Surrey, which cost £36,000. Everyone thought it was absolutely insane when George Harrison spent £100,000 on Friar Park in Henley. That was the most expensive house at that time that any musician had ever bought. John Bonham's farmhouse, which he bought and converted, never cost anywhere near that much. Plant never spent much on houses and Jimmy's house in Lewes, Sussex, cost about £100,000. When Peter bought Horselunges Manor in Sussex, it cost him about £100,000. Then the prices started to jump and hit the million pound mark."

When Grant eventually sold his Purley house to buy Horselunges Manor, he laid on a surprise for the new owners. The couple buying the attractive, neat and tidy red brick house arrived while Peter was in the throes of packing. "I'm in a hurry," he told them. "I've got a plane to catch. The thing is, I think I've left a package with £20,000 in cash somewhere in the house. I haven't got time to look for it now, but if you can find it, well good luck!"

Peter got on his plane at Heathrow and chuckled all the way to America. It was another of his wind-ups, and from time to time over the next few hours as he gazed down on the Atlantic Ocean from his first-class seat at the front of the plane, he laughed out loud at the thought of the new owners desperately ripping up the floorboards to find the non-existent treasure trove.

6

MR GRANT GOES TO WAR

"I would step on anyone who fucked around with my band – personally. I would never send in a heavy, I'd deal with it myself, just as I would go to any lengths to get the band the money they were due."

– Peter Grant

If there was one topic guaranteed to arouse Peter Grant's ire, it was the vexed question of 'bootlegging'. With the spread of more sophisticated mobile recording equipment in the early Seventies, it became easier for members of an audience to make good quality recordings of top rock bands in concert. Often these were fairly innocent ventures, intended solely for fans' own listening pleasure, but the more mercenary minded bootleggers were recording concerts to fuel a growing and illicit trade in unofficial albums. One of the first, and certainly the most famous, was *The Great White Wonder* that featured studio sessions by Bob Dylan and The Band. These tapes, containing several of Dylan's best known songs, were recorded at Big Pink, the group's farmhouse in Woodstock in upstate New York, and formed the basis of the first ever big selling bootleg album.

It soon became common practice for bootleggers to tape live gigs and manufacture vinyl LPs which were sold in plain sleeves by unscrupulous record dealers, usually back street record shops in central London or stalls in markets like those in Berwick Street in Soho, Camden Town or Notting Hill's Portobello Road. Many fans thought that such bootlegs provided an invaluable service, giving an insight into a band's career and supplementing the restricted official output. This was an opinion shared by many writers in the weekly music press, *New Musical Express, Melody Maker* and, especially, the more underground magazines such as *Oz* and *Friendz*. In some circles, it was even regarded as something of an honour to

Peter in the mid-Seventies, at the height of his career as the manager of Led Zeppelin.
(Bob Gruen/Star File)

The Rock And Roll Years: four of the Fifties acts that Peter Grant shepherded around the UK during the late Fifties and early Sixties, clockwise from top left: Gene Vincent, Little Richard, Chuck Berry and The Everly Brothers. *(Harry Goodwin)*

Peter Grant's first management clients, The New Vaudeville Band, with trumpet player and leader Bob Kerr, front row centre. *(Harry Goodwin)*

The Nashville Teens, whom Peter Grant worked briefly before he became involved with The Yardbirds. *(Harry Goodwin)*

Mickie Most, Peter Grant's friend and one-time business partner.
(Dezo Hoffman/Rex)

The Yardbirds in 1966, left to right: Jeff Beck, Chris Dreja, Jim McCarty, Keith Relf and Jimmy Page. *(Dezo Hoffman/Rex)*

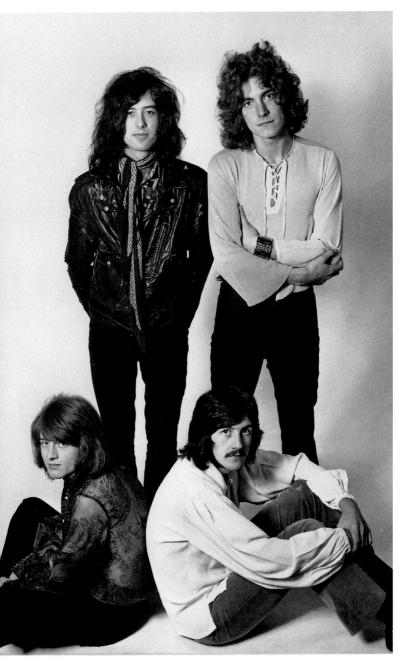

The Great Enterprise: Led Zeppelin, in 1969, at the start of their career; clockwise, from top left: Jimmy, Robert, Bonzo and John Paul. *(Dick Barnatt/Redferns)*

Peter Grant and Led Zeppelin accept gold discs for their debut album from Atlantic Records' Jerry Wexler. (*©Popsie/Chris Welch Collection*)

Peter with Bonzo, Jimmy and Robert at the *Melody Maker* Poll Awards in the Savoy Hotel, London, September 1970. (*Tom Hanley/Redferns*)

Peter on board the Starship, Led Zeppelin's private airliner, with Jimmy (top) and Robert (bottom). *(Neil Preston/Corbis)*

Peter with the gold single for 'Whole Lotta Love', the first of six hit singles Led Zeppelin released in America, though no singles were ever released in the UK. *(PA Photos)*

be 'bootlegged', since this demonstrated that a band was held in sufficiently high esteem that there was a clear demand for their live shows and outtakes to be made available illegally.

These were not arguments that appealed to Peter Grant when Led Zeppelin, now famed for their live shows, became prime targets for live bootleggers. In fact he was so outraged he took personal steps to prevent bootlegging whenever and wherever he could. His anger was comparable to the reaction of Metallica, whose music was copied and sold over the Internet by the Napster website in the year 2000. The thrash metal band took legal action. It's difficult to imagine quite how Peter Grant would have dealt with the new MP3 technology, but back in the early Seventies he tended to resort to traditional, old-fashioned, strong-arm methods. One notable confrontation occurred when a film crew tried to tape his band's performance at the 1970 Bath Festival without permission.

Said Peter: "Some people were trying to videotape the Bath Festival and they'd already been told beforehand they couldn't, so I had no qualms about throwing a bucket of water on to the tape machine which blew the whole lot up. Whoosh! It made a horrible smell and then it melted."

Grant knew that firm action had a two-fold effect. Firstly it nipped rip-off artists in the bud and secondly it reinforced his image as a fearless enforcer. "I don't believe in pussyfooting around," he said. "That's what the band hired me for. But as a supposed archetypal 'heavy' – most of these incidents have been on the spot situations, not the result of me sitting in an office and hiring a crew of heavies to go round. Let me put it this way. I would step on anyone who fucked around with my band – personally. I would never send in a heavy, I'd deal with it myself, just as I would go to any lengths to get the band the money they were due."

He was as good as his word. On the evening of September 4, 1970, Led Zeppelin performed a blinder of a show at the Los Angeles Forum which was taped by a member of the audience. There was something about the California sun, or the women who tanned themselves beneath it, that seemed to inspire Led Zeppelin to great things, and Los Angeles in particular would become their spiritual home-from-home. This particular LA show closed with a full-tilt rendering of Fats Domino's 'Blueberry Hill' which provided the title for the ensuing bootleg release, initially issued on the mysterious Blimp label as *Live On Blueberry Hill*. Within a few weeks of the show, this double LP would be sold from a small record shop at the top end of Chancery Lane, near High Holborn in London.

"This was a well-known bootleg outlet," says Chris Charlesworth, then *Melody Maker*'s news editor. "I got several boots there, Beatles, Stones, Who, and the man who ran it told me about the upcoming Zeppelin release. I knew it would make a good story for the paper." Charlesworth told *MM* editor Ray Coleman of the forthcoming Zeppelin bootleg and the story became the front-page lead in the following week's issue. "LED ZEP DOUBLE LIVE ALBUM DUE" *MM* informed its readers in bold type.

Peter Grant was not amused. He lost no time in assembling a small posse and paid a visit to the shop in Chancery Lane where he confronted the proprietor with a broom handle. Mickie Most and Richard Cole accompanied him on the trip. It was Cole's proud boast that he had 'connections' and if ever he needed any help, he just had to make a phone call to summon the required number of heavies to sort out a spot of bother. "I knew more people than Peter, but most of the time Peter and I could take care of it ourselves anyway. I remember we went to visit this bootlegger and gave him a couple of whacks with a broom handle and took all the stuff out of the shop."

"We did 'confiscate' some merchandise," Peter later confirmed, showing a mastery of understatement. During the confrontation he had implied that he was from Polydor Records who at that time distributed Atlantic in the UK. The proprietor evidently believed him.

"I heard they arrived just before closing time and waited until they were the only people in the shop," says Charlesworth. "Then Cole put the 'closed' sign on the door while Peter took an axe to the pile of Zep albums. I think he even chopped up a few Beatles bootlegs too, as a favour to them."

Interestingly, Grant and Cole had another accomplice that day: Peter's mild-mannered business partner Mickie Most. "All I had to do was stand on the sidelines, watching," he says. "I was the man of reason and Peter was the man of no reason! It was a nice combination. I remember that record shop. It was around the corner from our office and they were pirating Zeppelin. We got to hear about it so Peter and I went round and said, 'Have you got the Led Zeppelin album?' And the guy said, 'I can make you a tape for half price.' Peter got hold of this fellow and threw him against the wall, went behind the counter and smashed up the tape-copying machine."

Said Peter: "The funny thing was the guy rang me up the next day and said Polydor had sent these people down and it was disgusting how they'd treated him; he'd been terrified. He said one of the men had a beard, was six foot three, weighed 18 stone and he was really vicious. 'It just shows you what the record industry is coming to,' I said. He didn't know it was me who had come to the shop, so I told him: 'I think that's really disgusting of Polydor.' And he said, 'I knew you wouldn't approve.' The next day he rang back and said: 'Oh all right. I know you've made a fool of me.' 'Well we did have a laugh,' I said, 'because we tape recorded you on the phone!' We hadn't. But it was a good parting shot."

Peter had absolutely no qualms about his rough treatment of the record dealer. "Quite honestly it was a con on the kids because the albums they were selling were really crappy," he insisted. "They wore out quickly and they were charging £6 each. It was a liberty and when I found out where the source was I simply decided to go and do something about it myself."

It didn't matter what country Grant and the band were visiting. They'd cheerfully take the law into their own hands anywhere where they felt the code of Zeppelin was being transgressed. They didn't buy the 'free music for the people' ethos that was postulated by the likes of the Edgar Broughton Band either.

As leading lights in the hippie movement Edgar's trio had campaigned for a wider policy of free concerts, which was in keeping with the political theme of their material. They appeared at the first free concert in London's Hyde Park on June 7, 1969, which was headlined by Blind Faith, making their UK début, and was attended by over 100,000 fans. More than that turned up to watch The Rolling Stones a month later when their free Hyde Park show turned into a wake for Brian Jones. Free shows might have worked for the occasional supergroup in need of a publicity boost but it wasn't a practical way to run the music business. Nor were free concerts ever on Peter Grant's agenda for Led Zeppelin.

Many of the calls for 'free music' came from the continent, especially Germany where students felt increasingly obliged to create trouble at big rock gigs. When Led Zeppelin visited Germany in July 1970, Peter again took direct action against bootleggers. On this occasion he experienced a predictable backlash from those German youths who took the latest hippie slogans rather too literally, as was their wont in an era when hippie idealism seemed completely at odds with their aggressive tactics.

The four-day trip took place shortly after the Bath Festival and included concerts in Cologne (9), Essen (10), Frankfurt (11) and Berlin (12) and was regarded as a 'warm up' for their sixth US tour due to start in August. The author travelled with the touring party and saw both Zeppelin and Grant in action at first hand. Each night the band would try to relax in their dressing rooms before a show, betraying nerves and even a degree of stage fright. It was no joke facing thousands of baying Germans, some bent on causing mayhem, who waited in the darkness of the vast sports halls.

On the first night in Cologne Led Zeppelin played well but were distracted by the behaviour of the audience. There were only 4,000 fans inside the Sporthalle instead of the 7,000 they had expected – but outside over 1,000 politically motivated youths had gathered to demand free admission. When the mob was refused entry they took to smashing windows, causing DM4,000 worth of damage. It was the kind of riot situation that rock bands frequently endured during the turbulent early Seventies. In extreme circumstances even Peter Grant softened his approach if he thought the fans were getting a raw deal at such massive events. When Zeppelin played at the Montreux Jazz Festival for Swiss promoter Claude Nobs many were unable to get in to see them. In a welcome, albeit uncommon, gesture of altruism, Grant arranged for the fans outside to hear, if not see, the show. "It was so packed I had the idea of feeding the sound outside onto the lawn where loads of fans who couldn't get in had congregated," he said. "Claude loved that."

Back in Cologne, the German promoter, Fritz Rau, was visibly shaken and took the writer on a tour of the damage. He explained that after 9 p.m. they let in the fans although 1,500 refused to buy tickets even when they were reduced from 12 marks to six. "They think all concerts should be free," he said. Rau explained that Edgar Broughton had evidently stirred things up on a recent German visit by proclaiming that all music should be performed free of charge. It was a nice idea, although Edgar failed to suggest how touring bands that played for free would eat, or pay their crew, air fares and hotel bills.

Meanwhile, in the dressing room at Cologne, the head of security was explaining how they controlled the crowds to a bewildered and somewhat distressed Robert Plant.

"The police use sheep dogs instead of sticks," he said.

"But the kids don't come for trouble surely?" said Robert, betraying a modicum of sympathy for the fans that was in keeping with his own philosophy but wasn't altogether shared by the security man.

"Yes, and we use the sheep dogs!"

When it was time for Led Zeppelin to go on there were whoops, screams and firecrackers. "Christians to the lions," observed Jimmy Page sagely, aware that Zeppelin's set at the time included an acoustic interlude. "Shut up you noisy buggers!" said John Bonham as he headed for his drum kit to play the pounding intro to 'Immigrant Song'. These shows were like prize fights in a boxing ring. To achieve some sort of control over the crowd, the band had first to win them over with their music. It was a tall order that certainly sorted out the men from the boys in rock's premier league. Each show was an exhausting two-hour marathon, and at some the Zeppelin magic worked better than at others. Often they had to abandon the acoustic numbers. Exasperated, Robert would say: "If you are going to make a noise, we might as well go away – so shut up!" When he scolded them like children, the Germans and Americans in the audience gave affectionate, ironic cheers. The music usually won them over. There was no band more likely to convert a distracted, unpredictable audience than Zeppelin at their heaviest.

Between train trips, flights and hotel stopovers, Grant's men would indulge, not in the wild anarchy for which they later became infamous, but in quiet, civilised pursuits. Peter Grant liked to go hunting for antiques, accompanied by Jimmy Page, and the pair would spend their afternoons happily rummaging around in flea markets. Nobody bothered them. They looked like father and son on an outing. Peter was quite an authority on art nouveau and Jimmy liked to buy odd items of furniture, which he insisted on carrying onto airliners as hand luggage. They boarded one Pan Am Boeing 737 'City Jet' accompanied by a table and a mirror which had special seats booked for them under the name of 'Mr Carson'.

Zeppelin took delight in sending bills to the head of Atlantic in London, or cheerfully advising headwaiters in restaurants that 'Mr Carson will pay'. Mr Carson frequently had to disabuse people of this notion. One night in London's Speakeasy Club they even set fire to the pile of cash Phil had tendered to pay their bill.

When Zeppelin arrived in West Berlin on July 12 they visited the Berlin Wall, which was still standing and something of a tourist attraction, at least on the Western side. Young Robert Plant was shocked when he discovered that Berlin was entirely surrounded by Soviet held territory. Peter Grant climbed up a viewing tower and glared over the wall like a Mongol warrior. A few years later the entire Soviet empire collapsed.

The evening's show was at the Deutschland Halle and before the lights went down Peter wandered out into the crowds milling around the stage, working his way around the perimeter on the lookout for pirate recording activity. Not surprisingly, there were blatant attempts to record the concert being made by organised professionals armed with stereo tape recorders and microphones on boom stands. Several disgruntled 'engineers' set up in front of the stage soon found their tapes being unceremoniously confiscated.

Peter ripped one tape spool from a machine and began tearing it up. His hands full of mangled tape, his eyes glowering in fury, he began bumping the bootlegger away with his stomach, demonstrating a fascinating and effective offensive technique that he could only have learnt from his days as a wrestler. Even if the pirate had wanted to hit Grant, he couldn't have reached him beyond that huge and apparently ironclad belly. Indeed, Peter looked more like a buccaneer himself, with his shiny earrings, black beard and fierce demeanour.

The German was outraged that this manic Englishman was disrupting his private enterprise. He rushed off to find help and brought back a uniformed policeman armed with a stick and a gun in his holster. "Arrest that man!" he yelled into the policeman's ear. Peter glared at them both without saying a word. The policeman blanched and retreated, shaking his head. He wanted absolutely nothing to do with an ogre who looked like the biggest load of trouble since the Battle of The Bulge. The thwarted bootlegger was beside himself with frustration. Such incidents explained the warning notices that would appear on concert tickets in the future – "No recording apparatus of any kind may be brought into the auditorium."★

Peter would continue to wage his one-man war for as long as he managed Led Zeppelin. Many thought he was behaving like a dog in the manger or being overprotective, but Peter knew from his experience at the shop in Chancery Lane that this was not just a few fans trying to tape their favourite band so they could replay the concert at home. This was a concerted effort by local villains to make money out of Led Zeppelin, the act he managed and was therefore charged to defend against exploitation. Some unscrupulous pirates were even demanding the band's autographs and selling them on to real fans, or producing their own crude programmes and T-shirts.

★ Peter's efforts at this concert were to no avail. A 90-minute recording of this show survived Grant's onslaught and included versions of 'Heartbreaker', 'Dazed And Confused', 'Communication Breakdown' and 'Moby Dick'.

He could have ignored these activities, but in his heart Grant regarded it as a dead liberty. So it wasn't surprising to hear that he launched into a man wearing headphones that he spotted beside the stage during a concert in Vancouver, Canada, the following year. Peter saw him sitting down, twiddling the dials on a large piece of apparatus equipped with an aerial. Since the guy refused to identify himself and Grant thought the hall's official stewards weren't being sufficiently forceful in their investigations, he snatched up the mysterious black box himself and dropped it on the floor, smashing it to smithereens.

It turned out the secretive man was an official from the local branch of the Noise Abatement Society who promptly swore out a warrant for Grant's arrest. In the end, just like on TV, the Canadian Mounties came to the rescue, explaining to the noise buster that it was far from wise to mess with the man in charge of the world's loudest rock group.*

When the entourage visited Japan for the first time in 1971 there were more examples of Zeppelin's war on unwelcome recording. Recalled Grant: "The first time we went the Japanese record company insisted they record the show. They had a 6-track transistorised board, Jimmy was a bit worried about this, so the deal I made was that they could record it, if we could have the tapes and take them back to England and approve them. So Jimmy listened to them and found they were terrible. He took the tapes and wiped over them and used them again. So it was goodbye *Live In Japan*."

Peter would take his battle against bootleggers to the pages of the music press, expressing anger whenever the subject was mentioned and even issuing statements denying that such products were available. There were moments, however, when even the combined forces of Peter Grant, Richard Cole and their security gang couldn't combat the police, criminals and determined hordes of rioters. Perhaps it had something to do with its German wartime undertones, but there was just something about the name Led Zeppelin that seemed to spark off violence and hysteria among those who equated the band with anarchy, money and mayhem. Such people had little interest or understanding in the nuances of Jimmy Page's 12-string guitar technique or John Paul Jones' rhythmic interplay with John Bonham's right bass drum foot. The olive skinned people of those nations that sit at the edge of the Mediterranean have many fine qualities

---

* Curiously enough, Robert Plant had once been enrolled as a member of the Noise Abatement Society, in a publicity stunt when he was a member of the Band Of Joy.

but, as anyone foolish enough to drive incautiously in the Rome rush hour will testify, level-headedness under pressure is not among them. Thus, when Zeppelin arrived in Italy all hell broke loose.

The group had continued to make headlines and great music throughout their frantically busy first three years. They were grossing over $100,000 for shows at New York's Madison Square Garden and regularly winning the *Melody Maker* Readers' Poll as the world's top group. When they started one US tour with a show in Cincinnati their show was billed as 'The Greatest Live Event Since The Beatles'. By 1971 they were hailed as one of the biggest names in popular music. Tickets for all their shows everywhere sold out within hours.

There was therefore an atmosphere of feverish excitement when Led Zeppelin headed for the Vigorelli Stadium in Milan on July 5, 1971 during their second European tour. They were playing at a one-day rock festival organised and sponsored by the Italian Government, no less. The stage was set up on the grass on a huge football pitch. Five or six other groups went on before Zeppelin and all seemed to be going well. Then Led Zeppelin appeared, playing with all the enthusiasm and energy – and volume – that had won them tributes across the globe. It was simply too much. After a few numbers clouds of black smoke appeared at the back of the crowd. The promoter came onto the stage and asked Robert to tell fans to stop lighting fires. The group carried on playing for another 20 minutes but every time the audience stood up to cheer more smoke appeared.

As the show progressed amidst increasingly unpleasant crowd scenes, Jimmy and Robert realised that the smoke clouds were caused not by bonfires being lit by fans, but by tear gas shells being fired into the crowds by police. One canister landed 30 feet from the stage and the acrid-smelling gas drifted over the band themselves. Looking nervously over their shoulders, the four members of Led Zeppelin saw to their dismay that the backstage area was jammed with people and militia. Common sense dictated that they cut short the show and head straight into 'Whole Lotta Love', hardly a song to soothe the savage breast but their closing number nonetheless. Then, as Robert nervously broached his feelings way down inside, a fan threw a bottle at the police. It was the signal for a full-scale tear gas attack and riot. Abandoning their instruments, the group fled into a fume filled tunnel and locked themselves in their dressing room, while the road crew tried to salvage their equipment. Several of Zep's injured men had to be carried off on stretchers.

Not even the mighty Peter Grant could bump his way out of this one. He fled the scene with the group and stood by the dressing room door, ready to fell any unwelcome intruders. "The riot in Milan was a nightmare but I had once done four months in Italy as a tour manager with Wee Willie Harris back in the Fifties," he said later. "I knew what a dodgy place it could be. So I got all the money upfront and made sure we got the air tickets back in advance. Just as well because when we got to the gig there were water cannons and tear gas. Everybody just went mad. We had to flee and I'm not that good at running.

"But Mick Hinton (John Bonham's drum technician) and Richard Cole got us out and we barricaded ourselves in the medical room and stayed there until it all cooled down. Years later I bumped into the promoter of that gig in the toilet at the Café Royale . . . this guy saw me and pissed all down himself because he thought I was going to have him. I'd forgiven him by then though. You can't account for the actions of the Italian police."

In later life Peter Grant liked nothing better than to relive such stories. He may have been the manager of rock's biggest band but at heart he was still a roadie, a sort of super-roadie, a million miles away from today's besuited managers with their teams of lawyers, accountants and invest-ment advisers. He believed in leading from the front, supervising every gig, protecting his clients with his bare hands and brute strength. The road was his life and he craved its turmoil and excitement like Led Zeppelin's fans craved his band. He once stayed up with actor Rik Mayall until two o'clock in the morning telling him backstage stories . . . "Like the time Jerry Lee Lewis threw Brylcreem all over the audience. At least I'd had that great training as a tour manager, before Led Zeppelin. As the group got bigger and bigger I liked the idea of turning the shows into an event. That's when I came up with the idea of 'An Evening With Led Zeppelin'. People thought it sounded corny but it was like a line from a Thirties stage show, I guess it was a by-product of my days as a 14-year-old stagehand. I had learned my trade in the theatre. When I told the promoter that's how Zeppelin shows should be billed, they all giggled. But I was proved right again. Those big promoters like Jerry Weintraub loved it and Zeppelin shows really were an event. It was a golden age of touring."

It was also a golden age for Zeppelin albums. In November 1971 they released what became known as *Led Zeppelin IV* and it immediately ran into trouble. First they had problems with mixing the tracks and then they insisted on leaving the record untitled. There had been much argument about choosing a suitable name and after *Led Zeppelin III* it seemed a bit naff to call it simply *Led Zeppelin IV*. It was decided instead to choose a different symbol for each member of the band, supposedly representing their individual characters. As this was featured on the inner sleeve, the album was sometimes known to fans as *Four Symbols*. Jimmy Page was represented by the mysterious word 'Zoso' which he later stated wasn't a word at all. Robert Plant was symbolised by a feather inside a circle, John Paul Jones was given intertwining ovals and John Bonham had three linked rings, which, he suggested in characteristic down-to-earth fashion, resembled the logo of Ballentine's beer. The cover showed a portrait of an old man bent beneath the weight of a huge bundle of sticks. The rear cover shot showed slums being demolished to make way for high-rise buildings. Inside the gatefold sleeve was a drawing called 'The Hermit' depicting another old man holding a lantern and perched on a mountainside.

There was no information on the sleeve whatsoever concerning either the name of the group, the contents, price or even the record company. One worried Atlantic executive described it as 'commercial suicide' but he hadn't reckoned on the mysterious power of Led Zeppelin and the manner in which their fans related to them. This was something Peter Grant understood all too well, probably better than anyone by this time. Neither was there anything suicidal about the music or its prospects in the charts. For this album contained such classics as 'Black Dog', 'Rock And Roll', 'When The Levee Breaks' and the incandescent 'Stairway To Heaven'. 'Stairway' became the most played track on American radio, arguably the biggest rock ballad of all time. John Bonham's massive drum sound on 'When The Levee Breaks' was cited as a prototype for the rhythm-heavy dance music of the Eighties and Nineties.

But all that lay in the future. When the sleeve design was delivered to Atlantic it caused considerable anxiety. Peter was supremely confident that Jimmy Page had taken the right approach. "We had trouble initially but Ahmet Ertegun believed in us. It was a case of following our instincts and knowing that the cover would not harm sales one bit. And we were right again."

The whole world wanted Zeppelin but Peter was astute enough not to overspend on travel arrangements. "We went to Australia that year and the record company made a deal with Air India, so we got a round the world trip for £500. We went to Perth where the police raided us, but I slept through it all! Then we went to New Zealand where the gig was the biggest public gathering in the history of the island."

Despite the band's international fame there were still moments when they ran up against official indifference, or sheer ignorance, which stopped them in their tracks. One such incident became legendary after Grant's ultra cool response. He received a letter from Bernard Chevry, the organiser of the annual Midem Festival in Cannes, the trade fair for the music industry, informing him that 'Led Zeppelin and his musicians' had been selected to perform at the Midem Gala. The letter drew attention to the promotional advantages of this appearance, suggesting that it was an honour not to be taken lightly. As Midem was supposedly a gathering of the great and the good of the music industry, it seemed even more ridiculous – insulting even – that they had no idea that Led Zeppelin was a group, not an individual with a backing band. Peter's response was swift and devastating. He didn't reply to the letter, and instead took out a full-page advert in the edition of *Music Week* that was published during the week of Midem. The ad comprised a facsimile of the letter, reprinted in full, above which Peter had penned the inscription 'Mr Zeppelin regrets'. It was guaranteed to be seen by the entire European music industry and all those from elsewhere attending Midem. "I mean . . . Bernard Chevry, the guy who sent it, was a prat," said Peter, echoing the thoughts of just about everyone who read *Music Week* in Cannes.

But misunderstandings like this struck a raw nerve. For all their success Led Zeppelin were in many ways a secret society, an underground phenomenon understood and much appreciated by their multitudes of fans but largely ignored by the media beyond the cliquish music press. To a certain extent this was their own fault, the result of Peter Grant's uncompromising tactics. Tabloid newspapers have always been more interested in cheerful, publicity-hungry pop groups who top the singles charts and are willing to be photographed with dolly birds or jumping in the air with inane grins on their faces. Serious, contemplative rock musicians who concentrate on albums and want to discuss their musical influences simply don't appeal to tabloid readers. Similarly, their decision never to appear on TV precluded exposure in a medium watched by millions. Led Zeppelin were selling out big shows, collecting gold albums and doing the business, but in media terms The Rolling Stones, also tearing up America with a massive tour, were overshadowing them all the way. Mick Jagger and

Bianca, his sultry South American bride, had Led Zeppelin over a barrel when it came to charisma.

This was the reason why Peter decided in 1972 that perhaps he had better get another publicist. Bill Harry had already left the camp after John Bonham ripped off his trousers in a London pub, apparently the price Bill paid for refusing to arrange an interview for him. "To be honest, doing PR for Led Zeppelin was a strain," says Bill. "Bonzo leaned over and ripped the pocket off my trousers and all my money and keys went flying all over the floor. He ripped my shirt as well and I was absolutely furious. I said, 'I'm finished with you. I want nothing whatsoever to do with Led Zeppelin ever again. If I see you in the street, you'd better cross the road.'"

Peter Grant told Bill to buy the most expensive pair of trousers he could find and send him the bill, but it was too late. His PR wanted out. That same day Bonham and his drinking partner Stan Webb, guitarist with Chicken Shack, met up in the Coach & Horses in Poland Street and planned a day of mayhem. They broke down Bill Harry's office door, then tied up an executive of Chrysalis Records in sticky tape and left him bound from head to foot on the pavement in Oxford Street. Later they met up with Richard Cole and Phil Carson. Attired in Arab robes hired from a theatrical costumier, they borrowed a Rolls-Royce Phantom Six and drove to the Mayfair Hotel, where they claimed to be Arab princes. Booking themselves into the Maharajah suite they ordered champagne and fifty steaks, which they threw all over the room. In the melee that ensued they managed to smash a priceless terracotta statue of a Maharajah and horse. John Bonham was subsequently banned from every hotel in the West End. It was this kind of escapade that anyone relatively sane associated with Led Zeppelin, like Bill Harry, tried to avoid.

Peter Grant understood why mild mannered Bill Harry freaked out. But he just shrugged and blithely ordered up a fresh, unbroken PR. What arrived was B.P. 'Beep' Fallon, a genial little Irishman adept at talking his way into and out of tricky situations with all the skill of a leprechaun. He began his pop career in Dublin as a local DJ and TV personality and at one point engineered his own kidnapping as a publicity stunt. Visiting London in 1969 to interview John Lennon and Yoko Ono during their 'peace' period, he opted to stay on and seek work in PR. His ready wit soon endeared him to music writers in London, first as the PR for various acts handled by E.G. Management – including ELP, King Crimson and Roxy

Music – and later as Marc Bolan's constant companion and media adviser. His catch phrase was 'good vibes' and he had a not unpleasant habit of ringing up journalists and opening the conversation with the words: "I need to lay a verbal on you, man." He was also something of a ladies' man, rarely seen at night without an attractive companion on his arm. Jimmy Page, no mean judge of female beauty himself, looked kindly on 'Beep' and for a while they became fast friends.

"It really shook me up when our US tour seemed to be overshadowed by the Stones," Peter admitted. "So I got hold of B.P. Fallon. Beep came with us on the UK tour and we played at Greens Playhouse. Beep had a lot of make-up and glitter on and managed to get himself a good kicking outside the gig. John Bonham came up with a classic line. We came off stage and there's Fallon looking the worse for wear and John shouts out, 'Look who bopped the Beep!'"

Bill Harry merely had to put up with having his trousers ripped in public. B.P. Fallon had to endure having a pony and chickens deposited into his hotel bedroom at the dead of night, one of many practical jokes played on him during his tenure with the band. Nevertheless, he was a wise choice to help dismantle the wall of mistrust that existed between Led Zeppelin and their management on the one hand and the general media on the other.

As the band became bigger, so their responsibilities increased. The endless touring exhausted the young musicians. Jimmy Page, never the most robust specimen of manhood, was always in poor health anyway and the travelling and gigging didn't help. Robert suffered from sore throats and John Bonham began drinking far too much, which didn't help his temper. Only John Paul Jones, whose deliberate low profile cast him as Zep's 'quiet man', seemed immune to the strife. Quite often there would be fights between Robert and John when they wound each other up. Blows were even struck among the higher echelons of management. Such scenes were the cause of great alarm to eyewitnesses, but most incidents were hushed up and kept secret until many years after the band's demise.

One night in a Dublin hotel there was a pounding on the door of Peter's bedroom. It was gone midnight and John Bonham was in a great panic. "Peter, I've done something terrible. I've hit Robert!" wailed the drummer.

"Shut the fuck up and go to bed. We'll talk about it in the morning," responded Peter.

Worse was to come. Later the same night Bonham forced himself into the hotel kitchen to try to make himself a sandwich after the hotel chef refused to provide any more food. This led to a violent altercation, which had to be sorted out by tour manager Cole.

Says Richard: "It was when we were in Ireland that I broke Bonham's nose for the first time. The chef pulled a knife on Bonham and it was easier to knock Bonham out and quieten him down than attack the chef who had a 12-inch blade knife looking at me. So John then rang Peter and said, 'Richard has broken my fucking nose. I'm leaving the band.' Peter said, 'Fuck off then you cunt, and don't you wake me up again at this time of the night!' The next day we were drinking Irish coffees together."

Sometimes the tension grew so great that even Richard Cole and Peter Grant came to blows. "We had a strange relationship," says Cole. "I had a black eye from Peter and I nearly stabbed him one night. Oh yeah! It was a strange organisation. Actually, he hit me on the chin because I wouldn't go out with him one night. He'd had some trouble and had a big security guard with him and for some reason it was my fault. He caught me with a left hook under my eye. I had been out fishing and had this serrated fish knife with me. I punched a hole in his wall and was going to stick the knife in him. That's the way it was in those days. We did a tour once in Japan and something went wrong and Peter whacked John Bonham. The promoter called Ahmet Ertegun in New York and said, 'Oh, Mr Ertegun, the band has broken up. The manager has hit the drummer and the road manager has thrown a bottle at them.' So Ahmet said, 'Don't take any notice of 'em. They're like that all the time. They'll be all right in the morning.'

"There were always arguments. They'd argue over the petrol money for the Rolls-Royce. As if they needed twenty pounds! The other great one was Bonham went round to a petrol station and the guy who was filling up his car said, 'Oh, Robert's always in here filling up with petrol. What are you gonna do. Are you gonna give me in albums or pay me in cash?' John is puzzled and says, 'What do you mean?' And the guy says, 'Oh Robert always pays me in record albums.' It turned out that Robert used to ring Atlantic, tell them to send him four boxes of Led Zeppelin records and then he'd go round to the garage and use them to pay for his petrol."

Peter Grant: "There were always battles to get them to do what they were told, but I had to be firm. It was like my philosophy with every album that we should treat each one as a first album. You know, pay that much attention to the advertising, the sleeve, etc. They were always fantastic though. But part of our success was that we never hung out that much at the Speakeasy. We got together when we needed to and then did our own thing. That's why I always tried to make sure we didn't overdo the touring during the school holidays, so the guys could see their children. We didn't live in each other's pockets. We always delivered and everybody played their part. Of course there were odd rows. It's like what Bonzo said to Robert, 'All you've got to do is stand out there and look good. We'll take care of the music!' There were rows. One bloody amazing one in Japan, when Robert came off stage with a split lip. It was a dispute over money. He still owed Bonzo £70 petrol money from some tour years before. But that's how it was. But I always made sure they got on stage . . ."

Whatever else they got up to in Japan, the Hilton Hotel in Tokyo banned Led Zeppelin and their manager for life. But the chaps didn't really care as millions of dollars flowed in from tours and album sales continued to rocket. The group now travelled across America in their own private Boeing 720B jetliner, which opened up possibilities for new forms of aerial mayhem. It also enabled them to carry out a 33-date US tour armed with a crew of 30 and tons of sound and light show equipment, which earned them five million dollars.

Their blockbuster shows to thousands of adoring fans, their extravagant lifestyle and larger than life personalities all seemed like ingredients for a Hollywood movie. And that was exactly what Peter Grant had in mind for his next audacious project. At least there could be no fights, rows or dramas over such a worthwhile, artistic venture. At least, that's what they all hoped . . .

7

THE SONG REMAINS THE SAME: "WHO WAS THE GUY ON THE HORSE?"

"Jimmy needed Peter and Peter loved Jimmy . . . So having Peter on his side made him realise he could make anything happen. Yet the pair of them turned breaking appointments into an art form. They did just whatever they wanted at whatever time of the day."

– Film-maker Peter Clifton

Peter Grant had once harboured ambitions to be a movie actor. These were partly fulfilled as a young man, when he took small parts and acted as a double for famous stars. He certainly picked up a lot from the film world, not the least being the slight mid–Atlantic twang that comes from working with American crews. Even if he didn't make it as an actor, he enjoyed show business, especially the gossip and the humour. However, there would not be much to laugh about when Peter became involved in a major project that would take up more than three years of his time and lead to rows, abuse, tears and frustration. What he and Led Zeppelin wanted was a film that would celebrate both their music and their *raison d'être*. They finally got what they wanted, but only after an epic struggle that almost warranted a Hollywood movie itself. And Grant got his chance to play a leading role at last.

'The Song Remains The Same', the number which lent its name to Led Zeppelin's ill-starred venture into film-making, was the intriguing opening salvo from *Houses Of The Holy*, the band's fifth album, released in March 1973. A dramatic opus, taken at different tempos and including a long instrumental section delivered with breathless, clipped urgency, the song represented many of the best aspects of their work. There was something strangely moving and timeless about the mood of the piece, like Proust* set to music. The 'Song' was the most satisfactory item on an

---

* Marcel Proust (1871–1922), French novelist and author of *À la recherche du temps perdu*.

erratic album that saw Zeppelin making forays into reggae and soul, but included more inventive material like 'No Quarter' and 'The Ocean'.

It might have been the intention of the film-makers to capture some of the magic of the band's more intense moments. In the end *The Song Remains The Same* became simply a cinematic record of yet another stage performance, interspersed with backstage scenes and interludes devoted to the individual band members. With one exception, these so-called 'fantasy' sequences revealed little about their real lives and there was practically nothing about their inner thoughts or the band's creative process.

Yet *The Song Remains The Same* was a successful commercial venture. It was a box office hit and yielded a chart topping double soundtrack album, and it provided fans with a permanent record of the band in action at the height of their career. Some critics thought it a missed opportunity, but this was not for want of trying. The band, their manager and the directors and crews brought in to help realise their dream, all worked hard to make a movie worthy of Led Zeppelin's reputation. Yet there were moments when Grant wanted to give up and scrap the whole thing. Curiously enough, the real star of the film in many people's eyes, proved not to be the band, but their charismatic manager himself.

It was Peter Grant's performance, captured *ciné vérite* backstage while haranguing a hapless victim in a towering rage, that gave the film its most dramatic moment, more so than any of the comparatively tame events on stage. Grant is seen verbally assaulting a concert promoter whom he suspects of allowing a pirate merchandiser to trade within the venue where Led Zeppelin are performing. Vainly does the promoter protest his innocence, but Grant's tirade of abuse, a fearsome volley of four-letter words, renders him silent. The merchandiser, a minor character, cowers in the background, as Grant accuses the promoter of covertly sanctioning such activity in order to further profit from the night's gig. As he builds to a crescendo, Grant's anger is targeted not just at his present victim but at all American rock promoters and, finally, America in general, as if the whole country is out to make a buck at his expense. It's a chilling scene and it remains the only footage of Peter Grant in action, browbeating in the manner that only he could.

In many ways this scene reflects the mood of the making of the film, during which Grant veered from waging a charm offensive to simply being offensive, in his attempts to cajole, bully and goad those responsible for its creation. He wanted to stamp his authority on proceedings, take charge of the results and ensure that nobody else got too close to claiming credit, either financially or in terms of prestige. At least these were the thoughts and observations of Peter Clifton, the man later charged with the task of pulling the production together after various false starts and much debate.

He might well have shared these views with his predecessor, the hapless Joe Massot, who poured so much energy and effort into his original vision of the movie. Both Joe and Peter would suffer at the hands of their task-masters, although they would have to agree that Peter Grant had placed his trust in them and given them the facilities to make it happen. He held the purse strings. And he had the power to hire and fire. They grew to admire and respect him but the erratic, unpredictable nature of the small but powerful Zeppelin empire made both film-makers very nervous.

Joe Massot was a young American film buff, born in New York and living in London, who talked himself into the job of putting Led Zeppelin on the big screen and suffered the consequences. Peter Clifton, a witty, ambitious Australian, also living in London, was hired to take over the film production when Joe was summarily ejected from the project. He too would come to regret his decision to accept the job. Both men experienced humiliations and disappointments. Yet they learnt that it came with the territory when you tangled with Peter Grant, and both ultimately claimed pride in a project that has since taken on mythical status.

Massot was a friend of Jimmy Page's girlfriend Charlotte and he had seen Led Zeppelin in action at the Bath Festival in 1970, which placed the seeds of an idea for a movie in his mind. Peter Clifton had a background in pop and rock film-making and he had made an early stab at filming Zeppelin. He had brought his skills and energy to London from Sydney at the height of the Swinging Sixties. He admired artists like Jimi Hendrix and Otis Redding and understood the fickle but fascinating nature of pop music and the egos and excesses that accompanied its creation. Yet nothing prepared him for the experience of working full time with Led Zeppelin and their manager.

"Peter was one of the most extraordinary people I've ever met in my life," says Clifton, who now lives and works back in his native Sydney. Somewhat remarkably, he still regards Grant with great fondness, despite a long period of estrangement following the rows that accompanied the whole saga of making *The Song Remains The Same*. Reflected Clifton: "I never found it easy dealing with the group. They always had this enig-matic strength as musicians; that power they used on me and I found it very difficult to take sometimes. It was pure Led Zeppelin power – focused on me with no thought for manners or feelings. But very often it was because they couldn't see what I was trying to do."

There had been several previous attempts to film Zeppelin. These usually ended with their manager throwing buckets of water over the equipment, showing his innovative approach to the art of editing. Despite the early success of The Beatles with Dick Lester, rock and the movies just didn't seem to blend well. Few directors quite knew what to do with a static band on a poorly lit stage. Some, like Tony Palmer, who filmed Cream's last concert at the Royal Albert Hall in 1968, resorted to rapid zoom shots and trick effects that only succeeded in obscuring the group. Others went for the 'rockumentary approach' with interviews and scenes of roadies shifting gear. Grant, Zeppelin, Joe Massot and Peter Clifton all felt the need to do something different, something with vision. The problem was The Beatles were cinematic and had their Liverpudlian charisma and personality to win over moviegoers and critics. Ringo Starr was even hailed as 'the new Chaplin' after his cameo appearance in *A Hard Day's Night* (1964). Peter Grant was more likely to be called 'the New Al Capone'.

Joe Massot had been working in Hollywood on a rock western called *Zachariah* featuring Country Joe & The Fish and The James Gang before moving back to England in 1970. He took a cottage by the river Thames in Wallingford, Berkshire, in an area where many rock celebrities lived, including Jimmy Page. Joe had previously met his new neighbour, French model Charlotte Page, at a Cream concert in Los Angeles. Charlotte invited Joe and his wife to visit her at Pangebourne, where she shared their boathouse home with Jimmy. Joe became friendly with Jimmy and learned of his interest in antiques, art nouveau and, more intriguingly, the writings and philosophy of Aleister Crowley. Jimmy invited Joe to see Led Zeppelin at the Bath Festival and he was stunned by the band's performance. He also saw Peter Grant for the first time, throwing a bucket of water (one of several he must have kept handy) over the stage manager. He was given to understand that this was a ploy to discourage the next band, Jefferson Starship, from taking the stage before Led Zeppelin.*

---

* This is unlikely, given the strenuous efforts made to ensure that the previous band, Flock, departed promptly. In the event, Jefferson Starship appeared much later in the evening and were forced to abandon their set due to rain.

Two years later, Massot, having moved back to London, was looking for work as a film director. He spotted news stories in the papers about the progress of the band he'd seen at Bath and was amazed to find they were playing to huge audiences throughout America on a record-breaking tour. He also noticed they were due back in England and was seized with the idea of making a film of their tour. He tracked Jimmy Page down to his new home at Plumpton Manor in Sussex and explained his idea for a movie about the band on tour; complete with live concert footage and individual portraits of the band members. Page liked the idea and referred him to his manager. Massot worked out a budget, made some calls and went to meet Richard Cole at his Oxford Street office.

Richard was friendly and helpful but explained that he still had to convince his boss. Peter Grant eventually called Massot and turned down his proposal, on the grounds that while they wanted to make a film, they would prefer a 'name' director. Joe persevered however, even assembling a film crew, to show Grant he could be ready to travel to the States at the drop of a clapperboard.

The band returned to America and continued their tour. Then, on July 14, 1973, Grant called Massot and said he had decided it was a good idea for Joe to film Led Zeppelin after all. He'd got the job. He explained that the band had hired its own Boeing jet airliner, the Starship 1 and when they arrived in Pittsburgh on July 24, they would have their own police motorcycle escort, which he wanted filming.

Zeppelin was taking America by storm, earning thousands of dollars a night and selling out shows from coast to coast. Now was the time to capture all this excitement on film. However, Grant wanted to make sure that Led Zeppelin would own the film outright. They would provide all the financial backing and pay all the bills. Joe was ordered to fly to the States within two days, after he had rounded up his film crew. Among those he recruited was Ernie Day, who had been a camera operator on David Lean's epic *Lawrence Of Arabia* and Robert Freeman who had worked on *A Hard Day's Night* and *Help!*. They all agreed they fancied the idea of making a 'pop film' in America.

Massot flew to Boston to meet Grant and Cole. It was the first time he'd met Peter Grant in person, and found him wearing jeans and covered in Aztec jewellery. He explained that his lawyer Steve Weiss would handle all money matters. Joe's plan was to film events around the band in 16mm and the three major concerts at Madison Square Garden, New York, on

July 27, 28 and 29 in 35mm. It was expected that given the wages and the cost of film stock and equipment, it would all cost around $100,000.

The band and their management were very friendly but it was hard for Massot to get a proper contract. He said later: "Getting Led Zeppelin to sign anything or grant me any real power was to be very difficult. But I trusted them. What I wanted was to make a great movie."

Zeppelin were on a roll. Their show now lasted two hours and 45 minutes, and included such classics as 'Rock And Roll', 'The Song Remains The Same', 'Dazed And Confused', 'Stairway To Heaven' and 'Whole Lotta Love'. The concerts were so exciting that Joe wondered why the band hadn't been filmed before. Peter told him that they had commissioned a film at the Bath Festival but 'something went wrong' and the pictures came out blank. He didn't mention the bucket of water thrown over the ciné equipment.

Once the cameramen had arrived from London, Joe began filming some of the concerts as a test run for Madison Square. Engineer Eddie Kramer, using a 24 track mobile unit, would record the sound at the Garden concert. Joe had to emphasise to the group that they should wear the same clothes each night. All of them agreed to do this except John Paul Jones, which later provided the director with a continuity problem.

Massot was soon caught up in the extravagance and glamour of touring with Zeppelin – the fleet of Cadillac stretch limousines, the private jet with its seven-man crew, the girls, drugs and champagne. It was all very exciting, but nerve-wracking too when it came to extracting the cash from Richard Cole to pay the film crew's wages. They'd sometimes be kept waiting and threatened a revolt. But there was plenty to keep them busy, filming the scenes both inside and outside the shows, as young America went wild for the hottest band in the country. At the Baltimore Civic Center on July 23, 1973, they filmed cops chasing a half-naked intruder. This was also the setting for the scene in which Peter Grant berated the promoter. Amidst a flurry of abuse he more or less accuses the man of receiving kickbacks with the aim of squeezing every last nickel out of Zeppelin.

"We knew nothing about him. As soon as we found out about it, we stopped him," protested the man, believed to be one Larry Vaughan.

Grant is having none of it, not least because it was a member of his crew that discovered the illegal operation. "As soon as *we* found out about it more like," he rages. "It's fucking typical. As long as you can screw an extra few bob out of the group."

Meanwhile Massot hired some handheld 35mm cameras ready to shoot the big one at Madison Square. Their plans were almost aborted when the local trades union tried to block the film crew from working. Grant announced that the film was off but the last minute hitch was sorted out by the negotiating power of Zeppelin's attorney. The British cameramen were allowed in and filmed all three nights.

Years later Peter Grant gave his version of how the film had been put in motion: "We were in Boston in the Sheraton Hotel. Jimmy knew about Massot. We'd been on about the failure of the Stanley Dorfman film. So we got Massot and Ernie Day over and started filming. It turned out to be traumatic to say the least. They filmed three nights at the Garden and never got one complete take of 'Whole Lotta Love'. We always planned for it to be more than just a concert film."

Grant was quite keen to join in the creative process himself. "There was one idea I came up with. During 'Dazed' where Jimmy is playing really fast and the camera goes through his eyes to the black cop sequence – that was to show life going on around us – beyond the concrete wall."

On the second night of filming at the Garden an extraordinary event took place. Tour manager Richard Cole and attorney Steve Weiss had put $186,700 in $100 bills into safe deposit box 409 at the Drake Hotel on Central Park South. It was money set aside to pay wages and expenses when the tour ended. As it was the weekend, they hadn't been able to put the cash in a bank. Just before the band set off for their last show of the season, the deposit box was found to be empty. The police were called and a press conference was held. What became known as the great Led Zeppelin robbery was headline news. After an altercation with a photographer, Peter himself was arrested and charged with assault. The photographer, from the *Daily News*, had refused to stop taking pictures, so Grant took his camera, pulled out the film and handed it back to him. The photographer was outraged and pressed charges.

The band mostly took these events in their stride. Robert and Jimmy tended to laugh it off. The suspicion lingered, however, that someone from among the band's own staff had taken the money themselves. But the cash was never found and nothing was proved. Richard Cole, who had put the money in the box and held the key, took a lie detector test – and passed. Joe Massot was also questioned by the FBI about the group and his film project. They seemed convinced it was an inside job. At least the robbery provided a suitably dramatic episode deemed worthy of inclusion in the film.

Peter Grant recalled that night when he talked to DJ Steve 'Krusher' Joule in 1989: "I went to jail but I wasn't sentenced. In the film we used newsreel footage and you'll notice I had my arm outside of the police car. I thought it was funny because in America the police always use handcuffs and this time they didn't. We got fifty yards from the Drake Hotel and the policeman driving the car said, 'Do you remember me Peter?' I said, 'No,' although I wanted to say 'yes' to keep him happy. He said, 'It was a long time ago but I was a drummer in a semi-pro band and when The Yardbirds did a college tour, we were the support group.' Wonderful. Out of all the cops in New York I had to find him. That's why I had no handcuffs.

"He said, 'Don't worry. When you go down the jail and do your fingerprints, don't open your mouth because they'll hear you're English and they'll be on to you.' I went and sat down for 35 minutes. The jailer ran his stick along the bars and called out my name. 'Grant? FBI to see you.' When I came back, at least three guys stood up to give me their seat because if you are in jail and the FBI come and see you, then they think you must be a big shot. It was quite an experience. But you learn from these things."

After Madison Square everyone returned to England and during October 1973 Joe began filming the band on their home ground for the individual 'fantasy' sequences. Jimmy was filmed near Boleskin House that he had bought in Scotland and which was formerly owned by Aleister Crowley. This was in addition to Jimmy's 18th century manor at Plumpton, Sussex, which had 50 acres of grounds and lakes, on which swam a pair of black Australian swans. It was even more splendid than Grant's own Queen Anne style Sussex manor, not far away at Horselunges. Robert was filmed on his farm in Wales and John Bonham was pictured on his farm in Worcestershire and at a drag racing track. John Paul Jones was filmed at his home in Sussex.

Massot had his concept for the movie all planned out. "We didn't just want a concert film, we wanted to show them as individuals, but not in the traditional way with interviews. They wanted more symbolic representations of themselves. All the individual sequences were to be integrated into the group's music and concerts."

Joe wanted to capture the essential movement of the band on stage and reflect this in the individual stories. John Paul Jones was shown as the leader of a band of masked men terrorising a village, before returning to his home and family, where he read his children bedtime stories. The masked men were clearly an analogy for the group. Robert Plant became an Arthurian knight on a quest for a mysterious and very beautiful princess, while Jimmy Page was seen climbing a steep rock face to be confronted by a hooded figure, who turns out to be an aged version of Page.

Explained Massot: "Jimmy insisted that his segment be shot on the night of a full moon and it was quite difficult lighting the mountain at night." The scenes were shot in December and the area was covered in ice and snow. His crews had to battle their way to the location at Boleskine House, next to Loch Ness and try to complete everything in two days. Apart from getting Peter Grant to act, it proved to be the toughest assignment of all for the director and his crew.

John Bonham's scenes were much more fun. They showed him dressed as a Teddy Boy playing snooker, dancing with his wife, encouraging son Jason to play the drums and driving a high-octane fuelled hot rod at 240 mph. Peter Grant was shown driving a vintage car with his wife Gloria in a violent gangster sequence, which introduced the film. Dressed like Al Capone, or George Raft, he drove a 1928 Pierce Arrow together with his henchman Richard Cole who was armed with a Tommy gun. They pulled up at a big house and riddled the occupants with bullets.

Despite his youthful desires to be an actor, Peter Grant was not too sure about the idea of taking the role of a gangster. He was quite keen on being filmed with Gloria driving in their 1920s Bentley (one of his large collection of vintage cars) down country lanes. He was, after all, a family man, who hated being on tour so often, away from his son Warren and daughter Helen, both of whom attended the local village school.

In the end he agreed to play the role of a 'Rock Caesar' with Richard Cole as his henchman. Richard certainly looked the part in his hired pin-stripe suit and blank firing machine gun. However, Peter's two-tone shoes didn't fit and he felt uncomfortable smoking a cigar and wearing a tie. In the story the pair are seen driving to the bootleggers HQ where they fire some warning shots. Because the car tended to overheat, the crew had to load it on a trailer and film as if it were actually being driven. Later in the day the pair returned to shoot up the offices of the record pirates.

This was staged at East Grinstead Manor, a 65-room house the band had bought with the intention of turning it into a studio. In one of the scenes Peter had to have an angry conversation on the phone. Ironically, despite years of shouting and bellowing at people in real life, he couldn't summon the courage to do it in front of the cameras. He suffered stage fright and wanted to give up on the whole idea, becoming embarrassed, silent and morose. In the end, the scene was shot with Grant simply slamming down the phone. However, he enjoyed his next big scene, where he walks into the room after his henchmen have shot down the bootleggers, puffing his cigar. Grant also agreed to be filmed sitting on his huge four-poster bed, once owned by Sarah Bernhardt. But Massot began to sense that Peter was losing interest in the film, and more especially his own contribution.

By the end of 1973 the film footage was mostly in the can. Massot had accumulated thousands of feet of film and now faced the mind-boggling task of trying to edit it all together into a coherent movie. It almost broke up his marriage and drove him to a nervous breakdown. His first move was to buy a very expensive German made KEM editing console, which cost $25,000. It took a further three months before the machine could be delivered, and meantime Grant was growing impatient to see some results. Massot set up the machine at his London home. Just trying to synchronise the sound and pictures took months on end. Meanwhile Grant was unwilling to pay for the editing machine or pay any more of the mounting bills.

Massot then decided he would show a rough cut from the film, the section featuring 'Stairway To Heaven' at a preview theatre, with the idea of reviving interest in the project. It turned out the band didn't like seeing themselves on screen. Zep's roadies whistled in derision and the band began tearing the film apart. It seemed out of synch and full of anomalies. The viewing ended in complete silence. Then a row broke out over the long delay in completing the film. A private band meeting was called.

Next Grant called for a further screening and although he liked some of the action, notably John Bonham's contribution, he was against the back-stage scenes. Grant glared at the director across the table and said nothing. A week later a letter arrived from the band's accountant ordering Massot to stop all work on the film. From then on Grant wouldn't answer Joe's calls and Jimmy Page was also unavailable. Eventually Plant called and said the band wanted to see everything that had been shot over the previous two years. In the meantime Joe had not been paid and was in a state of high anxiety. It was vital that the group liked what they saw, after so much money and effort had been spent.

The band came to the screening in high spirits. John Bonham brought some takeaway fish and chips to eat during the show. Because the film still hadn't been finished, the scenes showing Jimmy Page dressed as a hermit climbing the mountain in Scotland were the first to be screened. Recalled Joe later: "I turned out the lights and just as the first shots of The Hermit came on John Bonham, who had a mouthful of fish and chips, let out a great roar of laughter. The sight of Jimmy Page in a long grey beard was too much for him." It was not an auspicious start. Page was mortified and berated Massot. Matters improved when the other fantasy scenes were shown, which the band liked. Joe himself thought he had created 'an amazing film' even though it was still in rough shape.

For a week after the screening there was total silence from Led Zeppelin. Eventually Peter Grant called on Massot at his house and demanded to see his portion of the film. He then told the director that the entire group had decided to bring in someone else to finish the film.

It was a bitter blow but there was nothing Joe could do. He didn't have a written contract. He was later offered a few thousand pounds to pay him off and a 'heavy' was sent to collect the film from his house. Joe had hidden the film in a friend's garage, but Zeppelin took away the KEM editing machine. Massot served a writ on Zeppelin and the next year was taken up with legal wrangles. It was finally sorted out after a meeting at the Mayfair Hotel in London with Grant and his US lawyer Steve Weiss. Joe was paid the money he was owed, after which he delivered the hidden film to the band's new office in Kings Road.

It was now up to Peter Grant to decide what to do with the Led Zeppelin movie. Peter Clifton's name was mentioned as a possible successor to Joe Massott. "I'm afraid with Joe it wasn't really what we had intended," said Grant. "We knew Peter Clifton because years back he'd come to us to do a film and showed Jimmy and I a load of clips in a viewing theatre off Wardour Street. They were shots of Jimi Hendrix that he had filmed. This was with a view to him salvaging the Dorfman film. But we didn't want to do that. So after it didn't work out with Joe, we searched for this Australian Clifton and found he lived in Holland Park. We offered him the salvage job of the Massot mess."

At the beginning of 1974 Sydney-born Peter Clifton, then 29, was preparing to make a reggae film in Jamaica and was actually about to leave for Heathrow when his phone rang. It was Led Zep's manager on the line. "I was taking my wife, child and nanny because we had done a house swap with some people in Australia," recalls Clifton. "I was going to make a film in Jamaica then go back to Australia and edit it there. I was going to leave England for six months. I had packed and sent my car back when Peter rang . . ."

Peter Clifton knew all about Grant's reputation and methods of doing business. "Most of the people in the pop business in those days, like Tony Secunda who managed The Move, were complete outlaws. I was the same as a film-maker, very much a maverick." He had a company called Star Films and made his entry into the pop world when he was commissioned to do a 13-part series on Swinging London in 1967. He filmed Otis Redding, Jimi Hendrix, Ten Years After, Cream and The Small Faces. "We had a helluva good time! Then I did a lot of stuff for *Top Of The Pops* and Immediate Records. I made these pop specials and sold them to Australia, which was starved of pop music in those days. I did some rock'n'roll documentaries but then I thought, 'Bugger these 16mm things, I want to go all the way,' which brought me to Led Zeppelin."

Clifton had already fallen out with Peter Grant once after having promised him he would get Page to approve a sequence for a film he was making for Columbia called *The Sound Of The City*. Led Zeppelin was going to be in one of the sequences, performing 'Whole Lotta Love' at the Royal Albert Hall. "I only had two 16mm cameras but through a lot of hard work I had made the sequence work. But because I'd made one tiny mistake and had put in a guitar that Jimmy didn't like, he wouldn't approve the film. They didn't have the balls to tell me, but I had to drop Led Zeppelin out of the film and I was really quite angry about it, because I'd spent all that money and lost face with Columbia. But I got Pink Floyd and Rod Stewart, which made up for it and somehow the film worked. Then I was off to Jamaica to make this reggae film when Peter called me and said, 'I want you to come into the office straight away.'"

En route to the airport with his family, Peter stopped in to see Grant. "I went upstairs dressed in my going-away clothes and Carole Browne, his secretary, who I used to call and call to get to speak to Peter Grant and who always put me off, said, 'Come straight in!' And there I was in his office for the first time. He took me into a side room and the four of them were waiting there."

Peter hadn't expected the entire band to be present. "Hi guys, I'm just off to Jamaica," he said. "Great to see you all – what's up?"

They looked at him in surprise and Peter said, "Well, we want you to make our film."

Clifton was nonplussed. "Why me?" he asked.

"Because you wanted to make a film on us for so long."

Clifton pointed out that they wouldn't approve his work before. Nevertheless, they insisted his editing was 'brilliant' and asked if he would do their film. It was explained to him that Joe Massot had been filming 'a documentary' about them. Clifton insisted that he wanted to do a full-length feature film. According to him, the band said, "We'll do whatever you want."

At this point in the meeting Peter Clifton made a momentous decision. The trip to Jamaica was put on hold and his family bundled off to the Churchill Hotel for two weeks while he sat down and wrote a script. It included the fantasies (that Massot had already shot) and was intended to have a real 'film look'. It had to be a feature film for the cinema, he told his new clients. "Otherwise it would have to be a down and dirty rockumentary showing groupies and stuff. They said, 'Oh no, no we don't want to do that,'" he recalls.

The band accepted Clifton's proposals and two weeks later he was driven down to Sussex for another meeting with Peter Grant at Horselunges. "He sent a car for me and it was springtime and all the lambs were out. It was very beautiful. I crossed the moat and into the courtyard. Peter finally appeared and we went upstairs and I was served ham sandwiches. I didn't realise it but Jimmy Page was hiding in the house at the time. I didn't see Jimmy and I didn't know he was there until much later. I gave Peter the thirty page script and he went off. They read the script which took a little time, while I was outside exercising, doing some stretches. Then he came out and said, 'Yes, that's just what we want.'"

Clifton then asked, "Can I have a contract?"

Grant: "No, but I'll sign your script."

Grant proceeded to sign the pages on behalf of Led Zeppelin, initialled the document, handed it back and said, "There you are. When can you start?"

Clifton asked for three weeks while he went to Jamaica and then Australia to sort out his business and personal affairs. "At that stage I told Peter I would do the job for wages, but I would like to own a piece of it. He said, 'Yeah, you'll own an equal amount with Led Zeppelin and me. That's an equal cut which will mean 17 per cent to you.' I said, 'That's great,' and he hugged me. I really fell for the man at that stage."

Clifton was about to experience the weird and wonderful inner workings of Led Zeppelin. His predecessor, Joe Massot, had formed his own less than favourable impressions of the way Zeppelin worked, stating: "As individual human beings Led Zeppelin were extremely sensitive and considerate, but as a group they were bloody difficult, if not impossible." It was now Clifton's turn to assess his employers. Indeed, he would write down his own thoughts at great length in the aftermath of the association and his essay makes uncomfortable reading. "The group that comprised Led Zeppelin, whether individually or collectively were the rudest, most arrogant and inhumane people I ever encountered in my 25 years in filming music," he wrote. "They were all dreadful and behaved appallingly! They were allowed to get away with their horrible behaviour due to their instant commercial success. I can say this with some authority after the ordeal of broken promises and daredevil tactics I put myself through because of my ambition to make the world's most successful rock'n'roll film. That ambition in 1974 revolved around their co-operation and commitment, which guaranteed the necessary funds. There was no question in my mind that Led Zeppelin was the most enigmatic of all rock bands. They never granted interviews or appeared on TV, never advertised a concert, and yet every one was sold out within hours of the release of tickets. Their popularity lay in myriad reasons; their indisputable talent, their sex appeal and sheer power. The nasty Seventies fitted them like an iron glove. It was Jimmy's band and what Jimmy said – or rather what Peter Grant said on Jimmy's behalf – was the way it was . . ."

Before reviving the Zeppelin film Peter Clifton had been working on *Sound Of The City* for Columbia and *The London Rock'n'Roll Show* starring Chuck Berry, Little Richard and Bo Diddley, which he had filmed at Wembley Stadium. "I was working for a man called John Heyman who Peter Grant respected and this was a big reason that I got the job. John used to manage Elizabeth Taylor and had his own film company and was a close friend of Robert Stigwood. He was very highly respected and he took me under his wing and I made a couple of movies for him. Peter Grant checked me out and John Heyman gave me the thumbs up, which I didn't know about. This was the way Peter Grant worked. He checked people out. This period was the absolute peak of Led Zeppelin's career – from 1974 until 1977. For the next three years we both wanted the same thing, which was to really portray Led Zeppelin as the most amazing band in the world. Because of that we had a symbiotic relationship. But my dealings with the band were on a totally different level."

Clifton wasn't necessarily a huge fan of the band's music. As with all recording engineers there came a point where overexposure took its toll. But he says: "If you loved rock'n'roll, you loved Led Zeppelin, although there were parts of the band's music that were very self-indulgent. There were also parts that were very moving. Most of the songs I used in the film I thought were fantastic, but if I hear any of their music now on the radio I can't listen to it, because I spent so much time with them. I can't even watch the film. I couldn't sit down and enjoy it with my friends."

Peter Clifton's name appears three times in the credits. He is listed as the director of 'a film by Peter Clifton and Joe Massot' and is also credited as 'director of editing', which was added, at his own insistence. He was allowed plenty of time for the project and took care to ensure that every shot had some significance. Despite this lassitude and the fervent desire of Peter Grant to make the film a success, the director claims he was beset with problems.

"I only met Joe Massot once. He was a nice guy. Peter Grant arranged for me to visit his home in Hampstead in March 1974 where I viewed his attempt at making a film on Led Zeppelin. It was a complete mess. There was no doubting Joe's talent, but he was in deep waters with this filming attempt and he did not have the strength to push the band members around. None of the material he had captured in 16mm or 35mm actually created sequences. There were a few good shots but they didn't match up, there was no continuity and no cutaways or matching material to edit or build sequences." Clifton explained all this in a written report to the band and said that a feature film was unachievable unless they started again and shot everything in 35mm with a new script. He would be able to use some of the Massot 'fantasy' material, like Bonzo riding his motorbike and drag racing car and Jimmy climbing the mountain, but they had to re-shoot establishing shots on location and in a London film studio. Clifton had to reassure the band he could do the job, but only with their co-operation.

"They were always fighting amongst themselves, but at least I had this luxury of time," he says. "To be honest the guys weren't really interested in the film. It was more Peter's idea. He had to sort me out, so I had whatever was needed to make the film. Every time I needed something I'd go to him and he'd make it happen.

"Jimmy would get very impatient with me, and Peter would come and really tick me off in the strongest way. But I was never afraid of Peter because he needed me. I grew up in Sydney and I could fight. Of course Peter could swat me down with one punch, but he would never do that to me. In fact he was incredibly good to be around because if you had Peter Grant on your side, then you had no problems. He gave you an extraordinary sense of security that I don't think anybody else has ever given me. And that's what he gave to Jimmy, because he loved him. Fortunately – he liked me!"

Clifton deduced quite early on that the relationship between Grant and Page was crucial to an understanding of how Led Zeppelin worked – even why it existed. More importantly, it revealed what motivated Grant and how the strength of the bond with Page affected his life. "They were very close and it was like Jimmy needed Peter and Peter loved Jimmy," says Clifton. "So having Peter on his side made him realise he could make anything happen. Yet the pair of them turned breaking appointments into an art form. They did just whatever they wanted at whatever time of the day."

Clifton soon found that you couldn't order Zeppelin around or expect them to jump to a schedule. He once hired a screening room in Soho and they turned up three and a half hours late. Columbia was paying the bill, so nobody cared. They just sat around waiting for the phone calls. " 'Jimmy is on his way . . . Robert is on his way,' we'd be told. Of course they'd all arrive at exactly the same time, so they had it all figured out. They were extremely self-controlled in that respect. Nobody had the power over them that Peter Grant did. When you were with him, you believed that you could pull it off. At one stage though he said, 'Look, we're gonna can the film.' "

Clifton responded by assuring Grant that he believed in the project so much he was prepared to re-mortgage his house to finish the job. Grant vowed to carry on and finances were secured.

The next task was to assess the rolls of film that had already been shot.

"The concerts were anything up to three hours long and the film was two hours and 17 minutes, but we filmed a couple of extra songs. Eddie Kramer engineered the sound and Jimmy Page listened to the tapes. He said, 'They're fantastic, let's make the film around these tapes.' What Jimmy didn't realise was that tape doesn't have sprockets. It doesn't have synch. Jimmy could never understand when he saw some of Joe Massot's footage, why we couldn't alter the synch."

This meant that the footage from one night didn't match another, so in effect, nothing matched. Most of the footage from the tour was on 16mm film, so Clifton suggested that they took bits of the Madison Square concerts like the long shots and wide shots and a couple of action shots and put them into complete reels with the soundtrack. Next came the most controversial move of all, one that would raise doubt and suspicion for years to come. Under conditions of the utmost secrecy, the band assembled at Shepperton Studios in Surrey, which they often used for rehearsals. The plan was to film the whole 'concert' again.

"I said to Led Zeppelin, 'If you are prepared to take the bits of Madison Square Garden including a couple of incredible action shots, I'll play you the soundtracks, project the bits on a huge screen in front of you and we'll put the cameras between you and the screen. When the shots come on, the soundtrack will be right, you play along and I'll shoot you again.'

"At first they couldn't believe I could do it and the trick was to work with an editor called David Gladwell, who had worked for Lindsay Anderson and later became a director himself. Between us we matched up these three nights from Madison Square Garden. We'd cut from Thursday to Friday and then to Saturday and back to Thursday. Jimmy never realised there were 12 to 16 edits on 'Stairway To Heaven'. I did that so I could grab a piece of Joe Massot footage. We had to be driven by the quality of the sound performance. In 'Stairway' we had three great guitar solos we could use."

Clifton was amazed that he'd managed to get Led Zeppelin to perform just for him and his crew. "In 1975 you were in awe of Led Zeppelin," he said. "I got them all on the stage together in their outfits and they suddenly realised they were back on stage together for the first time since Madison Square Garden. They started playing 'Black Dog' just for me and we all got such a shock. They were so hot and tight and fuelled up with you know what. There had been a huge argument just minutes beforehand and then suddenly they began playing and it was an extraordinarily electric moment between them. I knew then that I had them in the palms of my hands."

The editing took three months during which the band again became extremely impatient. Clifton protested that the work was really difficult and nobody would help him. As an aspiring young director, Clifton's all-time favourite film was *Lawrence Of Arabia*. Like Joe Massot before him, he took great pride in having Ernie Day as his editor on *The Song Remains The Same* because Day had worked on *Lawrence*. However, when Peter Grant met Day again at Clifton's own small studio and the latter ventured to offer an opinion, Grant greeted him with a glare and a roar. "And who the fuck do you think you are?" he yelled.

Clifton: "He would never speak that way to me, but when he entered the cutting room he abused the editors and cameramen on the band's behalf. It was to intimidate them and make sure they knew who was boss. The band was quite rude to me a couple of times, especially Bonzo who didn't like me very much. We finally finished the filming and I was flavour of the month, until I had a falling out with Peter. It was not over money, but how to deal with the boys. Jimmy was the most difficult because he was the most inarticulate and introverted. He once showed me Kenneth Anger's film *Lucifer Rising* which was half an hour long and quite hideous and about worshipping the devil, which I didn't want to have in my life. I didn't understand it or get any good vibes from the film. Anger had used Jimmy's wailing guitar in a singular sort of way on the soundtrack and Jimmy wanted to see it again. I said that unfortunately we had a 16mm automatic projector and it wouldn't rewind. He simply said, 'That's alright, we'll see it backwards.' So we watched it backwards without the sound."

Clifton and the guitarist sat and talked at great length after the screening and Peter began to feel he had been accorded a special privilege. "I think Peter had allowed me this sacred time with Jimmy in order to get to know him better. Peter had allowed me to get a little further into the circle. He was this huge, bull-like man but he was unbelievably sensitive. Because of the loose clothes and scarves and the long wispy hair, the big gleaming smile and the shiny white eyes, you sort of lost contact with his bulk and he became this other person – that you could bully and push around."

Clifton tried to explain that he wasn't trying to impose a 'Peter Clifton Film' on them. His idea was simply to make a film for the cinema. "I said if we don't do this now it will never, ever happen. I had to say this to them over and over again, because they kept pulling out! There was one scene where Jimmy Page was climbing a Scottish mountain and he didn't like those shots because it made his bottom look too big. He had done the climb during a full moon, but I had to shoot the scene again near his house in Sussex. By now I was speaking to Peter Grant three times a day about these problems and sometimes he was leaning on me. We had to shoot some scenes again and again. Peter would bring each of the boys in for a week and we'd edit those fantasies again. Peter Grant had created this incredible aura around them . . . which partially obscured the fact that they were *all arseholes*!"

Peter is quick to exclude John Paul Jones from this blunt assessment.

"Jones was very sweet actually and sparkled as a musician. They all had great respect for each other, which was a nice thing in a band. They were like a bunch of footballers, crude and rude. In fact they took a real pleasure in being rude to people. I remember them tying some girls up in their rooms at the Hyatt Hotel in LA. I walked into a bedroom only to find two of the guys asleep in bed together in their underpants. 'Excuse me guys, I'm trying to do some work here!' Then I walk into the next bedroom and there are all these groupies tied up. Dreadful girls. They weren't classy about who they hung out with."

It may have been Clifton's ambivalent attitude towards the band's lifestyle or simply the fact that he got a better room than them during one stay at the Beverly Hills Hilton. At any rate Zeppelin decided to give him the same treatment they meted out to anyone who got above themselves. He had a room right beside the pool, so Zeppelin decided to bring him down a peg or two by plotting revenge with the aid of Richard Cole. "They were really pissed off with me, so they got Richard to dump everything I had including the TV set into the pool. So I couldn't stay in the same hotel with them ever again and moved to the Beverley Wilshire."

When Peter Clifton finished the film he had good cause to stay even further away from the band and their manager. Events unfolded which soured his relationship with Grant for many years. "They sent Richard Cole round to search my room. He brought a big guy round with him and I couldn't fight them off. But I was prepared to, in order to avoid the indignity of having my room searched."

The Zeppelin camp suspected that Clifton was living at their expense in Los Angeles, which led them to believe he had his own, hidden agenda. It was, of course, all a misunderstanding, as he explains. "They had given me a limo which I had been using for three months while living in LA and mixing the film. Meanwhile I had just sold my other film *The London Rock'n'Roll Show* to Japan and the distributor wanted a 35mm print. So I went to MGM's laboratory in Zeppelin's limo to pick up the *Rock'n'Roll Show* film. I think the limo driver dropped me in it. Peter Grant called me up and said, 'What have you been doing?' I told him I had been working on our film. 'What *else* have you been doing?'"

Peter Clifton stuttered and denied he had been doing anything untoward, although he agreed he had been using the limo. Under interrogation Clifton's gaze wavered and he blinked. When he left the room Richard Cole told Peter Grant, "He's lying."

Clifton recalls what happened next. "They were really pissed off and that's when they came round to search my rooms. Somehow I had stolen the negative of our own film. This was the film I had been working on for two and a half years. As if I would have stolen it from the Technicolor lab. Could anything be crazier? It was nonsensical. The thing was, it was still *my* film at that stage because I had complete control of the negative and they didn't know where the negative was stored. But it was at Technicolor – of course. It was complete paranoia."

There was more to come. "After I had finished the film, I'd gone on holiday to America, and left my nanny at home in London with my wife and little baby son. That's when they sent Richard Cole around with their accountant and they got some sort of court order, which allowed them to search my house to see if there was any other Led Zeppelin film in there. I wasn't even in the house when they did this – and after we had been so close! I just felt my house had been violated. The nanny of course shouldn't have let them in – but she did and they grabbed a few bits and pieces of stuff."

They did find some footage, which seemed to be Led Zeppelin material. "What I'd done had been to create a present for all the boys after we finished the film. It was all the best of the home movie footage, which I was going to give to them. I had already given Peter Grant his copy. I had my son present it to his son Warren. So I tried to do the right thing, and then to be hit by this wave of paranoia . . . well I felt . . . 'You bastards, you c★★★★s.'

"We had gone through all those fights to complete the film and now they'd sent these heavies round to my house. But nothing surprised me at this stage and my conscience was clear. I hadn't done anything wrong. As if I would sell pirated footage of my own film. It was true they were very paranoid about bootlegging, but in my business, if I screwed one pop star I would be out of business! Anyone with any common sense would have realised that. I was friends with people like Mick Jagger and I had once worked with Jimi Hendrix. Would I jeopardise my reputation like that?"

After Clifton completed the credits for the film the management took away the film and changed it. He claims they removed the names of all the people who had worked on editing, make-up and effects. Clifton was furious but Peter Grant simply saw this as another personal victory. "The other thing about the film was the debate we had with Frank Wells (president of Warner Brothers) over the titles," recalls Clifton. "We wanted to bring in Po of Hipgnosis★ to do them again. We had a big meeting with all the Warners big shots where Frank said something like, 'We won't run out on you Peter,' and I replied, 'I know, because I won't let you get out of the fucking door.' It got sorted out in the end."

When the film was still only semi-complete it had to be shown to Ahmet Ertegun of Atlantic Records, for his approval, before it could be sold to Warner Bros for distribution. This prompted an episode which Peter Clifton now regards as his favourite Peter Grant story. "The film was only just finished, but nobody had seen it, not even the band. We had to show it to Ahmet and he was the one person that Peter really looked up to. Peter arranged a screening at the MGM Grand room in New York, which had a dozen huge leather seats.

"We waited until midnight before Peter gave the go-ahead for the screening. Ahmet had come from his wife's birthday party, which was why he couldn't make it until midnight. We hit the screening room at half past twelve and Ahmet arrived in his Rolls-Royce with his chauffeur and Peter and I came independently in two limousines. So we had two limos and a white Rolls-Royce waiting outside. We screened the film and it was very scratchy, no titles – it was hard work. By the time it was finished it was three o'clock in the morning and everyone was very tired.

"For Peter, it was like his first day at school. He was really sharp and cooking. Ahmet, of course, had fallen asleep several times during the movie. He woke up at the end and said to Peter, 'Who was that guy on the horse?' Peter was so shocked by this, because if the screening didn't go well, this was the end of the movie. If Ahmet didn't like it the movie was over. That's what we always understood. So Peter just got up, turned on his heels and walked out of the door. Ahmet looked at me beseechingly: 'What have I said?'

" 'Ahmet, that was Robert on the horse,' I told him. 'Oh, gee, well I nodded off,' he replied."

Clifton and Ertegun dashed after Peter Grant who was walking as fast as anyone had ever seen him. He had sped past the two limousines and the white Rolls-Royce and was heading in the direction of his hotel. "What'll I do?" asked Ahmet. The two men headed down the street, followed by a convoy of cars driven by the dutiful chauffeurs at walking pace. "It was a freezing cold night and we finally caught up with Peter at The Plaza and

★ Aubrey Powell, a celebrated sleeve designer.

was in tears. He said to Ahmet, 'How could you say that – we worked hard on this thing . . .' Ahmet tried to put his arms around him. He was ortified that he had upset Peter and said, 'I adored the movie, it's ntastic!' But at that moment you could see how much Peter cared about e film."

Yet Grant appeared less than enamoured of the finished product some ars later. "Some of it was okay. But what did we know about making ms? If it had been totally hopeless, we would have shelved it. I did enjoy e premieres and meeting all the film media." His final, damning mment on *The Song Remains The Same* was that it was "the most expen-re home movie ever made."

Says Peter Clifton: "When they felt I had failed to portray them actly the way they wanted they complained to Peter Grant who came er to my house in Kensington, into my basement film studio. This was nan I respected but didn't fear, although I feared what he might do to hers. I knew we had made a pact many years before, and remembered at spring morning at his medieval home in Sussex that features on the ologue of my film. That fateful morning Peter signed every page of my ript and budget for and on behalf of Led Zeppelin. He said, 'You are w one of us. You will receive an equal share of the profits.' We shook nds. I received nothing of course. But the production just about paid y rent for the two and a half years while I turned their three nights at adison Square Garden into a two-hour 17-minute, award-winning ture film. Peter Grant was a colossal character. He and Jimmy Page d a very special agreement. Peter made me swear that if I was going to ake the film, if anything went wrong I must remember that Jimmy was e first man into the lifeboat. But I never heard from any of the embers of Led Zeppelin again after the London premiere of the movie 1978."

As far as Grant and Zeppelin were concerned, the movie song had ded. But they left behind smouldering resentments among the film-akers and a few puzzles for movie buffs. Says Peter Clifton: "If you look the credits they wrote something very interesting. 'Musical per-rmances were presented live at Madison Square Garden.' It was some-nat ambiguous because the film was obviously done somewhere else!"

When he was asked about the provenance of the 'live' shots of Led eppelin at Madison Square Garden, Peter Grant did admit that they had deed shot some material at Shepperton studios, recreating the same stage set while the band donned the same clothes they wore at the actual gig. "Yes, we did," he said. "But we didn't shout about the fact."

Clifton reiterated that he used some of the 16mm shots by Massot which he blew up to 35mm. "His biggest mistake was that he shot some stuff on 35mm but he used 400 foot reels, because he was shooting with hand-held cameras. This meant there could only be one three-minute take at a time. And 'Dazed And Confused' was 27 minutes long."

The film ended up costing about £350,000 and, because they wanted total control and ownership, the five Zep partners decided to pick up the tab by borrowing money on personal guarantees from the National Westminster. "So they financed it with their own personal money," confirms Clifton. "Their chief accountant was there when they searched my house apparently, a woman like something out of a James Bond movie. I felt humiliated. It was a horrible feeling and I felt I didn't want to be friends with them anymore. I felt they had betrayed my trust. But I never betrayed their trust. It was just that they wanted a film about Led Zeppelin, made by Led Zeppelin and starring Led Zeppelin. So they left my name off the advertising and the posters, which was unbelievably hurtful because the film was so successful. Normally there is a credit for whoever made the film and to leave it off was ridiculous. My role was downplayed because of their unbelievable egos."

Once Ahmet Ertegun had mended his fences with Peter and reassured him that the film was 'wonderful', they were at last able to present it to Warner Brothers. The movie was shown to David Geffen and other executives at another, more successful screening. The project was approved and it was now deemed necessary to hold a high-powered planning meeting attended by all parties, including of course, the man who had made it all happen, Peter Grant. By all accounts the meeting turned into farce.

Clifton: "We had spent all this money to make the movie, so I said to Peter, 'We've got to get the money back so at least the boys can pay off their overdraft.' I said, 'You guys will get money from the soundtrack album, but get the money back out of the film straight away because you'll never see it. These films never make a profit.'"

Clifton advised Warners that Led Zeppelin had to be recompensed for the couple of million dollars they spent making this film, doubling the actual figure. "I did that deal to get them the money to pay off their overdrafts. Ahmet Ertegun approved it, so I showed Warner Bros the film and they said 'fine'. The deal was quite a big thing. David Geffen and Frank

Wells,* the president of Warners, said, 'Yes, we want it.' Then they called a meeting with Led Zeppelin, the film-maker – which was me – and all the Warner Brothers distribution people . . . it was a *big* meeting at Frank's office in Los Angeles, which was to take virtually the whole day."

Clifton turned up at the 11 a.m. meeting, having spent all morning trying to call Peter Grant at his hotel to find out what time he was due and to ask if any of the band were coming. "There was no sign of Led Zeppelin at all when we started the meeting. I could conduct the meeting about the technicalities – how to make the prints, the Dolby situation, etc. Then David Geffen and Frank Wells came in and everyone started looking at their watches and saying, 'Where's Peter Grant?' "

Clifton made an excuse and got out of the meeting to make a phone call to Peter's secretary Carole Browne. " 'Where the fuck is he?' I asked. I was told he was having a problem with Gloria."

It turned out Peter was still in London trying to resolve this family matter. Clifton was aghast. "He's in London? But everybody thinks he's here to make the deal,' I said. 'Don't worry. Richard's on his way,' they said."

Clifton's heart sank.

"At this stage Richard Cole was completely out of control," says Clifton. "He turned up at the meeting coked out, armed with bottles of booze and with another of the band's roadies. The pair of them hadn't slept for days. And this is Warner Brothers, not some party, right? They sit in a corner and start to mouth obscenities at the meeting. Richard is drinking and making all these inane comments, saying that San Francisco and Los Angeles are too close to release the movie there at the same time, because there'd be an audience spill over. The Americans are saying, 'Oh my God, where's Peter Grant?' I had to stand up and say, 'Well unfortunately Mr Grant is at a meeting.' After five or six hours of this, it became nonsensical, but we had to make the decisions without him. Frank Wells pulled me aside and said, '*Where's* Peter Grant?' I said, 'Look mate, I've gone through all this for two and a half years. This is how he operates and it's why he's so powerful. He just does exactly what he wants . . .'

"In fact he had just stood up one of the most important meetings in his life for personal reasons. I was really upset and having Richard Cole there – completely off his face – didn't help. I don't suppose he even remembers the meeting. But this was supposed to be the culmination of Led

---

* Frank Wells died a few years later climbing Mount Everest.

Zeppelin's great career. The movie! The meeting was in February and now Warners told me they wouldn't release the movie until November. There were tears in my eyes. I said, 'I've worked for four months to get the sound mix finished – night and day – how can you do this to me?'

"They then explained what they needed to make the film a success. They modelled it on *The Exorcist*, which they made very difficult to see for the first six weeks. You could only see it in one cinema in New York, then they released it across the country. This was David Geffen's idea – to make the film talked about. It was also Peter Grant's idea to make it difficult to see Led Zeppelin, so he was being really consistent when he didn't turn up at the fucking meeting! But when I saw him again in the last few years of his life, he had changed and become quite humble."

The long awaited film received its world premiere at Cinema 1 in New York on October 20, 1976. The theatre had to be equipped with a special quadraphonic sound system hired from Showco in Dallas, Texas. Richard Cole claims he had to threaten Warner Brothers distributors before they upgraded the system to ensure that the music sounded as good on the soundtrack as it would at a live concert.

Says Peter Clifton: "Obviously it was my idea to put a booster in there because I had done that quite a few times before. The band understood the need for good sound but they didn't know how to balance the tracks. I had to mark the projectionist's controls to show where the volume settings were with a chinagraph pencil. They needed me at the premiere because I was the only one who really understood the magnetic soundtrack system. Jimmy turned up at New York and told the projectionist to turn the sound up to full volume. If that happened, there would have been terrible phasing on the surround sound and distortion."

When the West Coast premieres were held in Los Angeles and San Francisco, the sound was less effective – 'absolutely abysmal' according to Richard and he recalls that the whole thing embarrassed Jimmy Page. Peter claims this happened because he wasn't invited to the West Coast premieres, but he did supervise the sound at the London premiere.

The premieres were attended by the members of Led Zeppelin but on the flight over to New York there was an incident in the first-class cabin of the plane after Richard Cole and members of the group had traded insults with Telly Savalas, the *Kojak* actor, and cutlery was thrown. Later that evening, the night before the premiere, Cole was ejected from Ashleys, the New York club, after having threatened *Melody Maker*'s Chris

arlesworth. "He was well out of it and he fancied the girl I was having
ner with," says Charlesworth. "He was trying it on with her and she
n't want to know, so I told him to fuck off. He tried to hit me but I
cked. The bouncers saw it all and threw him out. Robert saw it happen
and he was very apologetic to me. After all, I was a friendly journalist. I
n't done anything to offend them."

Charlesworth attended the premiere the next evening and went on to a
zy party at the Pierre Hotel afterwards. "I saw Richard there. He had a
r on his face that wasn't there the night before. Robert told me that
er had heard about the incident in Ashleys and had smashed Cole in the
e. Peter always wore all those huge rings with blue enamel so if he hit
it would have been like being hit with a knuckle-duster. It was very
midating to be around Led Zeppelin in those days."

Promotional material claimed that the film was "the band's special way
giving their millions of friends what they have been clamouring for – a
sonal and private tour of Led Zeppelin. For the first time the world has
ont row seat on Led Zeppelin."

ans welcomed the film but the critics were less accommodating.
bert Duncan of *Circus* magazine thought it had been written, pro-
ed, directed and edited "by junior college students who had just dis-
ered LSD". Dave Marsh in *Rolling Stone* wrote: "It is hard to imagine
other major rock act making a film so guileless and revealing. It is a
ute to their rapaciousness and inconsideration . . . their sense of them-
es merits only contempt." Despite the incident with Richard Cole,
ris Charlesworth in *Melody Maker* was more positive and said: "It has
n three years in the making but *The Song Remains The Same* is a classy,
surely enormously successful film."

Charlesworth: "After my review was published in *MM*, Robert Plant
ed me and thanked me and apologised yet again for Richard's behav-
r. I think he thought I'd give the film a bad review just because of what
pened."

Whatever the artistic merits of the movie, Charlesworth was correct in
eseeing its success. It grossed $200,000 in its first week and the double
ndtrack album topped the charts and went platinum. It has recouped
er Grant and Led Zeppelin's initial investment many times over. Now
ilable on video, it remains one of the most poignant and fascinating
facts from rock's golden age, not least because of the famous scene
olving Grant backstage.

Peter Clifton is quick to defend the movie. "Every shot was in there fo a reason. A lot of people still don't understand that film. Zeppelin let m get away with quite a lot. I even put the Drake Hotel robbery in there . . And there was that lovely sequence which Joe Massot shot, where Pete berates the guy for letting in poster sellers. Peter Grant says 'fuck' an 'cunt' eighteen times during that speech. Warner Brothers accepted th film but they said, 'You are gonna' have to bleep those words out. Get ri of them.'"

Clifton took the optical print and bleeped just the beginning of each o the offending words with a special pen. When the film was first screened the words were inaudible and the film was given an appropriate rating. Bu on every other print the cuss words were retained and came over loud an clear.

This was Clifton's final legacy to Led Zeppelin and there can be n question that his decision to retain Grant's foul language added immeasur ably to the final film – and to Peter Grant's legendary status. Whether the were grateful is another matter entirely. "I never did anything wrong, Clifton says today. "I never cheated them but when we finished the film the band more or less said, 'We've used him up, we've done the film. Let' get rid of him.' But with Peter there was a sense that we had shared thi . . . thing. It was like a war that we had been through together and h knew I came through for him."

Joe Massot also went to the premiere *The Song Remains The Same* i New York. But there was no first-class jet flight into the city, no blac Cadillac limo and no magnums of Dom Perignon waiting for him in plush hotel suite. He had to pay $10 to buy a ticket from a tout (scalper outside the theatre to see his own movie. As far as he was concerned whatever Peter Grant said, it was still *his* movie.

8

SWAN SONG

"Peter was able to achieve all kinds of things by employing his remarkable persona and that included that terrible stare of his. If he decided to stand up and move a bit too close to you, he could intimidate you with his body language."
— Swan Song executive Alan Callan

In the midst of the battle to produce *The Song Remains The Same* Peter Grant had another scheme on his mind. At the same time that he was keeping Zeppelin afloat and placating irate film-makers, he was busy planning a challenging new venture, the group's very own record label.

During the Seventies the major record labels had a habit of swallowing each other up, a practice that continued apace, until by century's end there were only a handful of multi-national conglomerates controlling the industry. However there was still room for talent spotting independent labels, and these 'Indies' gave sanctuary to many groups and artists whose music might otherwise have beeen overlooked. Another development was the growth of artists' own labels, widely seen as 'ego trips' or simply a means of maximising income from record sales. Such labels were often launched with the best of intentions, by bands that wanted to share their good fortune and boost the aspirations of artists they liked and admired. The Beatles had set the ball rolling in the late Sixties with Apple Records, about the only aspect of their Apple empire that succeeded. The Stones set up their own label, Rolling Stones Records, distributed through a new deal with Atlantic following their departure from Decca, and Elton John launched his own Rocket Records with a logo inspired by *Thomas The Tank Engine*. Led Zeppelin unveiled plans for their own label in January 1974, to be called simply Swan Song.

The move followed the expiry of the band's original five-year contract with Atlantic. Just as *The Song Remains The Same* had been a Zeppelin production under Grant's control, so Swan Song would represent another step towards artistic independence, not to mention greater financial control. Jimmy Page came up with the name of the label, having apparently considered several less attractive suggestions, among them Slut, Slag, Eclipse, De Luxe, Stairway and Zeppelin Records.

Peter Grant and Ahmet Ertegun put Swan Song on a sound business footing, with Ertegun's Atlantic records distributing the new label's product. Grant called a press conference to announce their plans just a few days after his right-hand man Richard Cole got married, at a ceremony at Caxton Hall, London on January 2, 1974. Richard had hoped to be involved in the management of Swan Song, but his ambitions were dashed when other, less volatile characters were appointed to take over the running of the label. Swan Song certainly had a classy image. The logo featured a pair of graceful swans, similar to the protected specimens of West Australian black swans, which swam on the lake at Jimmy's Plumpstead home. The label design was based on *Evening, Fall Of Day*, a painting by William Rimner.

Swan Song soon achieved impressive results and signed some formidable acts. Yet it never quite fulfilled its potential. It went through a number of label managers and seemed to lose momentum after being launched in the UK later in the year – on Halloween night – in a blaze of publicity with a party at Chislehurst Caves in Kent. The candle-lit party became a byword for Zeppelin's legendary excess with fire-eaters and magicians entertaining the guests, as well as strippers dressed as nuns alongside women in various states of undress rolling around in vats of jelly. Copious supplies of booze left partygoers speechless for days afterwards. Peter attended wearing a naval captain's hat and nodded in satisfaction as the nuns behaved like whores.

It was a fun evening, designed both to enhance Zeppelin's reputation as libidinous hedonists and stress their invulnerable position at the top of rock's premier league. But behind the scenes all was not well. Peter knew there were rumblings of discontent within the ranks, which if mishandled could seriously damage the operations. During the long drawn out making of the Zeppelin film cracks also appeared in Peter Grant's personal life, which began to affect his judgement, mood and attitude. The strain of running the entire operation was enormous and the band members also came under increasing pressure. Few outsiders appreciated what it was like to be constantly on the road and in the public eye.

Then, in late 1974, John Paul Jones, seemingly the most stable member
the band, told Grant that he wanted to leave Led Zeppelin. Recalled
ter: "He turned up at my house one afternoon and told me he'd had
ough and said he was going to be the choirmaster at Winchester
thedral. We had this heart to heart, during which we recalled a time in
stralia when I got very insecure and thought the band wanted to blow
out. Anyway, it turned out John said he thought it was the other way
und, that I was going to blow *them* out. I said, 'If you want to leave, well
u've got to do what you've got to do.' But I told him to think about it.
eanwhile we invented a press story saying that he was 'overtaxed'. It was
kept low key. I told Jimmy of course, who couldn't believe it. But it
s the pressure. He was a family man was Jonesy.

"By that time the security thing in America was getting ridiculous. We
rted getting death threats. In fact straight after the 1973 tour, following
e Drake Hotel robbery, there was a very serious one. Some crackpot
ter from Jamaica stated what was in store for us when we toured again.
got very worrying.

"That's how we lost a little of the camaraderie after that, when we were
America, because there were armed guards outside the hotel rooms all
e time. I think we even talked about wearing bullet-proof vests at one
ne. Bonzo told me to order extra large ones for him and me! We did
gh. But it was a serious problem. Then Jonesy came back refreshed and
dy to go again. That's when we finished the film and set up our next
oject, Swan Song."

Once Jones had been placated, the priority was to establish a head-
arters for the new venture and a roster of acts. Peter Grant was breaking
f his partnership with Mickie Most, which meant moving out of the old
xford Street office. Grant's friend Mark London, who co-managed
one The Crows, found the label premises in New Kings Road, London.
ys Mickie Most: "RAK moved to Charles Street and Peter decided not
come with us and wanted to do his own thing. He set up Swan Song in
elsea. I never actually went there."

As well as Swan Song operations, Zep business was also conducted from
e new address, but Peter increasingly did most of his work from home at
orselunges in Sussex, largely in order to avoid the long drive into town
rough traffic-laden streets.

Horselunges Manor represented the peak of Grant's ambition. A symbol
his success, it provided a place of refuge from the constant demands of

the music business. When he bought Horselunges in 1973 he took his mother down to see his latest acquisition and she just looked at him and said: "Peter, what have you done!" Recalled a friend: "One of the first things Peter did when he settled into the house was to buy his son Warren a frogman's outfit, so he could swim around the moat! Horselunges was a place he seemed to have known a long while. He got it through the property agent Perry Press, who found houses for stars. It was Perry who told Peter that Horselunges was up for sale."

Melody Maker journalist Michael Watts visited Horselunges to interview Grant and recalls the impression made by the magnificent house and its unlikely owner. "When I interviewed him in 1974 he lived in the most exquisite house I'd ever seen. It was a very old Elizabethan house set in these green acres and surrounded by a moat with its own drawbridge. Horselunges was full of lovely old tapestries and Grant collected art nouveau and art deco pieces.

"He was very big on antiques. I once saw him in an antiques shop in Kensington High Street and I went and said hello. He said, 'I spend a lot of time in here,' and he had a genuine appreciation of antiques. It was an enormous contrast between this rather oafish looking person and the very beautiful objects that he had in his house. There was also the contrast between his physical bulk and his tiny, petite wife who was a ballet teacher. She was like a little mouse next to his elephant."

In contrast to these splendours the working environment at Swan Song was decidedly drab. The Chelsea office came to represent the curiously low-key approach Grant liked to adopt in London. While in the States he was all for grand gestures, the motorcycle escorts, limos and private jets, somehow he knew this wouldn't cut much ice back home in the UK. He kept his offices deliberately dowdy and ramshackle. There were no potted palms, chrome furniture or leather seats in a prestigious tower block suite. Instead the offices, above the headquarters of the British Legion on a busy main road, were dark, gloomy and filled with second-hand furniture. Visitors found very few staff and often little signs of activity amidst the dust and cobwebs.

Yet when the label was launched there were high hopes and great enthusiasm from the band. Said Robert Plant: "The label isn't going to be like, 'Yeah, we'll have a label, far out heavy trip man' and just put ourselves on it. The label won't just be Led Zeppelin, that's for sure. It's too much effort to do as an ego trip. We're going to work with people we've known and liked . . . it's an outlet for people we admire and want to help. People like Roy Harper whose records are so good and haven't even been out in America. We want to take some artists who we think are fine and never let them down at any point . . . that's our intention."

Jimmy Page said that Zeppelin had been mulling over the idea for their own label for some time and thought it would reduce the kind of problems they had suffered with their own product. "We knew if we formed a label there wouldn't be the kind of fuss and bother we'd been going through over album covers. Having gone through what appeared to be interference on the artistic side by record companies, we wanted to form a label where the artists would be able to fulfil themselves without all that hassle. We didn't want to get bogged down in having to develop artists. We wanted people who were together enough to handle that type of thing themselves."

Jimmy could see one problem with having his own manager involved in the project. "There is one awkward situation with the label, which is that a lot of folk come along and seem to think that Peter Grant is going to be able to do everything for them. It's just one of those unfortunate things that he's there and they respect him, but he just doesn't want to know. He's got too much on his plate."

Page told reporters that the name Swan Song was at one time the tentative title of a long acoustic guitar piece he had written and was even going to be the name for an album, until it ended up on the label. "I think Swan Song is a good name for a record label, because if you don't have success on Swan Song . . . well you shouldn't have signed up with them."

Peter Grant was more specific about the problems that led to the creation of the label: "We first got the idea for Swan Song after Atlantic messed up the pressings for *Led Zeppelin II*. They ran off 100,000 copies, which jumped all over the place because they didn't follow Jimmy's instructions on the master tape. So we decided it was time for us to take control of our own situation and ensure Led Zeppelin were presented in the best possible manner." Grant stated that he would go to the pressing plant himself to check out the process. He discovered that vinyl records were dipped into vats of acid. For rock and pop records the vats were only cleaned every six months. However, for classical recordings the vats were cleaned out every ten days. So he persuaded the pressing plant manager to have Zeppelin's albums dipped into the classical vat, which markedly improved their sound quality. "We were determined to ensure that nothing went out with our name on it until it was absolutely right. We delayed the release of *Houses Of The Holy* for five months because the cover artwork wasn't right. Atlantic was going mad. But everything on our label got the right sort of attention."

Danny Goldberg, who would go on to a distinguished career in the US music industry, was appointed vice-president of Swan Song America. As an employee of the PR company Solters, Roskin and Sabinson, he'd already worked as the band's publicist in the States but Peter persuaded him to leave SRR to run the New York office from a high rise building on Madison Avenue. In May 1974 two extravagant launch parties were thrown in America, the first, costing $10,000, at the Four Seasons restaurant in New York. As they couldn't find any white swans to glide among the guests they hired a flock of geese – much to Peter Grant's derision. "Ya' think we don't know the fucking difference between fucking swans and fucking geese?" he raged at one Atlantic employee. "We all live on fucking farms, ya' cunt." Unfortunately two of the geese were chased out of the restaurant by Richard Cole and John Bonham and were run over in the traffic.

At the second party at the Bel-Air Hotel in Los Angeles, where the guests included Groucho Marx, Micky Dolenz and Bill Wyman, the lakes in the hotel grounds were already stocked with real swans. It was announced that artists signed to the label would include Bad Company, a band newly formed by former Free singer Paul Rodgers alongside his old drummer Simon Kirke, Mott The Hoople guitarist Mick Ralphs and King Crimson bassist Boz Burrell. As a legacy of Free's contractual obligations, they were already signed with Island in the UK. Others included Dave Edmunds, The Pretty Things, a female singer called Mirabai, whom they discovered in a New York club, and Scots singer Maggie Bell, formerly with Stone The Crows. The latter band, which Grant and Mark London had discovered in Glasgow and signed for management, had broken up in 1973, following the death by electrocution of their guitarist Leslie Harvey in an on-stage accident, a tragedy that deeply affected Peter Grant.

Peter claimed that he looked on Maggie Bell as his daughter and was very fond of her, but he wasn't able to devote as much time to her career as she would have liked. She always said that his first priority was Led Zeppelin. But she remembers that it was Peter who came up with the name for her best-known band. "When he first heard me sing, he said 'Cor, Stone The Crows!' He had flown up to Glasgow with Mark London and Richard Cole to see me and Les. They arrived at the gig in a big limousine with dark windows. They freaked everybody out. We all thought, 'Are they gangsters or what?' Ricardo was dressed like a pirate. He had a black and white striped T-shirt, black tight leather pants, a leather cap, a big earring and a red scarf around his neck. The club was packed out and we went down really well. We spoke to Peter and Richard after the gig but the guy who ran the club said, 'Don't think you are going with that big man in the flash car. I've got you under contract.' We told him to piss off. 'What contract?' Peter went off in his car and a couple of months later we went down to London and we were signed to him and Mark London for management and production."

The first time Maggie Bell saw Peter she told him he reminded her of Orson Welles in *Citizen Kane*. "He said, 'Yeah, do you want to be my little Rosebud?' He was absolutely enormous but always a very kind man. I was like a daughter to him, but looking back he didn't really know what to do with me. He managed loads of guys and my career suffered through that. But Peter did get a deal for me with Atlantic Records after Stone The Crows split up."

Maggie went to New York and stayed for a year, making two solo albums that were never even released, one produced by Felix Pappalardi from Mountain and the other by Felix Cavalari from The Young Rascals. "I paid for them but to this day I don't know what happened to them," she says. "I was told they weren't good enough, but believe me they were!" Maggie would later record her *Queen Of The Night* album with producer Jerry Wexler which was more successful.

"But I was a bit upset at having two albums rejected, which I thought were wonderful," she continues. "I didn't want to become a cabaret singer at 27 and I thought Peter failed me a bit. He was so busy with Led Zeppelin I could never sit him down to talk to him for an hour. No disrespect to Peter, but it was a sore point that I could never get to see him. I used to go to the Swan Song office, which Mark London had found for a ridiculously cheap rent. I remember when some elderly ladies came for the rent Peter would always get them some nice cakes to eat while they'd be downstairs in the basement counting the money. He had a thing about old ladies! 'Make sure somebody keeps an eye on them, because somebody could go in there and nick the rent money,' he said. I liked him for that."

Maggie got to know Peter's family and says: "His wife Gloria was fabulous. A lovely person. Helen, their daughter, looks like her mother. Gloria wore beautiful clothes and they were great together. She was there with him right from the beginning when they didn't have two pennies to rub together. I remember she came to the Swan Song launch party at Chislehurst Caves when it was pouring with rain outside and there was nowhere to go to the toilets inside. Peter and Phil Carson held up these two huge umbrellas while Gloria and I had to pee behind the limo! What a place to go to the toilet, eh? When she split up with Peter, she made her own life and nobody ever saw her again. But I had a lot of time for her because she was a good lady. She spent a lot of time with the kids and made sure Helen went to dance school. Gloria was very good at setting up house and I was very sad when she left Peter. It was a huge shock for him because he devoted a lot of time to his kids."

Maggie saw the kind of pressures her managers had to cope with on the flight from New York to Los Angeles between Swan Song launch parties. She joined a large entourage that included American rock press writers Lisa Robinson and Lorraine Alterman, together with Danny Goldberg, Steve Weiss, Richard Cole and Peter Grant. "We were going to the Swan Song launch in LA. We had the whole of the first-class compartment to ourselves but I remember Peter hated flying. He was absolutely paranoid. I sat between him and Mark London and the two of them both took a Valium 5 before they got on the plane and another Valium each just before take-off, so they could sleep during the journey. They kept saying, 'Now we're gonna be alright.' And as soon as the Jumbo jet took off Mark and Peter looked at me and said, 'It didn't fuckin' work!' But after a couple of glasses of champagne everyone was okay. We had dinner and we were just relaxing, when all of a sudden this guy comes up the stairs into the first-class section. He was some drunken American businessman. It was during a time when you could still smoke cigarettes on a plane and Richard Cole and me were just chatting and smoking to pass the time.

"This guy comes up and says, 'Put that cigarette out. It's bad for your health.' I said, 'If it's bothering you I will.' 'Oh, you're English are you? Are you with that bunch of degenerate guys downstairs? So you're in First Class. How do you people make your money?' He was really pissed off that we just ignored him. Peter and Mark were asleep by now. Two hours later the same guy comes back and he starts again. 'What do you guys do for a living?' Peter wakes up and says, 'Wot, who's that? Wassa matter?' And this guy is going, 'You've only got all these chicks because you've got money. It ain't because you're good looking!' Peter is awake now and says to the guy, 'Mind your mouth in front of these ladies.' He pushes the bell above his head and an air hostess and one of the stewards comes up and say, 'Is everything all right sir, can we get you anything?' 'Yes, you might tell this man to go and sit in his seat. He's being obnoxious and swearing in front of these ladies.' The crew could see we were taking up the whole front compartment of the plane and everyone went very quiet. Peter says, 'We're going to LA on business. This is not a pleasure trip.' And the guy starts calling us streetwalkers and English degenerates and he suddenly pulls a gun! So we all go 'Shit!' There's this loony guy pissed as a fart with a gun on a Boeing 747 half way to LA. He says, 'Do you know what this is?' Somebody else up front pushes another button and says to another air hostess, 'There's a guy up there with a gun.' So two guys and the pilot grab the guy and take the gun away from him. When we arrive in LA airport the FBI and the CIA are all there. Peter was wearing jeans and a silk shirt and a pair of trainers. We were all wearing casual clothes because we were going to California where it's hot! An official comes up and looks puzzled. He says, 'How many people are there in your party? What actually happened.' Peter explained he was taking a party of 12 on a business trip. 'This guy was being rude to the girls. This is Maggie Bell, a famous singer and the other girls are top New York journalists. We're going to Los Angeles to open up our new record company. This guy had too much to drink and he produced a gun.'

"The businessman was taken away in handcuffs and the FBI men were very nice to us. They wanted to know if we'd press charges but Peter told them just to let the guy sleep it off. Then as we went to collect our luggage the guy in handcuffs appears again and shouts, 'Have a nice day!' We all turn round, give him the finger and shout, 'You have a nice day too!' Peter wouldn't have done anything on the plane because he knew how serious and dangerous it could have been. He just gave him 'the look'. I was a bit frightened but Peter sure kept his cool."

Despite her respect and affection for Grant, Maggie still felt let down after she came home from America to a deathly silence. "It all went quiet. Nothing! I'd phone Peter and go down to his office and say, 'What am I going to do?' But he kept saying he had to find the right producer for me and time went by without much happening and he kind of lost the plot with me. He spent most of his time with Bad Company and Led Zeppelin. But then I never had a contract with him, only with Atlantic. I was on Swan Song too and we tried a couple of recordings with Dave Edmunds but the material wasn't right. Mark London got married and he left the company so it went quiet for me. But we stayed in touch. It was 15 years ago when I was living in Spain that I got a brown envelope in the post and there was this book with a picture of a motorcyclist on the front. I opened it up and there was a letter inside from Peter. It said, 'Here Mags, what do you think of the way I've lost weight – trying my best. I feel like a new person. Hope we can meet up soon.' It turned out the boys had bought him a big motorcycle and that was him on the cover. I never even recognised him, he had lost so much weight. He then used to ring me up at one o'clock in the morning and apologise for what had happened to me at Swan Song and how he'd never had any time for me. What could I say?"

Swan Song got off to a terrific start with their first release. Bad Company's début album topped the US charts and the single 'Can't Get Enough' was also a hit in both the UK and the States. Peter had helped put the new band together, went to their early rehearsals and accompanied them on their US tours. "I stood outside the hall, as I always did and just listened," he said of his initial introduction to the band. "Now I don't ever pretend to have the greatest pair of ears in the world but I heard them play 'Can't Get Enough Of Your Love' and I just knew they had what it took. Paul Rodgers, though, was probably the most difficult person I ever had to work with. He would always get himself into trouble and I'd have to pull him out."

Peter Clifton remembers a meeting with Paul Rodgers at this time that was besieged by visitors. "I was still in the middle of post production on the Led Zeppelin film when Peter Grant wanted me to interview Paul, who had just signed to Swan Song. When he turned up at my home studio it was in the early afternoon and I was busy editing, So I plonked him into my office and put on a film projector to show him some of my favourite clips. As the screening was about to start there was a banging on the door. An outlaw friend of mine from Australia called Jimbo had turned up looking for some action. I told him to wait for me upstairs. Again I started the screening and there was another knock at the door. Tony Secunda walked in. He looked after Procol Harum and now wanted me to launch his new band Motorhead. I asked him to wait upstairs with Jimbo and get into a bit of mischief while I finished the screening for Paul. In the middle of this, Peter Grant arrived with his cocker spaniel dog. I didn't hear him arrive but my assistant told him we were inside the screening room, but he couldn't come in as the door was locked.

"The dog started barking and Peter banged on the door with his huge fists shouting, 'Open up, open up it's the police!' Now Tony Secunda was a very paranoid guy and he and Jimbo were busy chopping lines. They grabbed Jimbo's huge bag of cocaine and poured it down the garbage disposal unit. By the time I got upstairs their faces were as white as sheets. When they saw it was a wind-up they began scraping the last of the coke off the blades of the garbage disposal. I wasn't in anybody's good books after that."

While Peter was busy launching Bad Company and overseeing the first British Swan Song release, The Pretty Thing's album *Silk Torpedo*, Led Zeppelin was off the road, which gave him breathing space. Meanwhile he kept an eye on developments at the King's Road office. Richard Cole was not impressed by the new venture. "I don't think Peter regretted starting Swan Song, although in my personal opinion it was a waste of time, if only for the simple reason that when you've got five people owning a record company, they could never decide between them what they wanted to sign," he says. "It was good they signed Bad Company to the label. That was a sure-fire winner. But they only ever signed two other bands, The Pretty Things and Dave Edmunds. I don't know how The Pretty Things got signed. It was just something from their old hippie days. And Dave Edmunds was a great rockabilly musician. Of course Maggie Bell was signed because Peter managed her. They also signed Michael Des Barres' band Detective. But the whole business was a nightmare. The office in King's Road had no furniture and there was never anyone there."

The first man appointed by Peter to run Swan Song in the UK was Abe Hock, a record promotion man from Los Angeles. "He lasted five minutes," says Cole. "It was difficult to get the five of the band down there to a meeting to make a decision or do anything. It never seemed to happen. That was all they signed in three years and once John Bonham died the whole lot dissipated."

Alan Callan, a former musician and a friend of Jimmy Page, succeeded Abe Hock. "I got to meet Peter and Jimmy in about 1968," he says. "When I first met Jimmy we were both quite young and Zeppelin was just being formed. People have sometimes described me as their tour manager or business manager, but I wasn't good enough to be their business manager. They asked me to do a very specific job, which was to do with the record label. Jimmy phoned me and asked me to work for them and it was a great job."

Alan travelled extensively with Zep and got to see Peter Grant exercising his authority in his own inimitable way. "I did four tours with the band. It sounds like Vietnam, doesn't it? I should have got a Purple Heart! I remember once when a senior member of their road crew was misbehaving. Peter got hold of this guy and showed him a ticket. He said, 'What does it say on this ticket? It says on the ticket, Led Zeppelin. And how much is it worth?' The guy says, 'Ten pounds Peter.' Says Peter: 'Does it have your name on it? No? Well just remember, nobody is coming to pay ten pounds to watch you and they certainly wouldn't pay ten pounds to watch me. Right? So cool down, get things into perspective and behave properly.'

"Everybody did some very extreme things in those days. Led Zeppelin were like four medieval princes cavorting across Europe, indulging in their every whim. All this stuff about Zeppelin – if you see it from the inside it all seems different. That was an incredibly honest and open view that Peter had about the band. I learnt a lot of things about him when I was on tour with them."

Callan soon discovered the source of Zeppelin's 'wild men of rock' image – it was to do with insurance policies. "When you are in America and you're going to play in front of half a million people and you are the centre of a huge industry that's worth a \$100,000,000, everybody needs insurance. The insurance companies say, 'Okay, we'll cover this tour provided you have guards outside every hotel and dressing room door, and you have police escorts on your cars to and from the gigs.' Eventually what happens is you isolate the musicians from the rest of the world. You stop them interacting, even amongst themselves. They can't knock on each other's hotel room door and say, 'Fancy a walk down the street and getting a pair of jeans?' If one of them is injured then the tour is cancelled and everyone has to get their money back. That's why the insurance companies started imposing conditions. So when the band went on the road they'd find themselves being locked into hotel rooms for months on end. This is where the room trashing came from, which led to that famous story about Peter Grant and the hotel manager."

Peter told the oft-repeated story himself: "We were in the Midwest and I said something to the hotel manager about the fact that it must be tough to have all the rock groups in there throwing furniture and TVs out the windows. He said they had something worse once and that was the Young Methodists Convention. Apparently they threw the carpets and everything out and the guy went into this rap saying, 'It's all right for you guys, throwing all your things out, but how do you think I feel?' So I said, 'You'd really like to do that too, wouldn't you?' And he said, 'Yeah, I'd love to do that.' So I said, 'Well, have one on us. I'll treat you. Do whatever you want.' And he went around and threw all the furniture out the windows and I went down to the desk and paid the bill, which was $490."

The famous motorcades, which seemed such an extravagance, were also part of the requirements of the insurance companies, as Alan explains: "People thought that when Led Zeppelin had six limousines and police motorcycle outriders that they were just being flash. What they didn't understand is that the insurance companies wouldn't let them all travel in the same car together. It was all done for a purpose. I remember being at one of their big shows at Madison Square Garden. I watched the show from the edge of the stage and then walked up the sound tower or the mixing desk and it was absolutely fantastic. One evening for some reason I had to go back to the hotel for a meeting. So I came down the tower, walked through the crowds and found the band's convoy of limos all waiting to go. I just went up to one of the cars and asked the driver if he could take me back to the hotel. He said, 'No problem, get in.' So I got in the front of the limousine and the big gates of Madison Square Garden swung open and off we went. The police outriders thought this was the signal that everybody was going. So the police bikes roar out and all the other limousines follow me. I'm now taking the entire motorcade back to the hotel for my meeting. I'm thinking, 'Oh no, G is gonna kill me!' The band were going to come off stage and there'd be nothing waiting for them. So I get to the hotel and I'm saying, 'You've all gotta go back!' And the police are saying, 'Waal, we've only been booked for one journey.' And I'm saying, 'No, this is terrible, you've gotta go back!'

"Peter found out and gave me a hard time. But he played all kinds of pranks on people, including me. I went to see them at one of their very early shows at the Royal Albert Hall in 1969, before I joined them. I'd bumped into Jimmy Page at Sloane Square and he told me to go to the stage door. He'd leave my name on the door and I could see the show. I thought there would be a support act and so I turned up at 8.30 pm. Of course they were the only act and had been on since 7.30 pm. I turn up banging on the stage door and I hear a voice saying, 'What the fuck do you want?'

"I've been invited to see the show."

"Oh yeah, what's your fucking name?"

" 'It's Alan Callan.' This was my first encounter with Richard Cole. He opened the door and he said, 'Peter and Jimmy are livid with you. They were waiting for you before the show and you never turned up. Peter is screaming, 'Where the fuck is he?' and Jimmy is furious you let him down. He's a mate of yours and you should have been here! Go up there, through those fucking doors and sit down!' I started walking up this corridor and they're all shouting at me and I'm absolutely petrified. I open this door and I'm on the stage. Jimmy comes over and says, 'What are you doing out here? Go and sit by Jonesy's bass bins!' So I sat on the side of the stage for the whole show and the place is going crazy. And afterwards in the dressing room Peter Grant is going, 'Ha, ha, ha – that'll teach yer!' "

Alan Callan saw Peter Grant in many moods and situations but insists: "What Peter most enjoyed in life was watching the artists he worked with becoming successful. Peter always wanted to create the perfect stage for the perfect performance. He wanted to take care of everything in their lives and he was an extraordinary man. There was a time when he wanted Mel Bush to be Zeppelin's promoter in the UK and Mel said, 'When do I get the contract?' Peter just stuck his hand out. That was the deal! Peter had this huge reputation for being intimidating. People quaked in their boots in his presence. But he had to use all the tools at his command and whatever circumstances demanded. In America he encountered lots of people who thought they were very tough and Peter's attitude was they weren't very tough."

Callan insists that in all the years he knew Peter he never saw him physically assault anybody. "He drew a consistent line in his relationships. People would say to him, 'I hear I've upset you,' and he'd say, 'Don't you think if you had upset me, you would have heard about it by now?' He once told me a wonderful story that he'd gone to the hospital because his hand was hurting and he was concerned that he had arthritis. So the doctor said to him, 'Mr Grant, do you use your hand in your work a lot?' 'No but I do a lot of this,' he said and prodded the doctor in the chest. Only Peter would talk to a doctor like that."

Alan didn't quake but he was certainly stunned when he was invited by Mr Grant to work at his behest. "They'd already set up Swan Song when I came along. First they had somebody from Warners, who ran it very briefly. Then they had B.P. Fallon their publicist as their A&R man – briefly again. Then they got Abe Hock from Motown who ran it for six months. Then one day I got this phone call from Jimmy who said, 'I'd really like someone we know on the inside. Call Peter and discuss what it's all about.' So I called Peter and he asked me to the office. We just talked and laughed about stuff and then he suddenly said, 'Okay, Jimmy and me and the boys have decided we want you to run the record label for us.' I remember thinking, 'God, this is amazing!'

"He asked me how much money I wanted, so I told him and he said, 'I think that's too much.' So I said, 'What do you think's fair?' He said a figure and I said, 'Why don't we split the difference.' And he said, 'Okay, right, let's go.' I then said, 'Well, when do you want me to start?' He said, 'Well, you've been here an hour. That'll do.' I actually started about two months before they were due to go on tour and he took me straight from his office down to Manticore where the band were rehearsing."

Manticore was formerly a cinema – and is now a supermarket – in Fulham. The Beatles had once rented it and it was now owned by Emerson, Lake & Palmer, who'd christened it Manticore after *their* own label, as their headquarters. Led Zeppelin also found it a useful place to rehearse, as it was nearer than Shepperton.

Callan: "Peter once said that the perfect office was any building with two staircases. That was so if somebody really boring was coming up the stairs, he could leave by the other staircase! I worked on three projects for Swan Song, none of which came to fruition. I wanted to sign Vangelis, and John Lennon and I wanted to make an album with Maggie Bell. My view of Swan Song was that it was uniquely positioned in that whilst other artists had set up record companies, the artists' own flow of income was mainly responsible for the outcome of that label. With Swan Song that was not the case. Atlantic were perfectly happy for the label to become a successful label in its own right and take the risks. I remember Ahmet Ertegun saying to me, 'Alan, if you'd signed a guy who shook matches and sung I'd be happy to pay the bill.' My original approach was to go out looking at bands, but I thought I'd have to be careful. We'd brought on Bad Company and Dave Edmunds, who were going to be successful, but we were going to struggle with The Pretty Things and we'd got Maggie Bell who hadn't done anything in four years.

"If we signed somebody completely new it would be perceived by everybody as somebody so far down the food chain it would never happen. So I thought the greatest statement Led Zeppelin could make about their label was to demonstrate that this was going to be a major record label and not just a vanity label. So I talked to Peter and said there were three artists that needed attention that we might get going. They were Vangelis, Lennon and Maggie. John Lennon was then living in New York and everyone was wondering if he'd ever make a record again. So Peter and I spent days at Peter's house sending messages to John Lennon, trying to get him to come back. We were trying to figure out a way to create something for him. In the end what happened was David Geffen just walked in and gave him a big fat cheque, and so we lost him to Geffen. Vangelis was with RCA and I thought his musical ability was fantastic and would be appreciated by the boys. It might have been a great meeting of minds."

It was frustrating for Callan that he couldn't get these projects off the ground and he also experienced some problems with Dave Edmunds. "There was some resentment from Dave Edmunds' management. It was like, 'Why do I have to deal with Led Zeppelin to be successful?' There was a kind of strange friction there. But Dave became successful and his talent was allowed to blossom. He was a studio man, producer, guitar player, writer, and arranger. I thought he was a great guy and yet he was conjured into this position where they thought they had to offend Swan Song in order to be successful. There was no need for that. Jimmy and Robert were committed to making sure his band was successful. Dave wasn't arrogant but the people around him were. It was just due to insecurity. They felt – well, 'I'm just as good as Peter Grant and Dave Edmunds is just as good as Led Zeppelin,' which was not true!"

Whenever business matters became 'boring' Peter was ready to forget the day's agenda and entertain his friends with stories of the good old days. "Peter grew up in a show business era," continues Callan. "It always amused me when he told me he was a stand-in for Robert Morley on *Crackerjack*.★ I could never figure out what Robert Morley had to do with *Crackerjack* and why he would be the stand-in! His introduction to show business was really quite extraordinary. I remember him telling me about Gene Vincent and the time Gene was firing a gun in Brighton or somewhere and the police surrounded his house. A gun going off in Britain in the early Fifties was something else. Somehow Peter got to hear about this and rushed over to Gene Vincent's house and charged up the front garden path while the police were shouting, 'Come away from there Mr Grant,

★ A BBC TV children's programme.

he's gotta a gun!' And G is banging on the door shouting, 'Vincent, open this fucking door! What are you doing you stupid bastard!' It turned out it was only a starting pistol. But nobody knew that at the time. There he was, with a bottle of Jack Daniels in one hand, a so-called gun in the other and the police thought Peter was a fantastic hero when he stormed up and disarmed him."

Another of Peter's tales from the rock'n'roll years fascinated Alan. "He told me a story about Little Richard playing the Lyceum in the Strand. Peter had been asked to take over as tour manager as the other guy was ill. Peter drove his Ford Zodiac 200 miles from Liverpool to the Strand Palace Hotel in London. He went to see Little Richard who said, 'I don't think I'll go on tonight.' Peter said, 'Whadya mean, you don't want to go on?' And Little Richard said, 'I really don't feel like it.' Peter said, 'Are you ill?' 'No, I just don't feel I have the right energy for a show tonight.' Peter looked at him and said, 'You look alright to me.' So Grant grabbed him, threw him on the floor, rolled him in a carpet and carried him round to the Lyceum and said to him, 'You're going on!' "

Many years later Alan Callan read an interview with Little Richard in *Rolling Stone*. "The singer was asked of all the amazing things in his life, what stuck out the most. Richard replied, 'The fact that my chauffeur in England now earns more money than I do.' And he talked about Peter Grant – his chauffeur – and the affair of the carpet and how wonderful Grant was and how much he came to trust him. 'This guy always made sure I got paid and that everything worked.' " In 1996, the year after Peter Grant died, Alan was in Atlanta and met Little Richard who said, "I was so sad to hear about Peter."

Says Callan: "Peter was able to achieve all kinds of things by employing his remarkable persona and that included that terrible stare of his. If he decided to stand up and move a bit too close to you, he could intimidate you with his body language. And yet it seems that everybody that really got close to him or had dealings with him, found he also had this extraordinary charm. He had such a great sense of humour, absolutely fantastic."

Callan still questions Grant's decision to run Swan Song from such a small office with just a telex machine. "But then Tamla Motown was started over a shop," he says. "The band did decide to buy a big country house, which they were going to turn into Swan Song offices, residential apartments and a studio complex. They ran into trouble trying to get planning permission. Then they didn't have time to get more detailed planning because they were going off on tour. Peter had this great idea they would lend the house to the local constabulary, so they could train their police dogs there. He was always thinking of these incredible ideas."

After its initial success with Bad Company Swan Song entered a slow decline from which it never really recovered, although all five subsequent Led Zeppelin albums were released on the label, starting with the double whammy *Physical Graffiti* in March 1975. The album's release was delayed due to 'artwork problems' caused by the elaborate cover design, just the sort of thing that shouldn't have happened on their own label yet entirely predictable considering the complex nature of the design.

Equally predictable was *Physical Graffiti* going gold and platinum on the day of release and entering the *Billboard* LP chart at number one. In America it earned some $12,000,000 in a year and revitalised the entire Zeppelin back catalogue which resulted in all their previous albums reappearing in the charts. The new Zeppelin album was their most consistent and impressive work since *Four Symbols* and was greeted with acclaim by the critics, enamoured of such new works as 'Kashmir', 'Houses Of The Holy', 'In My Time Of Dying' and 'Trampled Underfoot'. Even *Rolling Stone*, hitherto unimpressed with Led Zeppelin, changed their tune and featured them on the cover. Inside was a flattering profile by their youngest writer, Cameron Crowe. *Rolling Stone*'s about-turn probably had as much to do with timing as with Crowe's undoubted enthusiasm. The mid-Seventies was UK rock's golden age as far as conquering America was concerned. Bands like Zeppelin, The Rolling Stones, The Who, Pink Floyd, Wings, Black Sabbath, The Faces, Deep Purple, ELP and Yes, and artists like Eric Clapton, David Bowie and Elton John, all achieved extraordinary US success, filling giant arenas with ease and chalking up platinum albums with every release. It would never be the same again.

Physical Graffiti was perhaps Zeppelin's finest hour and certainly a peak moment in the Swan Song saga. Thereafter Peter seemed to lose interest in the label, which was eventually closed down and wound up after the demise of John Bonham and the break-up of the group in 1980. "In a way I was sad that it was wound up but on reflection it was too much for us to take on, what with me trying to manage Bad Company and Led Zeppelin," he would say later. "There were just not enough hours in the day. That's why I passed on managing Queen in 1975. I'd love to have done it but there just wasn't the time. What I regretted about Swan Song was not getting someone in to run it properly. We kept getting it wrong or I did. I couldn't trust people to make the right decisions. It didn't work with Abe Hoch and in America Danny Goldberg became another pain in the arse. I think if we'd have had Alan Callan in from the start it might have been okay. He was a good friend of Jimmy's and knew what we wanted to do. In the end he fell foul of Steve Weiss' ego problems. This all really brought home the situation I found myself in with the label and my home life. I tried to run it like a nine-to-five job, driving up to London for three hours every day. It just wore me out. Then I'd get home and Goldberg or Weiss would be on the line. It was too much.

"If I could have done a David Frost and jetted between New York and London, it might have been okay. But that was never on. That's not to say I didn't enjoy the success we had. I thought Bad Company were the perfect band for the label. That whole 'Can't Get Enough' era was so fresh. We had Maggie Bell doing quite well and The Pretty Things."

As a souvenir of Swan Song achievements Peter took pride in a framed *Billboard* chart with all of his artists listed during one week's appearance from early 1975. However the extra workload was getting too much, even for a man of his vaunting ambition. "It was just that even to do Led Zeppelin justice was a 24 hour a day job. Dave Edmunds and people like that – I just didn't have the time to oversee. Dave had Jake Riviera as a manager anyway, which brought its own set of problems. Of course, we also missed a few acts by not getting to hear the demo tapes. When we cleared out the office we found loads, including demos by Paul Young and The Q Tips."

Although Swan Song missed out on these talents the label signed an unknown singer songwriter called Mirabai. Said Grant later: "That was a perfect example of people making decisions I wouldn't have made and me having to support. That was a Goldberg investment that I persuaded Ahmet to bankroll. It was a similar situation to when I got him to take the Screaming Lord Sutch album that Jimmy and Bonzo had played on years earlier. Of course that wouldn't happen with record companies nowadays!"

9

"DID YOU ENJOY THE SHOW?"

*"You'd think by looking at him that he'd have this great bellowing voice, yet he had
a soft south London twang to him. He actually wasn't loud and he had a slight lisp.
He was just scary to look at and to be around."*
— Journalist Michael Watts

America was Led Zeppelin's happy hunting ground. It was certainly
where they found the most fun, excitement and rewards. As the Zeppelin
empire grew, so they seemed like a behemoth bestriding the land and
laying waste all opposition. Rich, powerful and immensely popular with a
generation of fans hungry for rock, they could do no wrong. As albums
turned gold and platinum and tours sold out overnight, the band and their
manager seemed hell-bent on enjoying a non-stop champagne party while
jetting in pursuit of the next audience to conquer.

Such was their success it seemed scarcely possible that within two years
the party would end amidst drama, tragedy and chaos. Yet the cracks were
already showing. Fame, adulation and riches were heaped on Grant and
his crew, but there was a price to pay in shattered nerves, damaged health
and broken relationships. There was also that strange effect described by
the Greeks as hubris, "an excess of ambition and pride, ultimately causing
the transgressor's ruin", which undermines the best efforts of those who
climb too high, too fast. For the moment however, there was nothing that
Peter Grant couldn't handle, with an oath and a smile.

His growling presence only added to the thrill of being around Led
Zeppelin. People still found him charming, dangerous and fascinating.
The growing problem, barely understood by himself or his entourage, was
that his pioneering methods and Wild West approach might not be
entirely appropriate now that Zeppelin was a mega-successful international business enterprise. The phrase 'corporate rock' was being heard.

The music business was now reckoned to be bigger and more important than Hollywood movies. It was time for the smooth touch and the gracious gesture, a time perhaps to adopt a more conciliatory approach and laid-back attitude. Instead, as personal problems mounted, unseen and unknown to most of the outside world, Grant became if anything more combative, volatile and suspicious. His temper, always fragile, became worse.

On his good days he appeared happy, relaxed and witty. He plunged into life on the road with as much fervour as the rest of the band. Yet his high spirits concealed a deeper malaise. When Zeppelin was off duty during 1974, he could contemplate the successful launch of Swan Song and the development of new talents within the fold, like Bad Company and Maggie Bell. He was secure in the knowledge that the vexed question of the 'home movie' was at last being sorted out. He also knew he had only to snap his fingers and the world would come running for another Zeppelin tour. He could sit back and name his price. As 1975 dawned he had good reason to be content. What could possibly go wrong?

At the beginning of the year the band were confronted by the news that they had to go into tax exile. Said Peter: "The 1975 tour of America was the start of our 'non-residency' in the UK, which we were only told about three weeks upfront. Our accountant Joan Hudson told us of the massive problems we would have if we didn't go. It was an 87 per cent tax rate then on high earners. Disgusting really."

As a result of this threat to their income the band had to live abroad for most of the year. It was a problem that faced many other successful British groups, including The Rolling Stones who began the decade in France. Zeppelin didn't want to leave the country and hated being 'exiles'. Plant and Bonham were particularly unhappy with the whole idea, and Bonzo waited until his daughter Zoe was born before he agreed to leave the country. It was explained to him that if he didn't, practically everything he earned would simply go to the Inland Revenue.

When the group weren't touring they moved to France and Switzerland for a period. Peter Grant chose to live in America and took a rented house on Long Island. Later the entire group moved to Jersey in the Channel Islands, which was the nearest point they could get to England. They rented a large house and spent most of their time drinking and socialising. These long periods away from home only served to destabilise relationships, put temptations in their way and further disrupt their lives.

Said Peter: "I had some problems myself that year and my wife was just fed up with it all and walked out on me. It was not a good scene at all. Jimmy's health was suffering and there were definite drug problems with one or two people, including myself. It was really hard for me, because I had to leave the kids and my divorce was starting."

Drug problems and a divorce? This was devastating news. It showed for the first time that the seemingly tough and invincible Peter Grant had a vulnerable side that all the bluster in the world could not conceal. How he would cope remained to be seen. In the meantime he had a show to put on.

Led Zeppelin returned to the fray, playing their first gigs in 18 months in Holland and Belgium on January 11 and 12, as a warm-up for their tenth American tour. Then came the first ominous blow to their confidence. Travelling up to London from his Sussex home, Jimmy Page caught the ring finger of his left hand in a train door at Victoria Station. It was a painful accident that caused Peter Grant to drop everything and rush to his aid. All 700,000 tickets for the US tour had been sold in advance and this relatively minor injury threatened economic disaster. But Jimmy carried on. He took a lot of painkillers and put his showcase number 'Dazed And Confused' on hold, until the broken finger had mended. There were other matters needing Grant's care and attention. John Bonham's fear of flying meant that he now hated touring to the extent that sometimes Peter had to drive him to the airport to get him on a plane to the States. He was much happier staying on his Worcestershire farm with his family and friends. It was undoubtedly this wrench from home that provoked the kind of misbehaviour that earned Bonzo such notoriety.

But there was work to be done. Led Zeppelin's public awaited. The logistics were awesome. The band that once had a couple of speaker cabinets and a drum kit was now using a 70,000-watt PA system and a huge lighting rig. They also introduced laser beams to the show for the first time. It required a 44-man crew to truck the equipment around the country. The group re-hired the Starship to fly themselves around the States, basing themselves at the Butler Aviation hangar at Newark Airport.

Once the troops were assembled the Zep army kicked off in Minneapolis on January 18. Such was the thrill of expectation the city of Boston had already banned the group, following riots at the box office, long before they'd even arrived in town. A typical day at Grant HQ would see his phone ringing constantly with streams of calls about everything from

Peter was able to strike terror into people simply by glowering at them. This was usually the precursor to what he termed verbal violence. *(Relay)*

Peter with Ahmet Ertegun, the head of Atlantic Records, in New York, 1974.
(Bob Gruen/Starfile)

Peter Grant in his milieu, watching over his charges on stage like a sentinel. *(LFI)*

Peter with Robert Plant at the Chislehurst Caves party to mark the launch of Swan Song Records in the UK, November 1974. *(LFI)*

Peter with John Paul, Robert and Jimmy, accepting an Ivor Novello Award in London, May 1, 1977. *(MSI)*

Richard Cole onstage in Oakland, 1977. *(Richard Cole Collection)*

John Bindon, the notorious London underworld figure whose arrival in Led Zeppelin's security team in 1977 would have disastrous consequences. *(MSI)*

Peter with Robert Plant and John Paul Jones, backstage at Knebworth, August 1979. *(Jill Furmanovsky/Retna)*

Peter kitted out in a tuxedo, the kind of garment he'd never have been seen in during the Seventies, at a Nordoff Robbins charity function in 1995. *(Rex)*

A slimmed down Peter at the 100 Club in London's Oxford Street, in September, 1995, two months before his death. *(LFI)*

Defiant to the last, Peter Grant delivers a verdict that suggests his attitude hadn't mellowed with age. *(AKI/Renta)*

Peter Grant's coffin is carried from St. Peter and St.Paul's Church in Hellingly, East Sussex, on December 4, 1995. *(Becket Newspapers, East Sussex)*

"Peter Grant changed the rules," said Robert Plant after Peter's death. "He re-wrote the rulebook. He was larger than life. A giant who turned the game upside down. Fierce, uncompromising with great humour." *(Corbis/SIN)*

ensuring there was fruit in the dressing rooms to fuel in the plane.

John Paul Jones, placated after his threat to resign, had decided to stay the course. He understood the nature of the beast and was prepared to put up with the stress, as long as he didn't get too involved in the wilder stuff. If he seemed mild mannered and quiet to outsiders, his role on stage remained a crucial element in the band's all powerful music. Whatever happened, he remained well disposed towards his manager.

Recalls Jones: "At its core, Zeppelin was quite a small operation and it was at its most fun when it was just a few people – us, Richard and Peter. Gee came to every gig. Yes he was tough with people. Basically, he hated artists being taken advantage of or screwed.

"Right from the early days he'd had guns pulled on him and people were always trying to arrest him while he was just trying to do his job. It was more civilised in England, but in the States in those days it was still pretty lawless. The promoters would just say, 'I'm not going to pay you.' He kept the worst of what went on away from us, so it wouldn't interfere with our playing. But I remember playing somewhere in Tennessee while Peter was arguing at the side of the stage with the local chief of police, who didn't have confidence in Robert to keep the crowd under control. Some bands would just send everybody wild and not be responsible. But Robert was always pretty responsible and he would never stir up a riot. If he saw trouble brewing, he'd as often as not, just stop and say, 'Look, we're not gonna play anymore.'

"I remember some places where the kids and the police were just using a gig as an excuse to have a go at each other. At one place nobody was paying the slightest bit of attention to us. It was just a big stand-off. Robert said, 'Look, if you don't all sit down, we're just gonna go.' After that we wouldn't allow uniformed police inside our gigs. Police outside, but not inside. They were just too provocative. I saw one police chief, whose feet literally left the ground, jumping up and down like a six year old screaming at Peter to stop the show. It was because the kids were standing on the concrete stadium seating. I think they took Peter downtown and he had to spend a few hours in jail because he wouldn't stop the show. He used to stand up for us and he hated people trying to rip us off. That's what led to that famous scene in *The Song Remains The Same* over the bootlegger.

"The hall managers would get kickbacks and allow these people in to bootleg the show. They thought they could do what they liked, but Peter stood up to them. Consequently everyone put it around that he was this horrible, hard man. And he wasn't at all. It was a tough job dealing with all those American guys. They all worked together and probably said: 'Okay, here comes a bunch of Limeys.' But in standing up to them, he wrote the rules. It used to be a 60/40 split of the proceeds from a show but it ended up 90/10 – in favour of the band. The whole concert business is based on those figures now. In the old days the band would do all the work and the promoter and the owner of the hall took all the cash, for doing virtually nothing. The band was the most important thing and he had to fight for that. Of course the promoters could see their whole way of life being threatened. And it was and they were right!

"As we know, Peter got all his experience from going round with The Yardbirds who had played every toilet in the world. They tried to rip them off, but he was a big fellow and knew that he could stand his ground. He wasn't armed and they could have just shot him. And they did have guns in some of those places. It was pretty dangerous. He brought pro-fessionalism to the business. He didn't need a gun; he could out-talk them. I never really saw him use his fists. He took a pride in out-talking people. His weight kind of backed it up because they thought twice about tackling him. But he used his brain, not his weight. It wasn't even as if he had to say, 'I'll send the boys round.'

"It was just him standing there and saying, 'If you don't like it, we'll go somewhere else.' I'm sure the word spread that this guy knew what he wanted and wasn't going to leave until he got it. A lot of Americans helped us, like Frank Barsalona. The bright ones could see what he was doing and could understand what he was getting at. Peter's whole thing was that if the band makes money, then everybody makes money. They saw that there was enough for everybody and you didn't have to screw everybody for the last cent. The band wouldn't come back, for a start. When you look at the long-term strategy, it all made perfect sense. He was a very smart man which wrong-footed them. They just saw a big guy and thought if they could move quickly they could get round him. But he had all that covered. He wasn't a 'muscle man' at all. The size made people think twice but it was his brain that did all the work."

John Paul explains that Grant fully understood the complexities of the music business, despite his frequent assertions that accountancy and law were 'boring'. "He knew all about contracts and when they were right or wrong. He could see the small print and also the spirit of a contract and just knew when it was geared up against the artist. He wanted to change the contracts and he understood how the business could be better. Record companies, promoters, other managers, were ripping artists off all the time in every possible way."

Former Swan Song executive Alan Callan agrees with John Paul Jones' view on Grant's traditional methods before the advent of computers and credit cards. "Peter always tried to make sure the band never got ripped off. You were coming out of an era when you got paid £300 for the night and you wanted it in cash. Advance ticket sales weren't done by credit card. People paid at the box office. The transition was quite late in time when you consider rock music started in the late Sixties. Peter had a very simple way of auditing. He would phone up the fire chief and say, 'How many people am I allowed to have in here?' And the chief would say, '38,000'. And Peter would get hold of the promoter and say that's what I want paying for. Peter wouldn't recognise the business today. It's all done electronically and Ticket Master would simply give him a printout of the figures from all over North America."

Once it got underway Led Zeppelin's tenth US tour would place huge demands on Grant's energy and resources. During the first few shows at Chicago Stadium, Robert Plant, normally a tower of physical strength, suffered an attack of influenza and struggled through the next shows in Cleveland and Indianapolis. However, the show scheduled for the Missouri Arena, St Louis, on Sunday, January 26, 1975, had to be cancelled. Plant rested at their Chicago hotel, while the rest of the band and entourage decided to take the Starship to Los Angeles for a holiday.

Chris Charlesworth, now *Melody Maker*'s US correspondent based in New York, saw a Chicago concert and was invited to stick around. "There was a band meeting to decide where to go," he recalls. "They paid for the Starship on a daily basis whether they used it or not and nobody wanted to stay in Chicago because it was so cold. John Paul Jones wanted to go to the Bahamas and Bonzo fancied Jamaica. Jimmy wanted to see some girl in LA. Then the pilot stepped in and pointed out that the plane wasn't licensed outside of continental America, so Jimmy got his way. All the way to LA we got roaring drunk and sang old English songs with John Paul on an electric organ. Peter Grant loved it . . . he was singing 'Any Old Iron' and 'My Old Man Said Follow The Van'. He was in a very happy mood."

Meanwhile John Bonham, who had been drinking vodka since before the plane took off, had fallen asleep in the bedroom at the back of the plane. "In fact he had collapsed," says Charlesworth. "I'd shared a limo with him on the way to the airport and Cole came and asked me whether I'd seen him take anything other than vodka. I hadn't but he was drinking it straight from the bottle, like water. The roadies undressed him and put him in a robe and left him on the bed. Then after two or three hours he suddenly woke up and came lurching down the aisle. He spotted one of the stewardesses who was wearing a very short skirt and he grabbed her round the neck. This girl screamed and Cole and Grant dragged Bonzo off the poor girl. The pilot came out and said, 'What's going on! You people come on this plane and behave like animals.' Grant was full of apologies and meanwhile Bonham was dragged back into the bedroom. Jimmy Page calmed the girl down and put his arm around her and said, 'He didn't really mean it, he didn't know what he was doing.' Very diplomatic he was, but the whole incident changed the fun atmosphere of the plane ride."

On the flight from Chicago to LA, Charlesworth sat in the cockpit at one point and watched the pilots at work. Then a pilot asked him if he wanted to have a go. "So I sat in his seat and held the stick for a few minutes. Then I went back into the plane and told G what I had done. 'That's nothing,' he replied. 'Bonzo flew us all the way from New York to fucking Chicago last week.'"

There was a reason for this apparent madness, as John Paul Jones explains: "Bonzo loved playing drums, but he hated being on tour. I remember in the early days he wouldn't go to bed until it was light. I used to sit up with him, just talking or listening to the radio. He really hated being away and he hated flying. So that was another thing that made him drink. We'd send cars to drive him to the airport and he'd been known to order the driver to turn round and take him back to Birmingham.

"His fear of flying actually got better, once we had our own plane. They let him sit at the controls of our jet liner and because he loved fast driving, he suddenly realised flying was a bit like driving his car. They let him do a few moves and I'm sure I can remember somebody coming out of the loo at the back saying, 'What the hell was that!' as the plane lurched. He came out of the cockpit with a big smile on his face and said, 'That's the fastest thing I've ever driven!'

"Like a lot of people with a fear of flying, once they feel they are in control then it's not so alien. Peter wasn't a great flyer either but John really hated it. He drank at the airport because he knew he had to get on a plane, and then when he was on the plane he'd create a bit because he was drunk. He was boisterous rather than abusive. He just got loud and we had to calm him down." Safely in LA the group stayed in the Continental Hiatt House on Sunset Strip and partied for 24 hours before flying all the way back to North Carolina. Recalls Chris: "The gig was really awful and everyone was very tired."

The show on Wednesday, January 29, 1975, was at The Greensboro Coliseum. It was a lacklustre performance, probably because Jimmy, John Paul and Bonzo had been obliged to rise at an uncharacteristically early hour to fly coast to coast (against the time zones) from Los Angeles to reach Greensboro in time. Robert, who flew in from Chicago, benefited from another day in bed and didn't have anything like so far to travel. Outside the venue a shortage of tickets for waiting fans caused more violence to erupt. This sparked off one of Peter Grant's most spectacular exploits. By the time he'd finished it looked like a scene from a Bruce Willis *Die Hard* movie.

Charlesworth: "It was a horrible gig and nobody wanted to do it. About five hundred fans attempted to storm the rear of the building, throwing broken bottles, stones and pieces of scaffolding. They even threw stones at the band's limos and three of the five limousines were severely damaged. The drivers of the other two – which were parked inside the building – wanted to take their cars away. Peter Grant wasn't having that . . . oh no . . . he was livid!" Only two limos had been able to drive into the arena while the other three had to park outside. Instead of having five limos to rescue the entourage from a riot situation they were reduced to two and their drivers also wanted to take their cars away, leaving the Led Zeppelin entourage stranded.

"They wanted the huge gates at the back of the stadium opened so they could drive out," continues Charlesworth. "Peter was called and he started shouting at the drivers, who said they had to go or else their limousines would get damaged. So Grant says, 'Alright, how much do you want for your fucking limousines. How much are they fucking worth? Forty thousand dollars each? I'll fucking buy them from you right now.' He carried a lot of cash around with him and usually had a hundred grand in his briefcase. The drivers protested, 'We can't sell them, they're not ours to sell.' So Grant says, 'In that case, I'll fucking steal them. I've offered to buy them and if you can't sell them, I'll just fucking take them.' The drivers said: 'You can't do that!'

" 'Don't be fucking stupid,' replied Peter. 'Of course I can do that. I can do what I fucking want, can't I? I've got twenty men working for me. You can't fucking stop me, ya' cunts.' So the upshot was all the people who had previously fitted into five limos now had to get into two. Grant said to the drivers, 'We don't need you. We'll drive the fucking cars ourselves.' Peter drove one and a guy called Magnet, a roadie for Deep Purple who was along for the ride, drove the other."

At the end of the set, Richard Cole came on stage with large red towelling robes for the band and they dashed off and jumped into the first car with Grant at the wheel. The stadium doors opened and a huge mob surged forward. Grant blasted a way through with his horn blaring and the crowd parted like the Red Sea. With a police escort, sirens blazing, the truncated convoy drove at speeds of up to 70 mph in a heavily built-up area. Grant led the way, driving through red lights and on the wrong side of the road. "After he'd driven the band and Richard Cole back to where the plane was waiting at the airport, he drove round and round the huge aircraft, tyres screeching, faster and faster," says Charlesworth. "When he finally came to a stop someone asked him why he'd done that. He replied, 'The band were placing bets on whether I dare crash it into the plane.'

"It was incredible to be involved in scenes like that . . . Peter was just unstoppable. When he got out he kicked the car really hard. 'Fucking useless pile of fucking junk!' he shouted. 'Way off tune . . . my old Bentley goes twice as fast!' We all just stood there laughing . . . totally exhilarated by it all. Then we flew back to New York and the band checked in the Plaza. It was a very tiring day. Unforgettable, though. When you rode with Zeppelin you rode high and fast."

Peter clearly enjoyed taking over the limo drivers' jobs. Perhaps it harked back to the days when he owned a minibus and chauffeured pop stars in the early Sixties. Certainly the episode at Greensboro wasn't a one-off. Peter Clifton recalls a similar incident during the making of *The Song Remains The Same*. "I always thought that Peter Grant was part swaggering pirate and part father figure. He was impulsive, wild, vengeful and uncontrollable. I remember when we were filming Led Zeppelin in Boston. We were backstage and there was a teeming crowd outside who pushed through the barriers at the end of the concert. They came right into the backstage parking lot and it was very scary. I packed up my cameras, but the limo drivers had bailed out. We were totally cut off. Peter grabbed one driver and said, 'You call your boss and tell him this car is now mine,' and he handed him his Gold Amex card. He grabbed Jimmy Page by the scruff of the neck, shoved him into the car and the other band members followed. Peter jumped into the driver's seat and floored the long black Cadillac. He drove like a maniac right through a fire hydrant, which exploded. He bumped over the gutter and onto the main road. I watched in amazement and awe as the limo sped out of sight."

During the next two months the band grossed a further five million dollars. It wasn't surprising the young rock gods were eager to let their hair down. They were richer than they'd ever dared imagine, especially Bonzo who'd worked as a building labourer. Now they could have anything they wanted and do whatever they pleased, all in the name of rock'n'roll. There were certainly plenty of people standing in the wings ready to help them enjoy themselves. Their PR Bill Harry recalls what it was like, before he bowed out of the Zeppelin camp, exhausted and with his trousers ripped courtesy of John Bonham's escapades. "We went to all these clubs in America and the places were flooded with groupies. It was always booze and mainly lager. Everybody had hangovers. But most of that was caused by sitting around in rooms for 15 hours of tension before a gig."

The promoter Bill Graham threw one particularly lavish party in their honour after a gig at the Winterland in San Francisco. The Winterland didn't have much space for entertaining, so he hired a suite at a nearby hotel. After the show they went to the suite. Suddenly the doors opened and two trolleys came in bearing naked girls with food placed over their bodies. "Bill Graham gave everybody foam cream to spray over the girls," says Harry. "The drinks were flowing and there were all kinds of orgies going on with people taking Polaroid pictures. Screaming Lord Sutch joined the party but he conked out on a bed. Somebody who had been bonking in the bath left the taps running and the water started going all over the carpets.

"After a couple of hours it leaked through the ceiling onto the floor below. Somebody complained to the management and the house detective started banging on the door. They used a pass key to get into the flooded bedroom and found Lord Sutch lying on the bed covered in Polaroid pictures of all the action."

During February the rampaging hordes of Zep played six concerts to 120,000 people in the New York area alone at Madison Square Garden and Nassau Coliseum on Long Island. The tour ended in March with three dates at the LA Forum. It wasn't until the end of the US tour that Swan Song finally released *Physical Graffiti* which should have been out months earlier. At least it was in time for the band's milestone UK concerts.

Led Zeppelin played five nights at the Earls Court Arena in London on May 17, 18, 23, 24 and 25 which went down as among their finest ever shows. British fans saw the full American show complete with lights and lasers. They played five songs from the new album. None of the ecstatic fans at Earls Court could know they wouldn't see their heroes again for another four years. It was their finest hour but it was already Led Zeppelin's swansong.

Peter saw these shows as 'keeping faith with the fans'. He chose Earls Court because he thought it was then the biggest and best venue in London for a big concert. He also liked the promoter. "Mel Bush did a great job with those dates and Earls Court was fantastic. Nobody sat behind the stage. We had the video screen and the whole Showco stage set up. It took half a Jumbo jet to get it over. Mel Bush did a super job in presenting those gigs.

"He presented us with souvenir mirrors afterwards depicting the 'Physical Rocket' idea used for the advertising. Mel told me that we had enough ticket applications to have done ten shows that month. There was a video of the shows, which Jimmy Page took when he came around to my house one day. They could be used for a video release one day. I just never really rated the idea of Zeppelin on the small screen."

Unusually for a new album *Physical Graffiti* had yielded much material that was instantly popular with audiences. Usually people clamoured for old favourites but they were stunned by two pieces in particular that marked a complete stylistic departure for the band. 'Trampled Underfoot' mainly featuring John Paul Jones on funky electric piano was a funky driving riff more in the spirit of Stevie Wonder than heavy metal. 'Kashmir' was even more unusual, a kind of Moroccan chant that reflected the interest Jimmy and Robert took in the music of the Middle East. Zeppelin was playing 'world music' long before the phrase was coined.

Even the critics liked 'Kashmir'. Yet its orchestral backing developed into a doomy, menacing soundscape that left some nonplussed, including their manager. Said Peter: "I remember Bonzo playing me the demo of 'Kashmir' and Jimmy running it down on guitar for me. It was fantastic. But the funny thing is when it was first finished it was decided it was a bit of a dirge. We were in Paris and we played it to Atlantic and we all

ought it was a dirge, so Richard Cole was dispatched to Southall in west
ondon to find a Pakistani orchestra. We put the strings on and Jonesy got
all together and the end result was just exactly what was needed. He was
master arranger."

Jonesy's skills were now so well respected within the music business that
e was accorded a high honour. Much to Peter's envy John Paul was
troduced to Grant's all-time idol, 'The King' of rock'n'roll Elvis Presley.
ecalled Peter: "Jonesy and Richard met him in 1974 during the launch
eriod for Swan Song. Richard had a watch and they had a swop. Elvis
ve Jonesy a watch with an east coast and west coast face. I met Elvis
yself in 1975."

Peter and the band went to see Elvis perform at one of his Las Vegas
ows. "We were sitting about twelve rows from the front of the stage. He
ad a big band with lots of singers. They did a number and the band was
ut of time and all over the place. Elvis goes, 'Stop, stop, stop,' and he
rns to the audience and says, 'We're gonna do that again because we've
ot Led Zeppelin in the audience and we want to look like we know what
e're doing up here.' I just went cold. It was the nearest I came to snuffing
I mean, what a compliment. And we went backstage and that's when I
t on Elvis Presley's father."

This proved to be one of Grant's funniest after dinner stories, which
oth he and friends delighted in recounting whenever a fit of nostalgia set
. "We were in this huge suite. Jerry Weintraub★ told me we'd only got a
0-minute stay and we were up there for two and a half hours. Bonzo and
lvis had been talking about hot rods and about how much kickback you
an get. And John was calling him 'El' and he says, 'I've had one El that
cked back real hard' and he pushes Elvis' shoulder and knocks him back-
ards. All the minders jump up but Elvis laughs and says, 'What did you
o that for?' And John replies, 'Well I've got to tell you El, I was in reverse
the time!'"

Meanwhile, as the evening wore on, Peter desperately needed some-
here to sit down. 'I suffer from a lot of back trouble and I was talking to
onnie Tutt and his wife. Ronnie was Elvis' drummer. Behind me was a
ng couch and I said to Ronnie, 'I've gotta sit down, cos my back's
urting.' I sat down and realised I had landed on somebody's legs. I
mped up and looked down and realised it was Vernon Presley in a white

US promoter who handled Presley's concerts and worked with Led Zeppelin in 1975.

suit. I said, 'I'm really sorry Mr Presley for sitting on you, but I guess if anybody is going to do that in this room, it's gotta be me.' Well, when we were leaving after two or three hours, we shook hands and said goodbye. Elvis said, 'It was wonderful of you to come up and visit me Mr Grant.' I said, 'Well I must tell you something Elvis, I've gotta apologise for sitting on your dad.' He looked me straight in the eye and said, 'Stick around kid, you might get a permanent job.' That was the best line anyone ever laid on me."

It was certainly friendlier than the response Grant got from the notoriously grouchy Bob Dylan. When Peter introduced himself to the harmonica blower at an LA party he said, "Hello Bob, my name's Peter Grant. I'm the manager of Led Zeppelin." Replied the great sage, "Do I come to you with my problems?"

Grant renewed his acquaintanceship with the Presley camp a couple of years later in 1977 when he began to negotiate with Colonel Tom Parker to see if he could finally induce Presley to come to Britain for the kind of tour that his UK fans had long dreamt about. It would have been a great coup. Peter: "I was talking to Colonel Tom just before Elvis's death, for him to come to England, but not as a promoter. He wanted me to advise him on where Elvis should play. Just before Elvis passed away I was living on Long Island just outside New York with Bad Company and that week he died, I was going to take the band to see him at Nassau County Coliseum. On the Sunday I was having lunch with Jerry Weintraub and the Colonel to discuss Elvis coming to England and who would be the best promoter. After seeing Elvis playing in Las Vegas and in New York I was sure he would have liked to get back to his rock roots."

Sadly Elvis passed away before this plan could come to fruition. Given Zeppelin's penchant for playing rock'n'roll, it would have been marvellous to hear the first great white blues singer with the greatest white rock blues band. After all, they got close when Zep backed P.J. Proby on an album. It all depended on whether Robert Plant would have minded playing tambourine for 'The King'.

After the May 1975 concerts at Earls Court Led Zeppelin became tax exiles once again and set up a temporary HQ in Montreux, Switzerland. Robert Plant had set off on a family holiday in Morocco and later he met up with Jimmy Page in Marrakesh for a drive through the desert in a Range Rover. From there they drove back to Europe and met up with the band in Montreux to plan a 33-date US tour due to start in August. Once business was done, Page and Plant left with their families for a holiday on he Greek island of Rhodes. Page went on to Italy and planned to meet he rest of the band in Paris to start rehearsals. But on August 4 Robert and is family were involved in a crash in their hired Austin mini car. His wife Maureen was driving the car and hit a tree, suffering a fractured pelvis and kull while their children Karac and Carmen in the rear seat escaped with inor injuries. Jimmy's daughter Scarlet was also in the car. Robert had ultiple fractures of the ankle and elbow. They were taken to hospital and hen airlifted back to London. Maureen spent several weeks in hospital nd doctors told Plant he wouldn't be able to walk again for at least six onths.

The band's plan for a round the world tour to fill in their tax exile eriod had to be scrapped while all attention was focused on the treatment nd recuperation of Robert and his family. Richard Cole recalls that Peter Grant told him, "This could be the end of Led Zeppelin."

Peter: "We had a second tour of the US all lined up as we were going to e away from England all year. I was in the South of France when I heard bout Robert's crash. It was a nightmare. We were trying to run the oper-tion from a house in Malibu, which was a crazy idea. There was a lot of ension about that period because we were all holed up in houses we idn't really want to be in."

Eventually Robert went to stay in Jersey in the Channel Islands with the est of the band, as it was nearer to England. On this visit to the island they ut on an impromptu show at Behan's nightclub. When the club owner nnounced to a small crowd, "And tonight, we present Led Zeppelin," obody believed him, until they came on stage.

In October the band went to Los Angeles where they rehearsed before arting to record their next album, *Presence*, in November at Musicland tudios in Munich, Germany. Robert had to sing while supported by a air of crutches with his leg in plaster. They spent December 1975 back in ersey, completing their year out. *Presence*, which contained the standout rack 'Achilles Last Stand', was finally released in April 1976.

Peter thought that the time recording the album in Munich was, "An phill struggle. It was difficult in the writing and rehearsing stage and then ve were pressured into recording it quickly. It was not one of my favour-e albums but there again it's got 'Achilles' which is a masterpiece. The ong 'Tea For One' sums that period up for me really. That was Maureen's ong. She used to come out to Munich at weekends and Robert was pretty epressed when she was away."

The album sleeve was quite a departure for Zeppelin. The design by Hipgnosis featured a surreal object called an obelisk placed in photograph of normal everyday situations like family snapshots. "The idea was to put into perspective whether the obelisk was real or just an illusion," said Peter. "The only time it becomes real is on the inner sleeve when you can see the shadow. On the sleeve it looks a bit stuck on. Our sleeves were often controversial. The Spanish authorities banned *Physical Graffiti* because it had a picture of a nun on the inner sleeve. They stamped 'censored' on it."

The band's tax exile period finished in spring 1976 and there were rumours that the band would play a small club like London's Marquee for their comeback appearance. "We were always getting offers but we weren't ready to do it," said Peter. "It was getting a bit worrying at that time. There were problems with Jimmy having squatters in his house we had to get rid of."

While Zeppelin were undergoing an enforced fallow period, another Swan Song act were having the time of their lives. Grant's signing Bad Company were 'doing the business' and he was especially pleased and delighted with their success. With their hit song 'Can't Get Enough' constantly on the radio the band were a hot property. *Melody Maker*'s Chris Charlesworth reported on their progress, often in the company of their now legendary manager. Chris remembers going to San Francisco with Bad Company for a show at Bill Graham's venue The Winterland, scene of many a British band's triumph. Paul Rodgers and friends were in Frisco with Dr Feelgood as their support act. They also played to crowds of 18,000 at the LA Forum.

Chris: "They were really making it big at this time. On the flight from San Francisco to LA in 1976, another private plane, I was sitting minding my own business when a roadie came down the aisle and whispered in my ear, 'Peter wants to see you.' It was like being summoned to the judge. I made my way to the private room at the back of the plane where he was sat with some of the band. There was lots of cocaine on a table and Peter offered me some. 'Did you enjoy the show Chris?' he asked, quite pleasantly, all smiles. 'Er . . . yes Peter.' 'Well, mind you say so in the paper. You can go now.' There was a big smile on his face but there was also a hint of menace. I wouldn't want to say, 'Oh the bass wasn't mixed too well and the drummer was a bit speedy and the show dipped in the middle.' It was not the place to say that kind of thing. The following night at the LA Forum Jimmy and Robert sat in with Bad Company. I had lined up a photographer to cover the gig but he was banned from the stage. Then when Jimmy and Robert got up, Richard Cole shouts at me, 'Where's your fucking photographer? This is your front page story!' "

In vain Chris spluttered, "But you told him to go away!" He eventually located the snapper and the picture duly made the front page of *MM*. "We got there in the end but there was always this paranoia. If they had been milder in their attitude at the beginning, there wouldn't have been all this stress at the end. I suppose they thought a photographer would get in their way. Yet they were often very indiscreet. A photographer once snapped Led Zeppelin at Rodney Bingenheimer's English Disco with scantily dressed young girls draped all over them, and *MM* printed it. I heard it didn't go down too well with their wives back home."

The Bad Company gigs coincided with a Swan Song summit meeting in Los Angeles and all of Led Zep bar John Paul Jones were in attendance. "I was in a limo on the way to the Forum with Plant when he opened the roof in the car park and stood on the seat, all bare chest and long curly hair. He looked out over the crowds and started saying something like 'my people' as if he was about to address them on matters of great hippy philosophical importance. Then someone in the car – probably Richard Cole – yelled, 'Sit down ya' fucking prat! You'll start a fucking riot.' "

When Bad Company's first album was released it became an instant hit. In fact it was number one in the charts the week Charlesworth saw them supporting headliners Foghat at the Schaffer Music Festival in Central Park, New York, in 1974. Jimmy Page joined Bad Co on stage for an encore, and the audience went berserk. It was a hard act to follow and many of the crowd began to leave, much to Foghat's distress. Jimmy Page, Peter Grant and Bad Company also left the park and it was on the way back to the hotel that Charlesworth witnessed the great 'Peter Grant Foot In The Door Incident'.

"Everyone was in a very good mood after the gig. There were two limos backstage for Page, Grant and us. Peter was getting into the back seat but the chauffeur was clearly overeager. He slammed the door shut and caught Peter's foot in the door. Peter just exploded! The language was terrible. 'What the fuck do you think you're doing, ya' fucking cunt!'

"The driver realised he had made a terrible mistake. Mistake number one was crushing Peter Grant's foot. Mistake number two was to say, 'I'm terribly sorry Peter.'

" 'Who the fuck told you you could call me Peter? It's Mr Grant to you, ya fucking cunt!'

"Peter went on like that all the way to the Essex House hotel," say Charlesworth. "You could have cut the atmosphere with a knife. He just didn't stop abusing this driver. It went on for 15 minutes or more, just relentless abuse. 'You'll never drive another fucking car again, you fucking useless cunt!' Even Jimmy Page seemed worried and we all sat there in embarrassed silence, not daring to speak while Peter shouted and ranted. The driver was really nervous and he was still getting grief, even when we got to the hotel. That poor man . . .

"The strange thing was that Peter came on like a tyrant and his enormous bulk backed him up. He could act like a vicious thug yet underneath he was as gentle as a kitten. I'd see him cry like a baby with tears in his eyes if someone said something nice, some genuine compliment. The more vicious the person, the more sentimental they become. I could never understand why he later recruited real criminals like John Bindon to work as a security man for him. Nobody was going to hit Peter or start a fight with him. If Peter asked for something in an intimidating manner, then ninety-nine per cent of the population would give it to him and the other one per cent are stupid. The real violence was completely unnecessary. He could simply be abusive and no one was ever going to argue with him."

Even so there were signs that Peter was growing increasingly worried and disturbed by inexplicable events that impinged on the band. He was brave and strong but he needed help. It was tour manager Richard Cole who brought in Bindon, a London villain with a taste for show business, to act as bodyguard to Grant and Page. Cole and Grant had intelligence, humour and charm to counteract their pseudo villainy. Bindon had few such redeeming features and his presence would subsequently have damaging effects on the band's image.

Swan Song executive Alan Callan could see how the mood of the times was changing. The free and easy good time party atmosphere was being replaced by something more sinister: "In 1975 there were all these death threats and security got really tight with guards licensed to carry guns travelling with the band. It was unpleasant but necessary. Peter had to deal with all this. The job of being manager of a band of that scale brought enormous pressure. People always wanted something from him and there was always someone who thought they could get a buck from him. People wanted to deal in merchandising. In those days we didn't make tour

T-shirts because we thought it ripped off the fans. Whereas today bands think that for every ticket they sell, they sell two T-shirts.

"Peter lived with enormous stress all the time and he was not only supposed to cope with the professional issues. He had to manage the personal affairs and relationships of a bunch of musicians. And that wasn't always an easy task. And he was there 24 hours a day for the band.

"I remember an incident where there was a guy in California who was making phone calls to Robert's parents in England, pretending to be a doctor and having the results of a medical test which showed some very negative effect on Robert's body. Peter's immediate reaction was to get the telephone company to switch all the calls to his house at Horselunges and speak to his friends in America at AT&T to have the calls traced. He'd get on the phone and pretend to be Robert's dad.

"It was an all-encompassing job. Peter's philosophy was very simple. You were either a friend or a foe. You were either somebody he could trust, or you weren't. If he could trust you, then you'd do business with him forever. If he didn't trust you, then you couldn't get anywhere near him. It was all about moments in time. I never found the guy threatening or intimidating. I thought he was a fantastically funny man to be around."

Alan loved the way Grant cooked up ways to cap a story. He experienced this one night at the trendy London club Tramp, in Jermyn Street. Grant was having dinner with Jimmy, John Paul Jones, Ahmet Ertegun, Mick Jagger, Keith Richard and Richard Cole. It was just after The Rolling Stones had left Atlantic and signed to EMI. "It was the first time Ahmet had seen them since the split from Atlantic," recalls Alan. "Peter said to me, 'At some point in the dinner, the question is going to have to be asked.' Then eventually Ahmet turns around and says to Mick, 'What was it that made you leave Atlantic and go to EMI?' and Peter kicked me under the table. Mick said graciously, 'Well Ahmet to tell you the truth, when we sat down to consider The Rolling Stones, we never thought we'd get to this peak. We look on this as our harvest period, when we went for the biggest amount of money we could get and EMI put the biggest amount of money on the table. That was the harvest we wanted.'

"Peter turned round and said, 'Oh, you should have signed with Swan Song. Alan gets our harvest up front.' I think he'd been rehearsing that line in his head all evening."

Whatever wit Peter was inclined to show when out on the town, the mood of paranoia and aggression at the heart of Zep's operations was on the increase, and the band's friends could not ignore the telltale signs and its effects on their manager. Says Callan: "One of the sad things about success and wealth is that it does become negative.

"In previous generations people who accumulated wealth bought land. What came with the land was a community. When you are a rock star or a businessman you buy isolation, you don't buy community. There used to be a whole feudal system that brought stability. When you are a rock star and you own a huge house and you go off on the road for three months, your wife is stuck in the middle of nowhere with very few friends and nobody treats you as normal. This kind of wealth brings you isolation. You own a great manor but nobody is allowed to knock on the front door. That puts great stress and strain on marriages. It did on mine and on Richard Cole's."

Managing Zeppelin put great strain on Peter Grant's marriage to Gloria and now he was about to endure the shock and pain of divorce, which undermined his confidence and sapped his good spirits. Alan Callan: "The years 1974 through to 1975 were very difficult for him. Gloria was living at Horselunges when it happened and then he moved and went into isolation for a while. The situation was exacerbated by the fact that the rock'n'roll business is not a nine-to-five job. He said it was 'five years of fun and 25 years of hanging about.'"

Peter Grant separated from his wife Gloria in 1976 following a breakdown in their relationship exacerbated by the constant touring and absence from home. The split became permanent when Peter discovered his wife had found somebody else to share her life. His loyal lieutenant Richard Cole observed the drastic effects of the catastrophic marital collapse on Grant's mood and temperament. "It was during the time when we were editing the Zeppelin movie and I used to have to fly over to Los Angeles every couple of weeks because he wouldn't leave LA. They kind of left me in charge. Gloria was very down-to-earth and quite a small woman. Moving into those big houses was a bit overwhelming for her. It was like, 'Oh my God, what's all this?' I think all the Zeppelin wives were a bit amazed to find out that the men they had married turned out to be multi-millionaires. They were all married before they became successful, apart from Jimmy. John was with Pat, Robert was with Maureen and John Paul Jones was with Mo and Peter was with Gloria. So they were all happily married. And it wasn't too hard to live with success. They all got nice cars! Bonham was the most generous. John Paul Jones didn't drive a car in those days. He had a Rolls Royce and a chauffeur."

What went wrong?

"Well basically everyone was doing coke. Peter was pretty straight. He'd have a drink and that was it. But what happened was one day he had a toothache. He was moaning about it so much I said, 'Well put a bit of this on it, that'll cure it.' So I gave him some cocaine to stick on his gum and of course that did cure the pain. And from then on he started to get into coke. And of course in the music business, if you're waving a bag of coke around, the women come running. It was very strange. To get to the band the girls would even climb up the outside of buildings. I'd have to keep them off but I was a scaffolder, so I wasn't worried about heights!"

Many wondered how such a strong-willed man like Peter could have got into drugs.

"Well a lot of strong-willed people get into drugs! The drugs take over and that's all there is to it. The pattern of his life changed. Whereas Peter would call his wife every day, once he got into coke, the phone calls didn't come at the usual time every night. Gloria sussed something was going on. Once that happened, he was finished in one sense. He kind of fell apart after that and never really recovered, I don't think. He became a different person. A nastier side came out. There he was, one of the richest men in the country and certainly the most powerful man in the music business and suddenly your wife runs off with a hired hand, who was in charge of the cows! It was a terrible blow to his ego and he never got over it. My own relationship with him didn't change that much, simply because I was getting divorced from my wife for the same reasons."

When Peter first discovered what was happening back home, he seemed to take it with a degree of phlegmatic good humour; but then he had his own peccadilloes to conceal as Mickie Most recalls:

"Of course away from the band the rest of his world was his wife Gloria and the two kids, Warren and Helen. I know what happened. He finished a tour and instead of coming back he said, 'I'm just going to sleep for three days and then I'll be back refreshed.' In fact he was with some other woman for three days and Gloria found out and that kind of put the cat amongst the pigeons. Gloria ran a little dance school for the local kids and she had her life well organised while Peter was on the road, battling away.

"She wasn't sitting at home saying, 'Oh, where are you Peter?' She got on with her life in the nicest possible way. And when she found out about this other stuff it kind of jaded the relationship. Then when Peter went away on tour again they took on a new guy to work on the farm they owned. Peter said to me: 'When I came back from the tour I was having breakfast and sitting at the breakfast table was this farm manager. And he didn't get the burnt sausage. Then I realised something was up.' What he meant was the favourite doesn't get the burnt sausage. You know what I mean? If you are staying in digs with a glamorous landlady, you know who is giving her one because – he never gets the burnt sausage! It was one of Peter's many original expressions. He tried to repair the problem with Gloria, but she had fallen in love with the guy, so it wasn't a question of a fling between friends.

"She said, 'I'm in love.' And that kind of killed Peter off and took a lot out of him. It all came at the wrong time. He was having problems with Led Zeppelin because of their drugs and booze. I went to Paradise Island in the Bahamas and Jimmy Page was there and he never came out of his hotel room in two weeks. I also went to his birthday party when he had a big house out in Windsor, which he bought from Michael Caine. They had roast pigs on spits and all sorts and he never turned up. He never even turned up for his own birthday party. So it was all a funny time.

"You led an unusual life being in Led Zeppelin. They were touring continuously and they lost their sense of reality. Add to that taking sub- stances and it's a bad mix. You're living in a world where nobody says 'no' to you. The record companies, the tour promoters say 'yes' to everything. 'I want five girls with 80-inch breasts.' They'll be there. 'I want a red, white and blue Cadillac.' Anything you want, it will be there. My point is that nobody says 'no' and of course that is very unhealthy. You can almost commit murder. Rape. Pillage. Driving cars into swimming pools at parties. It's a terrible thing really. There was an element of fun about it, but in retrospect, looking back, you see how silly it all was.

"I remember being on the road with Zeppelin and saw the way they treated people. This reporter came to see them and they started pouring beer all over him and insulting his girlfriend. There were times when it got out of hand. And I'm sure if they look back on it, the guys who were responsible would probably say they wouldn't behave that badly if they could live their lives again.

"I know it came with the territory, to be outrageous and do things you knew you could get away with, but there was something unpleasant about it all. It might have seemed fun at the time but in retrospect, it wasn't very nice. Most of the people in rock bands were just normal guys who didn't want to be sheet metal workers or go down the coal mines. Nobody would turn up in a Rolls Royce and say, 'I want you to sign me. I've got a band but we don't need any money.' That never happens. They always come from the wrong side of the tracks. It was an option in the Sixties. You liked music; you bought a guitar and learned to play it. All of a sudden you've got your friends around you and they can play a bit. That's how it developed. Even The Beatles started off as a skiffle group and ended up being the best musicians, singers and writers we'd ever seen. You need to be a very strong character for success not to go to your head *or* you have to have very strong management.

"It's hard to control a group because there are four people there who are all different and basically they are not mugs. Every one of Led Zeppelin could play and they were all wonderful musicians and Robert Plant sang like an angel. They all had this wonderful ability and there was nobody along for the ride. They were hard to control but Peter had a unique relationship with them. The problem with that is it always turns nasty in the end. It always turns sour. Nobody knows why. It's not one particular thing that happens."

Most does not buy the view that Grant and Zeppelin had an indestructible bond. "There's far too much sugar in it. When Led Zeppelin started Peter was like the fifth member of the band. He would kill for those guys and he made sure they never got ripped off for one programme, one ticket or T-shirt. He was really meticulous. For him it was like a matter of life or death or even more important than that. So I figured that their relationship was so unique and they were so tight that eventually it became very claustrophobic. I think by the end of their fourth album everybody wanted some air and freedom. The relationship had started off being very healthy and then it became unhealthy and that happens a lot.

"My relationship with Peter Grant was very close and then drifted apart because he changed as a person through the tremendous hard work and success and all that goes with that. He had a personality change and of course the split-up with Gloria was like the nail in the coffin. Then he was kind of morally broken and he wasn't the Peter Grant that we all knew and had a good time with. He never said anything to me that was abusive and not correct but he became very secretive, which he never was before. There were always secret phone calls going on and you felt a bit uncomfortable around him."

Grant fought to cope with the break-up of his marriage. Despite jokes about 'burnt sausages' he was consumed by anger and, as Richard Cole recalls, seemed bent on revenge, although quite what he proposed to do about Gloria's new beau was never made clear, even to Richard. "He called me up and I went down to Horselunges one day with a shotgun," he recalls, "and a few other guns locked in the trunk of the car, while he decided what he wanted me to do with this guy. Gloria was talking to him and he was trying to find out what was going on."

The pair approached the house but Grant, who was in an agitated state, appeared stymied by his own moat and drawbridge. "The house was on an island with a moat around it and I was on the outer perimeter," says Cole. "Peter wanted to get back into the house. I had pretty good judgement and figured if I climbed up this tree, I could get onto a branch and then across the moat. Unfortunately the tree was rotten and the branch snapped and I fell into the middle of the moat." The incident ended on a fairly peaceful note but Cole says that a fortress state subsequently pervaded Grant's beautiful home.

Observes Alan Callan: "I don't think Peter ever got over his divorce from Gloria because he was the kind of person who believed that marriage and friendship was for life. I don't think he ever recovered from the fact that something he'd held so dear was taken away. It was a great personal tragedy. He eventually won custody of the children, Gloria left and he ran the house properly. He did everything he possibly could, but as far as he was concerned, within his life, he had failed. And he was not a man used to failure.

"When things went wrong, all his life he had been able to find a solution. If you worked with him and you had a problem in your life, then he'd solve it for you. Then suddenly there was this problem in his life and he didn't solve it."

In the midst of all this there was the unspoken fear that the band he helped create wanted to get rid of him. Strung out, nerves on edge, it wasn't surprising that he'd launch into blistering attacks on anyone who got in his way, offended his pride – or slammed a door on his foot. Peter Clifton, still busy working on *The Song Remains The Same* during this traumatic period, could see the way Grant was beginning to succumb to emotional turmoil and was resorting to drugs.

"When I first met him, his marriage was happy but by the end of the film-making, everything had collapsed. He began to drug himself into a stupor and wouldn't get out of bed. Peter was living like a king in this great bed at his house and he wouldn't get up. Gloria loved him . . . she really loved Peter. But she told me that Peter loved Jimmy more than her. He was the only person he really loved. I remember when Jimmy hurt his hand in the train door and I was with Peter when he heard the news. We were working on something to do with the film and he just got up and left like a shot. He wanted to look after Jimmy. I always felt that if ever there was a problem, Peter would protect me and I guess that's how Jimmy always felt."

Journalist Michael Watts thought it more likely that Grant's peccadilloes caused the rift more than any excessive loyalty to Jimmy Page. "He behaved very badly and that's why they got divorced. There was certainly a soft side to him but I think in life people's actions and their personalities can, to an extent, be dictated to by their appearance."

The complex, multi-faceted nature of Grant's personality left him confused about his real feelings and intentions, just as those outside of the inner Zeppelin circle were confused – or scared – of Peter Grant. Power and money simply exacerbated those characteristics and personal traits that might otherwise have been manageable.

Watts: "Because he was a quite villainous looking character I think he decided at some point in his life to play up to it. If you're in the wrestling ring, it's very easy to portray yourself as 'Count Massimo'. The other contrast about him was that you'd think by looking at him that he'd have this great bellowing voice, yet he had a soft south London twang to him. He actually wasn't loud and he had a slight lisp. He was just scary to look at and to be around! The pop business has moved on a lot since his day. It is de rigueur to paint the manager as the bad guy and that's how he would appear in a movie of his life. But rock bands aren't like Led Zeppelin anymore. They're not as big and in any case accountants run the music industry. There's less room for mavericks like Peter Grant. Kids aren't interested in rock, only dance music and rap and most rap figures are scarier than Peter Grant could ever hope to be. Some of those guys have committed murder and next to them Grant was a pussycat. You're talking about people who take fierce drugs, carry guns and have taken part in serious crimes."

Richard Cole could see that the man who once terrified others was now becoming frightened himself, in the wake of his separation and divorce. "Because of the cocaine he was taking, Peter became very paranoid and his place was full of surveillance cameras. He was always calling the police out. He was convinced there were people waiting for him outside. I remember one day he wouldn't let the police in the front door; he made them come in through the window. And he was sitting there with a sawn-off shotgun under his seat and I'd got an axe under mine. Who were we expecting? No one! It was pure paranoia. We were doing so much coke. There weren't any blokes coming down to see us. Either Peter knew all the boys, or I did! We both knew guys like John Bindon, but I had a lot of different contacts from Peter, because I lived in America and I worked for a lot of people there – let's say. My connections went back a lot longer, before my time with Led Zeppelin."

These connections – and Grant's paranoia – would soon lead to the notoriously violent outburst that abruptly ended Led Zeppelin's reign in America. They had started the decade with high hopes and aspirations. Now they were about to endure 'the wrong goodbye'.

10

THE WRONG GOODBYE

"He was always bad vibing people and he was just not a very nice person to be around. That's why it was not really a comfortable situation to be involved in, because you never had faith in the consistency of his behaviour."

— Drum technician Jeff Ocheltree

When Caesar crossed The Rubicon, a small river in ancient Italy, in 49 B.C. he passed beyond the limits of his province and became an invader, thus precipitating war with Pompeii. Peter Grant crossed his Rubicon when he declared war on the personal fiefdom of one of the most powerful men in American rock politics. The results would be devastating.

When powerful men lose self-control, they expose weakness. In the case of the manager of Led Zeppelin, his greatest skill had lain in his ability to coerce, intimidate and use personal charisma to achieve results. It was only when Grant resorted to real personal violence that he lost face and respect, those twin assets that are unspoken and indefinable, yet more valuable than any number of blows and punches.

It all came to a head during what should have been just another concert on yet another money-spinning, successful tour. 1977 was a strange year, which did not augur well for popular music culture. It was a time when sections of disaffected British youth had suddenly begun to question the validity of super powerful rock groups, who flaunted their wealth and seemed to delight in trampling everyone underfoot. There was a growing movement to wrest back control of rock'n'roll and place it in the hands of the untutored, impoverished 'kids on the street', from whence it came. Punk rock was the new force already capturing headlines in the London music press. Led Zeppelin were prime targets for the new rebels with a cause, who loudly proclaimed they wanted to sweep away the 'boring old farts' and the 'dinosaurs of rock'. It was into this atmosphere of aggression and disrespect that Zeppelin blundered like an untethered balloon, blown by the forces of an ill wind.

Violent events involving Peter Grant and his band on one side and US promoter Bill Graham and his men on the other in July that year were a defining moment. It was the day when the pioneering spirit of rock music died, amidst the thumps and grunts of a sordid beating inside a backstage trailer.

The previous year had been a time of consolidation for Zeppelin, during which they celebrated their past achievements with the release of *The Song Remains The Same* and pointed to a more diverse musical future with their latest album *Presence*. As far as most of their public were concerned the band still seemed untouchable; giants of rock who earned millions and whose word was law. In reality, of course, they were just as vulnerable and uncertain about what life held as any other participants in a great artistic enterprise. Despite all the hype and all the uproar that seemed to surround Zeppelin, the bottom line was they were sincere about their work and were always seeking ways to improve and change.

Unlike the gaudy glam rock bands that followed in their footsteps, creativity was always more important than the Rabelaisian lifestyle they were supposed to pursue. Jimmy Page and Robert Plant were gifted men, who took pride in their craft and were well versed in the roots and origins of the folk and blues that provided Zeppelin's seed corn. John Paul Jones and John Bonham were consummate professionals and equally creative. All four were admired and respected by their peers, and together they had created a band whose influence was felt for years after its demise. Whatever happened during the latter part of the band's career, nothing could detract from their achievements. Yet ironically, the man who helped them bring it off almost brought them down, by misuse of the very methods that had previously worked so well in their favour.

Led Zeppelin had been out of action since May 1975 and there was an eagerness to get back into playing live. January 1977 was taken up with rehearsals, although Page and Plant also took time out to visit London's thriving new punk rock clubs to see The Damned. The following month, just a few days before the band were due to start their latest American tour, Robert suffered a bout of tonsillitis.

Once Plant had recovered, the eleventh US bash began on April 1 at the Dallas Memorial Hall. They had some 51 dates scheduled in 30 cities and they expected to play to some 1,300,000 fans. Grant and Cole based the band in hotels in Chicago, New York and Los Angeles and once again the entourage commuted between cities on the Zeppelin Starship. Peter recalled his mood during the build-up to the tour. "It was a really hard time for me because I had to leave the kids and my divorce proceedings were starting. John Bonham was also uptight that year and we took Rex King out to be his whipping boy."

Apart from Page suffering from food poisoning and the occasional riots by fans desperate for tickets, the tour seemed to progress smoothly. Despite Grant's continuing anti-pirate crusade, bootleggers managed to record many of the concerts.* The recorded evidence of these sold-out gigs showed performance levels strangely below standard. Fans who eagerly taped their shows spoke later of guitars out of tune, lyrics forgotten and drum breaks muffed.

At the Pontiac Silverdome on April 30 they played to 76,229 people, the largest audience ever assembled for one rock band. During these blockbuster shows Jimmy Page experimented with his Theramin, a unique electronic device played without touching the instrument, which made a splendid addition to the violin bowed guitar he used during 'Dazed And Confused'. Recordings made at the Pontiac Silverdome captured the audience egging on their heroes. According to one review the sound was like 'An immense battlefield with its constant firecracker outbursts.' Robert Plant could be heard introducing John Bonham as 'the greatest drummer in the band'.

During May Zeppelin took a two-week holiday and Peter Grant went to Grosvenor House in London to receive an Ivor Novello Award for the band's 'colourful and energetic contribution to British music'. It was a time for honours and plaudits. The music business clearly held Grant in the highest esteem and was grateful for his efforts in helping to create such a lucrative industry.

On May 18 they resumed the US tour in Birmingham, Alabama, and journeyed through the Southern states. They arrived in Florida on June 3, but the show at Tampa Stadium had to be cancelled after 20 minutes due to heavy rain, which began to leak into the electrical equipment on stage. Some 70,000 fans began to cause a disturbance that resulted in a ban on the group returning to Tampa Stadium. It was the first major 'blip' of the tour,

---

* Peter was still suffering a year-long ban from entering Canada after his fracas with the noise-monitoring engineer he thought was a bootlegger.

but there was worse to come. Grant admitted later that the booking had been "a big mistake. Possibly one of our biggest, and all because we never realised there should be a rain date. It had been dreadfully wet for days in the area with rain like we'd never seen."

Peter should have realised that if an outdoor show was rained off, a sup-plementary 'rain date' had to be booked, which the band was then supposed to honour the following day. But Grant wasn't concentrating. His mind was on other things and his health was poor. "Somehow we missed the detail on this one," he admitted. "It wasn't until we were on the plane flying from Miami to the gig that Richard Cole showed me the ticket which said on it 'An Evening With Led Zeppelin June 3: Come Rain or Shine', i.e. no rain date. I stormed off to blast Terry Bassett from Concerts West. Steve Weiss our lawyer should have caught it in the contract."

As was his wont, Grant was always ready to 'blast' others about a job he should have taken care of himself. Yet when asked about the litany of disastrous events that year, Peter was unusually forthcoming about the Tampa debacle. It was almost as if he preferred to talk about a storm and a riot than more painful events closer to home. "I should have sent Richard out to check the place," he admitted. "But he'd been sorting out some trip for Robert and Jonesy to visit Disneyland with the kids. All sorts of trouble. If Richard had gone he'd have seen that they'd set up a canvas roof instead of a metal one, which we always demanded. So when we got to the site there was something like 1,000 gallons of water resting over the drums. I had to make a decision about them going on. There was a lot of pressure. When they were about to go on, the rain stopped. There were 70,000 fans gathered and we had to get it on somehow. So I decided to let them start. There was a great big rain cloud looming overhead. I thought at this rate it would be us who would be leaving under a big black cloud and sure enough, after three numbers it started pouring. I signalled to Robert to wind it up and off we ran. One funny aside to this was Robert told me later that as he was coming off stage, my son Warren shouted to Robert to pick up a Frisbee he'd thrown. As you can imagine Robert told him in no uncertain terms to leave it there!"

The show had run for just twenty minutes before it ground to a halt. Police with riot gear moved in and began hitting and kicking protesting fans. Over a hundred fans and 17 police were injured in the ensuing fracas. The Mayor announced later that Led Zeppelin would be banned from ever appearing in Tampa again 'for the health and protection of police and citizens.'

Reporter Jack Lyons described the scene in *Rock Scene* magazine. "It all started innocently enough; fans drove from as far away as New York and Georgia, waving to each other with one thought in their mind – Led Zeppelin. The much publicised concert began as the rock group hit the stage at 8.20 p.m. 'This is our first trip to Tampa in four years,' said bare-chested Robert Plant, his huge penis bulging in his pants. 'It's good to be back.' The band had barely played 'The Song Remains The Same' before lightning ripped through the sky and rain poured in a drenching torrent. 'We have to stop or our equipment will blow up,' yelled Robert."

While pressmen were trapped amidst the unfolding chaos, the band fled to their cars waiting backstage, with Grant and Cole shepherding their charges to safety. "Getting out was a nightmare," recalled Grant. "We had to wait at the airport for John Paul's wife Mo, who had travelled out in a separate limo which had spun off the road. It was another typical 1977 mishap all round. Now we would get the blame for all this and there was a town council meeting coming up at the weekend. So I put our view forward, which was the truth. I took a double page ad in the *Tampa Times* or whatever it was, stating that in no way were we to blame and that Concerts West were taking responsibility. The way we rushed it through is that I knew Colonel Tom Parker's son-in-law ran an ad agency, so we got him out of bed early on Sunday to get the ad in for the first thing the next morning. So, no matter what the council said, we were in the clear for all to see."

Another problem loomed. It seemed $10,000 had gone missing from the band's funds. Grant was worried. After the Drake Hotel robbery, it seemed Zeppelin money was leaching away. There were no prizes for guessing where the money went or what it was used for, but said Grant: "There was a query over some of the expenses Richard had handled, but it all turned out to be an accountant's error, thank the Lord. I mean, if it had been just a thousand dollars I could have lived with it. It might have been down to someone putting something on his expenses, but $10,000 was a bit different. The thing is, it wasn't my money, or Richard's. It was the band's money and I was paid to be responsible for it."

In the midst of the riots and the mystery of the missing cash, the Zeppelin magic worked for all those who loved their music. Said Peter: "One positive memory of '77 was that I came to realise just how much it all meant to people. It was during our stay at the Plaza in New York, which we used as a base to fly out to the surrounding gigs. Our stint at Madison Square was still some weeks off. Every night outside the hotel there were scores of fans surrounding the limos and it was just amazing. Then we announced the New York dates on Scott Muni's radio show. Woosh! All tickets gone. The tariff for that Madison Square Garden stint showed that our advertising costs were nil. The tickets sold out purely from demand on the streets."

Even Grant was impressed by the way the band's success just kept escalating. "The loyalty of the fans astounded me. There was no hype, no MTV promotion or anything like that. It was all down to pure demand. At that point I really did wonder how much bigger all this could get. From those humble beginnings in 1969 to this level in the space of seven years was just astounding. And the music was still wonderful. I remember the first time Jerry Weintraub (promoter) saw Jimmy Page on stage. He said to me: 'Is that guy gonna live?' Jimmy was faking it a bit, which he often did for a laugh with the others. Being on stage was where it all happened for Jimmy."

Even if Jimmy was 'faking it' there was no doubt he looked ill and seemed painfully thin, unable to eat solid food and with flecks of grey beginning to appear in his black, tousled hair. He attempted to boost his health by eating bananas and taking more protein. The rest of the band stayed with their diet of horseplay in hotel suites. One eyewitness at the Ambassador East Hotel in Chicago spoke of seeing "a room with wall-to-wall hamburgers, Cola drenched bed sheets, French fried plastered walls, mustard smeared mirrors, a 16-piece telephone and gutted cushions where the furniture used to be."

Peter Grant turned a blind eye and pulled out his chequebook. Still agonising over his divorce, Grant kept his distance from the usual Zeppelin frolics. As long as he delivered the band and they delivered on stage, he remained proud and happy. Amidst all the media frenzy that now attended their every move, the group were determined to give value for money.

The best shows lasted over three hours with an extra long acoustic set and each member of the band had their chance to shine, including their bass and keyboard player. Recalled Grant: "Jonesy was doing incredible versions of 'No Quarter' at this time. I wasn't surprised there were a lot of bootleg albums from that tour because one night Benji LeFevre lost some of our sound desk tapes. I never did bollock him for it; I just put it down as one of those things. In fact in the early Eighties I was disappointed and hurt by his plan to become Robert Plant's manager, which all went wrong in the end. I used to phone him up and I'd never get a return call or any communication. Silly really."

As Zeppelin grew in stature and esteem, so the world beat a path to their door. Peter Grant was most impressed when even the Soviet Union began to take an interest in their activities. "1977 was also the year I had a meeting with the Russians. I was invited to dinner at the Russian Embassy and the entire guest party came to the gig. It was utterly amazing." The Russians came to one of four gigs at the Capitol Center, Landover, Maryland, at the end of May. "They really knew their stuff. I was in the limo with one of the wives and she said, 'What's the sound like for your group?' and I said, 'Very good,' and she added that when they saw The Rolling Stones the previous year there was 'no bottom to their sound' because all the amps were hung above the stage. Amazing! They met the band beforehand and during the gig, instead of watching from the box, they all went to sit at the side of the stage. Jonesy then played variations from Rachmaninov during 'No Quarter' and the Russian guests were just blown away. We planned to go to Russia but after Robert's tragedy, we had to scrap it. It was a shame because we could have been one of the first rock acts to go to Russia. Elton John went instead."

Peter was all smiles and full of old world courtesy when dealing with his VIP guests. Those who worked for him, however, noticed that at other times he was irascible, suspicious and hostile. He seemed to particularly dislike some of the young Americans who worked for the band during their US tours and formed the impression they were only there for the ride. One such new recruit was drum technician Jeff Ocheltree. He had been working for Billy Cobham, the drummer with the Mahavishnu Orchestra, when John Bonham had spotted him at a concert at the Crystal Palace Bowl, in south London.

Intrigued by the idea of a 'drum tech' whose sole job was to tune drums and ensure the boss had a good sound on stage, Bonham offered Ocheltree a job as his personal assistant, even though he already employed long standing pal Mick Hinton to do this task. A couple of weeks after a formal meeting at Bonham's LA hotel, Jeff Ocheltree got a phone call from Peter Grant and was asked, somewhat grudging as it turned out, to come on tour with Zeppelin and work as John Bonham's official drum technician. It was the dawn of the era of greater expertise among road crews, but this did not impress the management.

"We did a bunch of dates," recalls Ocheltree, "and there were moments when I thought, 'What the hell am I doing here?' I had Peter Grant coming up to me and saying, 'What are you doing anyway?' So I said, 'Well I don't think you'd understand if I told you.' Of course that would tick him off. I said, 'I'm tuning the drum.' He said, 'Aw you don't know how to tune a drum. That's what John Bonham does.' Peter left me alone for a while, but then he started coming up to me and saying, 'I understand you are being paid in dollars. Well, you are going to be paid in pounds from now on.' So I said, 'That's great.' And he looked at me and said, 'Oh, you are a sarcastic fellow are you?' I said, 'What is sarcastic about being paid in pounds? That's your sterling – that's your money.' And he said, 'Precisely.' Then he said, 'I don't really see why we need you and Mick Hinton.' So I said, 'Well, I don't want Mick to get fired.' 'What do you mean by that?' 'Well, you don't need both of us but I know you need me.' Then I thought, oh, that's the wrong thing to say. So I apologised to him. Peter then said, 'Well I just took that as another of your sarcastic remarks.'

"Peter once heard one of the road crew guys complaining about the lack of security on stage. Let's face it; Peter Grant *was* the band's security. But if some fan wandered on stage or somebody became threatening, they had to take care of the situation. When he overheard the crew complaining he got really mad and left the stage. Then he came back with this great big heavy bag and he threw it down on the stage. He said to us, 'Get over here.' We ran over and he said, 'Open up the bag.' Inside was a bunch of brand new frame hammers. He said, 'Use these for your security. I don't want to hear another word.' So later that night I looked down and saw Jimmy's roadie hitting a fan on the fingers with a hammer.

"I thought, 'Oh my God, they took this literally.' The road crew felt very threatened by Peter and very intimidated. To this day some of the guys will not talk about Zeppelin. It's very strange, isn't it?

"Peter remained suspicious of me. He thought I was scamming the band. He said, 'You're just trying to make some money off them.' I said, 'Really? You think that this pays that well? You think you're overpaying me? You just don't understand what I'm doing.' I remember a couple of times him threatening me and having John step in to say, 'Hey, wait a minute.' He explained that I was just trying to get Bonzo a great sound every night. But I didn't think it was cool that he had to stand up for me, like that.

190

"Peter Grant had a real temper problem. I knew a guy called Beauford Jones, a sound engineer who worked for Showco, who was asked to cover the Bad Company tours. On the first day he goes into the dressing room to get a Coke. While he's pouring it Peter Grant comes in and says, 'Who the hell are you?' and grabs him by the neck and squashes him against the wall. Beauford told me later: 'I thought I was going to die. I was gasping for air. I told him I'm just the house mix guy. I'm mixing the sound.' Grant said, 'Don't you ever go into the band's dressing room and take anything out of there.' He was always bad vibing people and he was just not a very nice person to be around. That's why it was not really a comfortable situation to be involved in, because you never had faith in the consistency of his behaviour. He had too much power and he viewed himself as a tough guy who was taking care of business. To give him credit he was a genius in certain marketing ideas. He went to Madison Square Garden and said, 'Hey, I'm renting this place for three or four days. You get your people out of here, I've got my own staff.' And he brought Led Zeppelin posters over from England to sell in New York. He didn't want anyone in America getting their hands on stuff he thought he could take care of himself. He knew what he was doing and so did Bill Graham. Until he disrespected Bill Graham so badly, the two of them could have gone on to do even greater things. Bill Graham was a tough guy too and he was not afraid of Peter Grant one bit. Peter Grant intimidated a lot of people because they knew he was actually physically tough. But Bill Graham wasn't scared of him."

During June the band played six nights at Madison Square Garden, New York and a further six shows at the Los Angeles Forum, always a Zeppelin stronghold. Once again audiences went wild and thousands were left still begging for tickets. The following month they began the last leg of the tour at the Kingdome, Seattle, on July 17, followed by a somewhat disjointed performance at the A.S.U Activities Center, Tempe, Arizona, which was disrupted by blasts of yet more firecrackers thrown by a noisy audience.

Afterwards the band headed back to California to play two dates for Bill Graham at the Oakland-Alameda County Coliseum near San Francisco on July 23 and 24. Within a few days, what had been a successful and generally good-humoured tour would come to an abrupt halt amid violence and tragedy. It started when a minor backstage incident escalated into something much worse. Peter's son, now aged eleven, was enjoying the adventure of going on tour with the band.

Says Warren: "I went on the 1977 tour for quite a few weeks and travelled on the Starship. It had Led Zeppelin painted on the side and I remember sitting in huge seats and seeing the bar – of course. At the back there were circular beds with curtains around them, where they could kip – or whatever. I'm sure they weren't just there for kipping! I flew on it quite a few times."

He was allowed to roam freely around the backstage area at Oakland, which was ringed by security men. He then spotted the small wooden identity plaques hung on the doors of the large trailers or caravans, called Winnebagos, which were used as dressing rooms at big outdoor events. A row was sparked when Jim Matzorkis, one of Bill Graham's security men, spotted Warren attempting to take down the 'Led Zeppelin' sign from one of the trailers as a souvenir. Unfortunately the guard allegedly slapped the child on the back of the head while remonstrating with him. (He later denied having hit Warren.) John Bonham, who was taking a break from his drums during the show, saw the incident, came across and kicked the guard in the balls. He then returned to the stage to carry on playing. Later versions of the story suggested that both Grant and Bonham had carried out the attack simultaneously. Certainly when Peter Grant heard what had happened to Warren, he became incandescent with fury. Someone had dared hit his son? He wouldn't allow anyone to get away with such a liberty.

He confronted Bill Graham and demanded to see Matzorkis, promising Bill he wouldn't 'get physical' with him. As it turned out, he had no such intentions. He and bodyguard John Bindon lured the guard into showing his face and, while Richard Cole kept watch outside, the Londoners beat the man up. All hell broke loose backstage when it became known what had happened but the band was still expected to complete the next day's show. Led Zeppelin would perform only if Graham promised not to take legal action against the perpetrators, but as soon as the last show on July 24 was finished, the four culprits, Grant, Bonham, Bindon and Cole were arrested and charged with assault and battery. As well as the charges of battery a civil suit was filed against Led Zeppelin seeking $2 million in punitive damages. Three employees of Bill Graham brought the suit and charges on July 25. Zeppelin's lawyer Jeffry Hoffman confirmed that all four men would plead innocent.

In the bitter aftermath the rock press delivered its verdicts. *Rolling Stone* led with a coldly factual story headed simply 'The wrong goodbye: Led Zeppelin leaves America'. More details began to emerge of the Oakland Incident. It seemed that bad vibes had been building up between Grant and Graham's rival security men all afternoon.

Said Graham: "There were really two incidents, both of which happened after the Saturday concert was over. The first involved Peter Grant and his security man John Bindon. As they left the stage, Jim Downey (one of Graham's road crew) said to Grant, who looked very tired, something like, 'Do you need any help?' From what I can tell offence was taken to that statement. Bindon struck the stage crewman and his head was bashed against concrete. The second incident involved Jim Matzorkis, a stage security man. He was taking a wooden plaque with Led Zeppelin's name on it off their dressing room door to put away for the next show. A young boy asked him for the sign and Jim said, 'No, we need it for the next day.' It turned out the young boy was Peter Grant's son.

"Matzorkis was putting the sign in a storage trailer when Grant, Bonham, Bindon and Cole approached him. 'You don't talk to a kid like that,' said Grant. 'Apologise or I'll have your job.' Bonham also told him to apologise and then kicked the guard in the groin. Matzorkis fled and hid in a trailer."

Graham then told how Grant's men then went looking for Matzorkis. During the search Richard Cole allegedly hit Bob Barsotti, the promoter's production manager, on the back with a four-inch aluminium pipe. Graham went to speak to Grant in his trailer to try to clear the air and stop a dangerous situation from getting worse. "I said, 'I don't know what went on, but if there are any apologies due, I extend them on behalf of my company.' Peter just said, 'I want to speak to this man.' I said, 'Peter you are a very big person, give me your word – nothing physical.' He said, 'Bill, I give you my word.' I went over to the trailer where Jim was hiding. I said, 'Jim, it's okay, it's me. This is Mr Peter Grant the boy's father . . .' Before I could finish the sentence, Peter blasted Jim in the face. I tried to stand between them but Grant forced me to the door of the trailer and this other man came in and then Grant forced me out and locked the door. I tried to open the door, but their people came over and guarded the door. Matzorkis worked his way to the door while they were hitting him and he was able to get out. His face was a bloody mess."

Matzorkis was taken to East Bay hospital for treatment for cuts, bruises to his face and lips and a broken tooth. During the assault the American security staff employed by Graham became so enraged they threatened to get handguns locked in the trunks of their cars and use them. Bill Graham restrained them by promising he'd take proper legal action, then waited until after the second show was over the following day before making his move. This was regarded later as a sign that he was only interested in making money out of the band. But Graham insisted he was more worried about the idea of 60,000 fans turning up and rioting if there was 'no show'. Indeed, the second concert went ahead only after Graham signed 'a letter of indemnification' which promised he wouldn't take any action against Zeppelin. The band's lawyer presented the document to him only half an hour before show time, while the band was waiting at their hotel. They didn't actually say they wouldn't play but the inference was plain. No signature, no show. Graham was advised the letter was not binding, as the promoter had no legal right to act on behalf of his security man and in any case it could be shown he was acting under 'duress'. So he signed it anyway and asked his production team to cool down. At one stage plans were hatched for Graham to sign with his left hand, to prove he was under duress and his men even planned to steal the document to prevent it being delivered. But these ideas were abandoned when it was realised that the letter was 'not worth the paper it was written on'.

The show on Sunday was a very low-key affair. Uncharacteristically, Jimmy Page sat down for most of the performance and Robert Plant made a point of thanking Bill Graham "for everything he has done for the musical events."

The following day armed police from the Sheriff's department arrested Grant, Bonham, Bindon and Cole. All four were questioned, charged with battery and released on $250 bail. The criminal charges were followed by the civil action, which dragged on for months.

"I could never in good conscience book them again," said Bill Graham. "For these people to assume that might makes right takes me back to Nazi Germany and I've blocked pretty much of my childhood out.* I cannot help but wonder how much of this in fact went on in the past with these people."

At the time the Zeppelin crew understandably tried to play down the incident. Jimmy referred to it as 'a few whacks backstage' and their Swan Song press officer said it was all 'bullshit'. Whatever the truth about what

* Members of Graham's family had died at the hands of Nazis in concentration camps.

had gone on inside the trailer, it left a nasty taste in the mouths of the American public. Certainly the media was not impressed and there was a genuine feeling of shock that a member of the band could have been involved in quite such an over the top assault.

The story made headline news around the world. It was later confirmed that Grant had also punched stagehand James Downey after the concert and that John Bonham had been involved in a fight with the production man Robert Barsotti. There were rumours that Zeppelin's men had actually murdered someone, something that even people who had been close to the band believed for years afterwards. It was of course simply malicious gossip.

Most of the band were completely unaware of the fighting backstage, but word soon began to reach them. Their natural reaction was to believe that it was all the promoter's fault for allowing a security man to hit Warren. John Paul Jones was concerned by events backstage, but his main priority was to protect his own family who had accompanied him on the tour. "It was basically a fight between their security and our security. I saw cops running and Cole running across a few tables, but he was often doing that. I thought, 'What's he up to now?' It was only later in the day when the police arrived at the hotel that I heard what had happened. In fact I had a motorhome booked, which was parked in the street outside. I was going to drive my family up to Seattle for a few nights.

"Suddenly there were sirens wailing and police zooming through the hotel lobby. Me and my family got into the service elevator, went down to the street and jumped into this motorhome, which I had never driven before. I just headed for the freeway. We snuck out the back, so I didn't get arrested! We were already packed and ready to go when the police arrived. In fact I had no idea what it was all about at that time. I think they sent the Highway Patrol looking out for us. But we were heading up to Oregon. After a couple of days holiday I called in and they told me what had happened. It was one of those things. The security guys get bored at these gigs and somebody took offence at something. I seem to remember that 'Bill Graham never forgave us' but I don't remember Bill Graham ever being a huge, close buddy of Led Zeppelin. I always thought he was weird. He never spoke to me. The first time we turned up at the Fillmore I remember him just screaming and shouting at everybody. He was quite an unpleasant person. I remember saying, 'Oh, who's that?' 'Oh, that's Bill Graham.'"

Bill Graham's own his account of the story made it clear that as far as he was concerned Grant and Bindon were the main instigators of the attack. Grant himself remained tight-lipped on the subject for years and would only say: "Oakland was a nightmare and very heavy. It was a flashpoint situation that got out of hand. It could have got a lot worse. It was just a very regrettable incident. But we were up against Bill Graham's security guys with their gloves filled with sand. We didn't want to get into that. There were wives with us and we had brought our kids with us for that part of the tour."

Richard Cole admits that he was involved in the violence but not in the direct assault on Matzorkis. "I wasn't in the caravan, I was standing outside, whacking people who were trying to get in with a bit of tubing. The four of us got arrested. We were lucky really because they sent a SWAT team round and each of us had an armed guard on our door and an armed cop. And of course each of us had bindles of coke. The dangerous part was that somebody could have been seriously hurt. If somebody had knocked on the door and said, 'Police, open up,' they would have been told to fuck off, because we'd have thought it was someone joking with us. We didn't know that because of Bill Graham's power in San Francisco, he had been able to speak to the police department and he took the armed guards off our doors.

"But a guy called Greg Bettler, who was one of our security guys and is now a police commissioner in Cleveland, happened to be in the lobby when the SWAT team came in and he knew one of them. He said, 'Hey what are you doing here?' And the guy said, 'We're going up to get those mother fuckers Led Zeppelin.' Greg said, 'Just a second, I work for those guys, what's going on?' and so they got talking and our man said, 'Do me a favour, don't do anything stupid. I don't know what you've been told, but these guys are fine.' So they had a meeting and instead of coming up to the room they called us on the phone and said, 'We've got a problem. We've come to arrest Richard Cole, Johnny Bindon, John Bonham and Peter Grant.' Lawyers were called in and we were held in an open jail. Bill Graham was rubbing his hands that he'd got us locked up. We were due to fly out and normally all the limousine drivers were billed, but they said they'd been asked to take cash only. We could have been nasty about it, but that's how they make their living and it wasn't their fault. We just paid the cash and how they dealt with their boss was their business."

It was extraordinary that Grant had picked a fight with Bill Graham's

employees, or rather just steamed in without thinking of the consequences. As the man who had set up America's best-known rock venues,
The Fillmore East in New York and the Fillmore in San Francisco,
Graham was a powerful and influential figure, arguably the most powerful
rock promoter in America. He was also feared for his temper and no nonsense approach to dealing with adversaries. At the same time he had been
responsible for helping many British acts achieve success in America by
showcasing them at well-organised gigs. Richard Cole understood the
need to keep on the right side of his organisation. "I'd known Bill Graham
since The Yardbirds days and he ran the best shows in the world. I did a
lot of Fillmore shows with different bands and he was one of the first
promoters that actually took care of bands. He always put food and drinks
in the dressing rooms and he always had the best sound systems and light
shows. He was a professional promoter.

"Sure, obviously there was always arguments between Peter and Bill
about money – because one is the promoter and the other is the manager.
But there was never an ongoing battle from the first day we met Bill
Graham. It was just this one particular show where it all went off because
the guy slapped Warren, Peter's son, on the back of the head. Then Peter
Grant heard about it and that's what set it all off. Apart from that, we'd
never had a problem with Bill Graham. He and Peter would shout and
scream at each other and he'd say things like, 'I hope you fall into your
moat and the crocodiles eat you alive.' But it wasn't real venom – it was
just vocal venom! It wasn't malicious. The guy who was beaten up survived
and the offence was knocked down to a misdemeanour and the record was
scrubbed. Once we got out of jail we rounded all the troops up, jumped
on the plane and got the hell out of town. We went to New Orleans –
where we were gonna be given the keys to the city! Led Zeppelin was
going to be the first band to play at their new stadium."

Nevertheless, Bill Graham's crew were still seething long after the
second show and planned to pursue the band to New Orleans, where a
25-man posse armed with guns would extract a bloody revenge. If it had
happened, it would have been the worst disaster in rock'n'roll history.
Mercifully their action proved unnecessary.

However, the band's run of bad luck was not over. "We had just gone
into the hotel and there was a message at the desk for Robert Plant to call
his wife," says Cole. "Robert then told me he'd heard his son was ill."

Robert was informed that five-year-old Karac had been taken ill with a stomach infection back home in England. He was driven to hospital for treatment. Then came worse news. Remembers Cole: "It couldn't have been much more than two hours later that his son had died." Karac had died of complications resulting from a virus infection. Plant immediately quit the tour and returned home

"Robert asked that John Bonham and me fly back to England with him to take care of him. And so at the funeral there was only the three of us sitting on the grass outside afterwards. Jimmy was in Egypt and couldn't get there and Peter was out at Long Island with his kids. John Paul Jones had already arranged a holiday with his wife. When John Paul Jones went on holiday I was the only person he'd give his phone number to, which drove Peter mad. I couldn't reach him because he was travelling in a hired camper van, and so we had no way of reaching him. The instructions were not to disturb him unless it was an emergency. Robert was very hurt about it."

Robert's father later made a poignant comment about the death of Robert's son: "All this success and fame . . . what is it worth? It doesn't mean very much when you compare it to the love of a family."

With the 1977 tour now cancelled the Oakland show on July 24 was Led Zeppelin's last ever appearance on American soil. Indeed it wasn't until 1979 that the band would play in public again.

The Oakland outburst is perhaps better understood in the context of Peter Grant's own personal crisis. If as Richard Cole says, the use of cocaine was rife, then it would have had the effect of inflating the user's ego, making him feel agitated, aggressive and all-powerful. The presence of a real London thug, the notorious John Bindon, only added to this dangerous cocktail of emotions. With Grant still seething over his divorce and surrounded by 'heavies' goading him to present a show of force, it took only a gesture or some imagined slight from some entirely innocent party to provide the spark. He wanted a fight. He needed to give someone a good hiding. The victim who presented himself as an unwitting target for this pent-up frustration and anger had simply tried to stop his son from taking a souvenir that was needed the following day. Such violence might have escaped unnoticed or unremarked if they had been two Teddy Boys in a coffee bar in Soho in the Fifties. Instead Grant and his cohorts were in America under the glare of the media and at the mercy of gun toting US cops. They were also disrespecting the American music industry that had welcomed them to their country and made them rich. Altogether, it was not a wise move.

Many were left wondering why Grant had found it necessary to employ John Bindon, a former TV actor, as a bodyguard. After all, Peter had managed his own security perfectly well for years with a glare and the butt of his stomach. The effect on Grant's own prestige and image of his association with such a notorious thug was insidiously damaging. People who once rather admired the man with the patched elbows began to instinctively back away and avoid contact.

John Bindon was the son of a merchant seaman who had fought his way up from the back streets of London. He was raised in a council flat in Fulham and left school at 15. He could barely read or write and spent time in Borstal, the young offenders institution. He also served 15 months of a two-year prison sentence for assault. Determined to 'go straight' he met British film director Ken Loach, who was looking for an actor to play a wife-beating thug. Bindon seemed perfect for the part and appeared in Loach's 1967 movie *Poor Cow* with Carol White and Terence Stamp. He played Carol's 'swinish husband' Tom, a petty thief who is sent to jail. More film roles followed. He played 'Moody' in the controversial Mick Jagger movie *Performance*, a gangster flick so realistically violent that it dismayed leading man James Fox. Bindon went on to appear as a drug dealer in *Quadrophenia*, the film based on The Who's album of the same name, and was a tough guy in the TV cop series *Softly Softly*. Having tried to break away from the reality of a life of crime, Bindon found himself playing criminal roles in all his movies. Playing rugby for the London Springboks and – irony of ironies – the Law Society seemed a good way by which to burn off his natural aggression. It was said that he was particularly impressive when playing against the Metropolitan Police. He was even awarded a medal for bravery in 1968, when he rescued a man from drowning in the Thames.

Bindon developed a reputation as a playboy and his good looks and physical strength made him especially appealing to women. He once met and was photographed with, Princess Margaret, while on holiday in Mustique. It did nothing for the Princess's prestige, especially since at the time he was wearing a T-shirt bearing the legend 'Enjoy Cocaine'. He also had affairs with the model Vicki Hodge and a *Playboy* publicity girl. In his case it seemed the lines between show business and the underworld were never so finely blurred.

Peter Grant later tried to explain how and why he'd brought Bindon into the Zeppelin camp. "John Bindon was a friend of Richard Cole's. I had decided I wasn't going to do much clubbing and John was an aide who ended up looking after Jimmy quite a lot. He had once looked after Ryan O'Neal and looked after Tatum. He had a lot of good points. He took care of my situation and he took care of Jimmy."

The 'good points' were lost on Bill Graham as he pointed out in his book *Bill Graham Presents: My Life Inside Rock And Out*. It wasn't until the publication of this book in 1992 that Graham told his side of the San Francisco story, a chilling and damning testimony, backed up by statements from his employees, including the injured Jim Matzorkis. In prefacing the episode Graham stressed how the band always drew an aggressive, all-male element* to their shows, but even so, he still liked their music. "They were a great rock'n'roll band," he allowed. He recalled how they had worked their way up through the ranks and that he'd frequently put them on at the Fillmore East and West. He described their manager as, "A bull-necked man who wore huge satin shirts with ruffled collars." He noted the denims specially made for an oversized man, the long stringy hair and scrubby beard and the silver jewellery and big rings on his fingers.

Graham described how on the Friday afternoon before the two weekend shows Led Zeppelin's tour manager had rung him and said, "We need some money." It was late in the day but he would go to the bank and see what he could get. They were demanding a $25,000 advance on their earnings for the shows – in cash and up front. Graham knew they would make hundreds of thousands of dollars as both Oakland stadium shows were sold out, but he couldn't understand why they needed money so urgently. He spent some hours going round the city getting the cash together, mainly in single dollar bills, which he carried in a large shopping bag and three shoe boxes. He went to the band's hotel and walked past a security guard into their room where he saw and recognised a local drug dealer. "Then it hit me for the first time. This was *drug* money." Graham said he felt like walking out and taking the money with him, but then he shrugged and realised it was their money and he had no right to withhold it, even if he strongly disapproved of their actions.

---

* Not strictly true, as anyone who's seen *The Song Remains The Same* will testify, since it features many a girl transfixed by Robert Plant.

On the following day, the Saturday, the band was late on stage. Although they were twenty minutes overdue, it was actually the earliest they had started any show on the tour. Graham confessed that he didn't like what he had been hearing about Grant's recent behaviour. "What I didn't like about Zeppelin was that they came with force. I heard how they muscled promoters to get better deals and had shaken them down for money. And then what they had done with the money. I heard about the ugliness of their security, how they were just waiting to kill. They had these bodyguards who had police records in England. They were thugs."

Graham's own road crew eyed up the 'Limeys' with great suspicion. Said one: "They were evil people. Just the *worst*." One of the Americans, Jim Downey, recalled how he was standing by the steep ramp up to the stage when Grant and Bindon walked by. When he said something like, 'It's a long way up that ramp,' Grant took offence and Bindon went over and knocked him out. "The next thing I remembered was waking up on the ramp. I never saw it coming." Other members of the road crew held off the two men with a chair. Meanwhile the row with Jim Matzorkis was developing. Said Matzorkis: "After the show on Saturday I noticed this young kid pulling these wooden plaques off the trailer doors, which had the names of the acts on them. We still had another show to do and so we really didn't want the signs stolen. I told him in a manner which I thought was courteous that he couldn't have the signs." A brief argument ensued and Matzorkis just took the signs away from Warren. "It wasn't a violent act. I just took them away and didn't think anything of it. It really was not a major incident."

He was storing the signs in another trailer when John Bonham came up to him and called his attention. Said Jim: "Peter Grant was with him who kept saying, 'You don't talk to my kid like that. Nobody does. I can have your job. Who do you think you are? I heard you hit this child.'"

Matzorkis tried to explain it was all a misunderstanding and just then Bonham came up and kicked the man in the crotch. He fell back into the trailer but was rescued from further attacks by some of the band's bodyguards, who got between him and Grant and Bonham. Matzorkis seized his opportunity to escape and ran off to hide in another mobile home outside the perimeter fence."

The matter was reported to Bill Graham and he and Peter Grant met up to try to resolve the issue. They spent twenty minutes arguing and debating, while Graham tried to calm Grant down. The latter insisted on

meeting 'this man' and eventually Graham – rather foolishly – led him
the trailer where Matzorkis was hiding out in fear. Said Bill: "Hey Jim
Here's Peter Grant. I know it was a misunderstanding and I want you guy
to get together. I opened the trailer and went in first to where Jim w
sitting. I said, 'Jim, Peter is the father of the young man.'"

It seems that the guard stretched out his hand in greeting. Grant grabbe
Matzorkis' hand and pulled him towards him. "He took his fist with all th
fingers covered with rings and smashed Jim in the face, knocking him bac
into his seat. I lunged at Grant. He picked me up like a fly and handed m
to the guy by the steps. That guy shoved me out. He threw me down th
steps and shut the door. Grant and one of his guys went inside with Ji
and I couldn't open the door. I heard Jim say, 'Bill! Help me, Bill!' And
lot of noise."

Matzorkis also told how Grant and Bindon threw Graham out of th
trailer and, while Bindon held him in a full Nelson, Grant worked hi
over, punching him in the face with his fists and kicking him in the groi
"It was horrifying having this three hundred pound guy just beating th
crap out of me," he said. The victim tried to crawl under a table and the
to his disbelief and terror, Bindon began to try to gouge his eyeballs ou
"When he went for my eyeballs, that got every bit of adrenalin going an
somehow I got to the door . . ."

Outside Bill Graham was running up and down trying to get help whi
Richard Cole guarded the door of the trailer with a length of pipe. One
the Americans, Bill Barsotti, claims he shouted at Cole, "You lime
cocksucking sonafabitch" which drove him so wild he chased after hir
leaving the way clear for others to get into the trailer. It also enabled Ji
Matzorkis to escape, bleeding from the mouth and face. "Our guys wer
just showing up when I got out. Bill and the others were deciding wheth
they were going to shoot their way in. Our security guys never carrie
guns but they all had them in their cars. They had gone to get their piec
out of the trunks. For all they knew, they were killing me in there. If
hadn't been able to get out, they might have."

In the council of war that followed, the American security men told B
Graham: "Before the show tomorrow, after the show tomorrow . . . we'
gonna *do* those guys." Bill said he wouldn't try to stop them unless l
could come up with a better way. He dubbed the Zeppelin men "viciou
fucking wild animals" and said, "I'll fly 25 guys of your choice to Ne
Orleans, the next stop on their tour, and you can do them there."

The Wrong Goodbye

When Zeppelin's lawyer approached Bill Graham the day after Matzorkis was taken to hospital the latter referred to 'that minor altercation'.

"What minor altercation?" yelled Graham. It was anything but minor as far as he was concerned. There then followed discussions about the waiver that would supposedly indemnify the band against all lawsuits. While Graham appeared to agree to the plan he held meetings with his lawyer and also got the band's limo drivers to keep a watch and report on their activities, to make sure they didn't skip town. He promised his security men that although he'd sign the waiver, he would ensure that they would seek retribution. "We're going for jail. We're going for financial retribution for the guys who got hurt. If we do it the other way, we'd be taking the law into our own hands."

That afternoon the band made their way to Oakland-Alameda County Coliseum under heavy escort, arriving an hour and twenty minutes late. Graham considered they were 'behind enemy lines'. No one spoke. No one greeted them. No one smiled at them. After the show was over the band got into their cars and headed out of the stadium surrounded by their entourage. Bill Graham stared at Peter Grant through the window of his limousine and said nothing. It seemed to him that Grant was saying, "See who I am? I can do anything I want." Graham, however, knew that within 24 hours he would be arrested. It seemed the band were going to stay on in San Francisco on the Sunday night. The limo drivers were instructed to tell the promoter of their every move. The next morning Bill went to the Hilton Hotel where they were staying and found the place full of off duty cops from Dallas acting as Zeppelin's security men. The hotel was swarming with guards, police and detectives all searching for the culprits. It could have been another ugly scene but the men the police wanted to arrest finally gave themselves up. As Bill Graham watched he concluded it was, "A pretty sight. I watched those guys walk through with their hands cuffed behind their backs. That was worth everything. I saw them with their heads bowed down and their tails between their legs.

"As far as I was concerned every one of those guys in the band was accountable for that shit, because they allowed it to go on. And we weren't the only ones it happened to. We were just the *last* ones." Bill had heard all about the hotel rooms and restaurants they had trashed and the waiters and people in restaurants they had abused. Although the fans remained loyal, the music business was glad to see the back of them.

Grant, Bindon, Bonham and Cole got bail and went back to England

203

and then a suit was filed for two million dollars. Zeppelin offered to settl
and then the day before a criminal trial was due to start they pleaded *no
contendere* and reached a settlement with the judge. The civil case went o
for a year and a half and was eventually settled out of court. Bill Graha
was disappointed. He wanted to see them all go to jail. He said later: '
didn't like those people. I didn't like their influence on society or the
power. Back then Zeppelin were kings of the world. They fucked wit
promoters by cutting costs and cutting corners. When I think back to th
whole incident, I think about that dealer sitting in that hotel room in
cowboy hat, waiting for his twenty-five grand. They surrounded them
selves with physical might and they were ready to kill at the slighte
provocation. If it hadn't been that way before, they took on that demean
our because of the power they represented."

In the aftermath the band were clearly embarrassed and upset by th
whole affair. As Robert Plant said of events at Oakland, "It was an absolu
shambles. It was so sad that I would be expected to go on and sin
'Stairway To Heaven'. People now know how I feel about that song. I ha
to sing it in the shadow of the fact that the artillery that we carried with u
was prowling around backstage with a hell of an attitude. It was a comin
together of these two dark forces which had nothing to do with the song
that Page and I were trying to churn out."

Years later when Peter Grant read Bill Graham's frank account an
judgement on him for that dark day in California, he burst into tears an
wept.

11

THE LAST HURRAH

"I don't want to be thought of as a bad person."
– Peter Grant

Peter Grant and Led Zeppelin returned home to England in a state of shock. Their last hours in America were nothing short of a humiliating disgrace, which left even their most ardent supporters in the music business stunned and disappointed. The Oakland incident became the talk of the industry. Bill Graham was held in enormous respect throughout that industry, and he enjoyed good relationships with booking agents and concert promoters everywhere. Sympathy for Graham and his staff was mixed with anger, the prevailing attitude among most Americans within the rock fraternity being that Zeppelin and Grant "had it coming". Sooner or later, they felt, something like this was bound to happen, given their increasingly aggressive behaviour. However, the fans were angry with Graham for causing John Bonham in particular to be arrested and for refusing to rebook the group. Hate mail deluged the promoter as a result, although few of those expressing their outrage knew what really happened backstage at the Alameda County Stadium.

Generally there was a feeling of sorrow. So much good music had been played and yet so much goodwill had been dissipated. Said one commentator later: "It seemed quite extraordinary that after all the massive, overwhelming success Led Zeppelin achieved in America, it should all have ended in California like this – Jimmy Page sitting down for their last show, Grant and Bonham led off in handcuffs, John Paul Jones doing a runner and poor Robert's son dying. No scriptwriter could have come up with a more dramatic, tortuous final scene. The later events – Knebworth, the band's last European tour and even John Bonham's death, seemed like a postscript. The sad thing about this whole ugly episode was that the people

involved were probably so out of it on heaven knows what, that the
didn't really know what they were doing and couldn't remember muc
about it afterwards – not that that in any way excuses them for their trul
dreadful behaviour. One cannot help but muse on the fact that of the fou
people arrested, Richard Cole is the only one left alive and he – of a
people – is now a teetotal, born-again Christian."

"Maybe the power that we had went to our heads along with the drug
and the alcohol," admits Cole. "Do I regret what we did? I don't believ
in all that shit. You either did it or you didn't. You have to pay the conse
quences and that's it. I've been sober for 15 years and the only time I'v
been arrested since is for a speeding ticket! I haven't been in a fight fo
15 years either."

Cole admits there were outbreaks of violence around the all-powerfu
supergroup right from the start of their tumultuous years together. "O
yes, there were fights on the road. Because of my background I could se
things coming a lot quicker than most people. The band never reall
understood when there was trouble brewing. All of a sudden they'd se
my fist go out and someone drop to the ground. They didn't realise the
were sitting with some guy's girlfriend and I could see by his eyes that he
coming over to do something. Before he got there, he'd be put away
Often the band wouldn't even know they were nicking someone's girl
friend. The girl would come over and the boyfriend would get pissed off.
was very good at divining their intentions and stopping them before an
trouble started. It was the way I was brought up.

"There was a guy who pulled a knife on John Bonham once in a men'
room. I happened to be there at the same time and I saw that he'd got th
knife half out of the sheath. I smashed his head against the porcelain. Spl
his head open. The band wouldn't see all that because most of the tim
they were oblivious to trouble. I was watching them all the time. Some
body once said I had the fastest reactions they'd ever seen. If somebody go
within 18 inches of my head, I'd most likely head-butt them or if the
were three feet away I'd give 'em a karate kick under the chin. You'd hav
to stand well away to avoid those lethal blows."

Whatever charges the righteous might level at Richard, he cannot b
accused of being pompous or hypocritical. His first priority was always t
protect Peter Grant and the band, and he remained doggedly loyal to h
employers whatever the circumstances.

However, when Bill Graham's posthumous account of the Oaklan ncident was first published, Peter Grant rang his friend Ed Bicknell, the manager of Dire Straits, at his office in some distress.

Bicknell: "He was in tears on the telephone. He was really crying. I thought something tragic had happened. He said, 'It's terrible, this book has come out and it tells the full story.' He gave me the details and I said to Peter, 'This sounds pretty bad, is it true?' And he said, 'Yes, it is, but I don't want to be thought of as a bad person.' Towards the end of his life he had his regrets. If one says he wanted to 'make things right' that sounds too simplistic. But he really didn't want to be thought of in that way, and he was very upset. The only thing I could offer was the thought that it was tomorrow's fish'n'chip paper' and that's where we left the matter. But Oakland was a source of great regret."

A grim fate awaited most of those involved in the backstage beating. In November 1979 the former actor and security man John Bindon was in the news again when he walked free from the Old Bailey, acquitted of murdering a man during a frenzied knife fight and brawl at the Ranelagh Yacht Club, in Fulham, London, the previous year.

It was alleged he had gone to the club to carry out a contract killing, a claim that he always denied. He said that he had gone to the club for a drink armed with a hunting knife, because he was told an 18-stone man he referred to only as Mr X might be there and that he would need to protect himself. He said that Mr X had told him 'his days were numbered'. Friends of Bindon, however, assert that he was 'absolutely fearless' and would never have been afraid of anyone'.

At the club Bindon became involved in a fight with one John Darke, a known police informer. The latter was left dying with nine stab wounds while Bindon had his face slashed and throat cut. He managed to crawl away and was taken to a friend's house, where he was bandaged and patched up before being taken to Heathrow and put on a plane to Dublin. Despite bleeding from his wounds he managed to get through passport control and onto a flight to Ireland. Once in Dublin he hid for three days before being treated at St Vincent's Hospital, where a priest gave him the last rites. He later gave himself up to the police and in court denied that he had gone to the club specifically to kill Darke.

In 1993 John Bindon died from cancer at the Chelsea and Westminster Hospital. He was 48. Asked about his death, Peter Grant replied: "I didn't know anything about it until the *Evening Standard* rang me for some quotes. I was very surprised, but I hadn't seen him in years."

Bill Graham, who had instigated the arrest of the Zep men, died in helicopter crash on October 25, 1991. The promoter was on his wa home after a concert by Huey Lewis & The News when the helicopte in which he was a passenger collided with an electrical tower just afte take-off.

Like his adversaries Peter Grant and John Bindon, Bill Graham had le an extraordinary life. Born in Germany in 1931, his real name wa Wolfgang Grajonca and he had fled the Nazi persecution of Jews b walking to France at the age of seven. He was smuggled out to Lisbon, an placed on board the *Serpa Pinto*, a refugee ship bound for America. H arrived in New York in September, 1941, and was adopted by an Ameri can family, who gave him the name William Graham. His first job wa waiting tables but when he arrived in San Francisco in 1966 he becam involved in the burgeoning music scene and began managing bands an promoting concerts. Although he closed his famous Fillmore venues i 1971, he continued working as a promoter, working with Bob Dylan an The Rolling Stones. He also helped organise the American Live Ai concert in 1985. After his death a memorial concert was held in Golde Gate Park, San Francisco attended by 500,000 and featuring Santana Jackson Browne, CSN&Y and the Grateful Dead.

In the aftermath of Oakland, nothing more was heard from Led Zeppe lin for many months. It was assumed in most quarters that this was the en and they had broken up. Then, in October 1977, probably at Peter Grant' urging, Jimmy Page issued a statement, explaining that Robert Plan needed time to be alone with his family. He insisted there was no questio of the band splitting up.

In February 1978 the case against Grant, Bonham, Cole and Bindon wa heard in California. All four men pleaded *nolo contendere* through thei representatives. This meant they would be liable to conviction in th criminal case without having to appear but would still be able to den charges brought in any civil action by Bill Graham's men. They wer given suspended prison sentences and fines ranging from $500 to $750. I meant they could not now be presented with the civil lawsuits and Bil Graham could not get them to court.

Said Graham later: "I can't believe that anyone can go into a trailer an kick the shit out of someone and then the judge says, 'Tut, tut, just b good boys from now on.' The real issue in the long run is that the onl thing it cost them is something they have plenty of. So they'll never learn

They should have had to appear publicly to be charged, just like other mortals." Graham complained that they hadn't been made to face up to charges in a court of law which might have made them "think twice about beating people up." He added, "They didn't have to give up anything that mattered to them. At worst, in the next couple of years, they'll just be careful that they're not seen."

Graham wasn't to know it but Led Zeppelin was never to be seen as a band in America again, and it wasn't until May 1978 that they even began working again, rehearsing at Clearwell Castle in the Forest of Dean, near Wales. It was the first time they had played together for ten months and it was mainly a symbolic gesture, designed to draw the team together again. There is a curious, perhaps apocryphal, tale that explains how Robert Plant came to rejoin the band. During the intervening period Jimmy Page and his friend Roy Harper had worked on music together. The singer/songwriter lived on a farm and had acquired some pedigree sheep. Roy gave an interview to a farming magazine about the sheep, and when the interviewer turned to Harper's musical career Harper hinted that perhaps he might become the singer in Led Zeppelin – or at least in a group with Page – since Robert Plant was apparently no longer interested in the band and Page wanted to work again. Plant, who also lived on a farm, subscribed to the same farming magazine and read the interview. Horrified that Harper might be taking his place, he contacted Page for the first time in many months. Their friendship was renewed and Zeppelin effectively reformed.

Peter Grant, meanwhile, had retreated to his palatial home in East Sussex to lick his wounds and contemplate the disturbing events of the previous year. He was under pressure from all sides. He had the burden of trying to run Swan Song and he had to deal with the public relations disaster in America. He also had to face the likelihood that his chief source of income was about to be cut off. Added to that was a custody battle for his children and the worsening state of his health. It was perhaps not surprising that in the midst of all this he suffered a mild heart attack. He was ordered to lose 151 pounds in weight and was told not to drink spirits or take sugar, which would in any case exacerbate his diabetes.

Peter: "It was in early 1978 that I had a heart scare and that really did worry me, but after a period of recuperation, it got better. It was all down to pressure. My divorce really did knock me for six." Grant had plenty on his mind. He was aware that his failure to be at Robert Plant's side during his bereavement was a source of distress to the band's sensitive and emotional singer. He explained later: "We were still in New Orleans when Robert phoned me from Scotland, just after the funeral. I couldn't get back as I was trying to sort out the cancellations of the 1977 US tour dates. In New Orleans the radio stations were playing Led Zeppelin records 24 hours of the day, which was meant to be a tribute to Robert's loss.

"When Robert phoned me I just said, 'Let me know the situation when you're ready.' He obviously needed a break. I didn't think it was the end of the group at the time. And I didn't think Robert would say he didn't want to sing 'Stairway To Heaven' again, which is what he kept saying at rehearsals. After that I knew it would take a while for him to recover after the tragedy. But I also knew he would eventually come back to the fold.

"Even so it was a long, uphill battle to get Robert to work again and go to the rehearsals at Clearwell. Robert kept saying he'd do it and then back down again. But Bonzo was a tower of strength. We had a meeting in the Royal Garden Hotel and they started talking about Bad Company and Maggie Bell and all that, with their Swan Song hats on and I said, 'What the fuck are you talking about? You should worry about your own careers.' I suggested going to Clearwell Castle because Bad Company had just been there. Robert said he'd just like to do some jamming, so that's what they did. And it was okay. I went down there and things were looking up."

Robert also began sitting in with friends and local bands and he sang with Swan Song artist Dave Edmunds during a show in Birmingham in September 1978. John Paul Jones and John Bonham took part in a 'super session' organised by Paul McCartney at Abbey Studios. They played on two tracks that appeared on the Wings album *Back To The Egg*. It was all part of the healing process.

In November Led Zeppelin reconvened and began six weeks of serious rehearsals and writing sessions for their ninth album *In Through The Out Door*. For tax purposes it would have to be recorded outside the UK. In December they went to Stockholm to begin work on the album at the newly opened state-of-the-art Polar Studios, owned by legendary Swedish pop group Abba.

Said Grant: "Abba came to us and offered the use of the studio. It was actually a slog to do the album. We used to get the noon flight out on Monday and then return on Friday for the weekend. It was cold and dark all the time in Sweden. They were difficult conditions but Jonesy was great. He put in so much effort. But that was Led Zeppelin as four people, bonding together to lift each other up."

John Paul Jones admits that although life with Zeppelin was becoming very fraught, especially during its last tour of the States, he remained committed to their music. "We had started to play bigger places and I must admit they weren't that much fun," he says. "When we played at the Pontiac Superbowl everyone said it was like playing a soundcheck in the dark. Presumably the crowd were having a good time but we couldn't see them. Even the crush barriers were sixty feet away, so I never saw anybody. There was no vibe in the place and you begin to think, 'What are we doing this for?' As it became bigger and bigger, so it became less fun. The core of the band started to break down a bit as well. We began to see the other members of the band a bit less.

"We just operated at different times of the day. Robert and I moved in the daylight while Bonzo and Page tended to move at night. We got out of synch. When we did *In Through The Out Door* in Polar Studios, Robert and I tended to operate in the daylight and we'd turn up at the studios and sit there looking at each other, waiting for the others. The band had started to fragment, shall we say. I actually thought we should have gone back to the States to tour, but we never did."

Richard Cole well understood the reasons for the slow disintegration of the band and the escalating problems faced by their manager. He knew the situation was exacerbated by the insidious spread of drugs. "I would say we became slightly fragmented. I was always close with Bonham but I wasn't that close with Robert. What happened was Peter started dabbling in heroin. I was as well. I remember going out for dinner with Planty and Jonesy one night and they were reading me the riot act.

"I felt like saying, 'You should speak to the others, what do you keep talking to me for?' When you are a heroin addict you don't depend on one person to get your drugs for you. You need about seven different people around, y'know? It wasn't as if I was the only one who used to get the drugs for them. They had their own people as well. It was getting pretty disastrous. If they were rehearsing, one of the guys would miss three or four trains to get to the studio. He would have a car waiting at Victoria station to drive him two blocks and the car might be waiting for six hours.

"They would also have to send two Phantom Six Rolls Royces down to Peter's house because he would say he was gonna leave, but sometimes he never left the house for weeks. They had to have two drivers down there, one asleep and the other one staying awake, in case he decided to leave. The costs were rising and it all started to add up. They'd have a heli-copter sitting on the lawn for two days waiting to know if they were going to go somewhere. Peter had a fling with heroin as well, because nobody was doing anything.

"We used to have suites at The Sheraton [in Stockholm]. We'd leave on Monday morning and catch the last flight home at 5 p.m. on a Friday evening. Jimmy would take the master tapes to his home studio and do all the overdubs over the weekend before he'd fly back on Monday morning. There was a lot of argument between them because the only people who turned up at the studio on time were Jonesy and Robert. Jimmy always resented the fact that when the writing credits came out, John Paul Jones was on every credit, because he had been working all the time.

"I think Jimmy kinda thought Jonesy was trying to take over as pro-ducer, which he wasn't. He was just making use of the time until the other two turned up. The truth of the matter was we never turned up until the middle of the night until we had scored. The other two got there when they were supposed to and just messed around doing stuff."

Cole admits that heroin use within Led Zeppelin's circle went back to before the incident in San Francisco. "It kind of really started after Robert had the accident in Rhodes," he says. "Then some of the band went to Malibu colony. I wasn't with them, but I think some people were doing a bit of heroin out there. I was back at the office in London while they were being tax exiles. Then we went to Munich in November to make *Presence* and it was freezing cold there. Bonham wouldn't do his tax exile trip abroad because his wife Pat was having a child. So he said, 'Fuck the money. I'm going to stay with my wife.' John and I flew to Munich from London and the others flew in from Los Angeles. When we got there, they'd been there two days before us and it was very cold. But one of the crew was laughing and giggling. I said, 'You don't seem worried by the cold.' And he said, 'No, we've found the solution,' and he pulled out a bindle of heroin. So I said, 'That'll warm us up,' and off we went.

"It kind of escalated after that. Although on the '77 tour we weren't doing it much. In fact I don't think we did heroin at all. In my case, I flew back early with John and Robert to the funeral to make sure he was all right. Then somehow or other I started getting into it regularly. Basically there was nothing to do. Peter had a house out in Long Island, which he rented in the summer. It kinda carried on for the next three years."

In February 1979 Led Zeppelin returned to Stockholm to mix the new album. At the same time they were still winning popularity polls, were voted the World's Best Group and Jimmy Page was the World's Best Guitarist. As far as the public was concerned they could do no wrong. Despite the music media's preoccupation with 'punk rock', Led Zeppelin topped the album charts.

In May it was announced the band would play at an open-air concert in August at Knebworth, Hertfordshire. This would be their first live UK date since 1975 and their first gig anywhere since July 1977. The feeling was the band would now put the past behind them and rebuild the trust and faith of their audiences.

Most fans and doubtless their manager felt a sense of relief that Robert Plant was ready to start singing again after all the trauma of the previous years. Freddie Bannister, who had given Zeppelin the headlining slot at the Bath Festival in 1970, promoted the show. When the first date sold out, with 150,000 tickets gone in a matter of hours, a second date was added.

Grant decided the band should get ready for the big one by going back to their roots. Led Zeppelin would play a warm-up date in Copenhagen, which was the scene of the first ever Zeppelin gig back in 1968. They played two shows on July 24 and 25 at a small theatre and included two songs from the new album, 'Hot Dog' and 'In The Evening', as well as favourites from all the past albums. Eyewitnesses said that the first performance was very poor, but things improved during the second show.

The first Knebworth concert was held on August 4 with a bill that included Fairport Convention, Commander Cody, Chas 'n' Dave, Southside Johnny & The Asbury Jukes and Todd Rundgren's Utopia. Grant wanted to ensure the great comeback event was given full technical support and the American company Showco installed a 100,000-watt sound system and 600,000-watt light show. A huge video screen was also erected so that the audience could see the group in close-up. Nobody could miss the action. Zeppelin played a three-hour set and even included 'Stairway To Heaven' as one of their four encore numbers.

The second show took place a week later with much the same supporting cast, but with the addition of Keith Richard's New Barbarians, who came on late and played rather badly. Although Zeppelin played professionally and at full bore, the vast audience took some coaxing to respond after a day of listening to music. Sometimes it was possible to hear a pin drop between numbers and there was an eerie feeling of 100,000 strangers standing in a darkened field in the countryside watching an unfamiliar band dutifully going through its repertoire. Many in the audience were seeing Zeppelin for the first time and didn't quite know what to expect or how to react. What was missing was the old interaction, the communal sense of excitement and joy. There was none of the screaming pandemonium that had greeted Led Zeppelin at the Bath Festival nine years earlier. However the band's spine tingling performances of 'Stairway To Heaven', 'No Quarter' and 'Trampled Underfoot' were eventually greeted with roaring applause.

Despite some less than complimentary reviews the band had achieved its aim and lived up to expectations. It looked like Zeppelin were back in business. Peter Grant was also back in business, making sure he got the full amount due from the promoter. He pulled out all his old tricks to ensure the cash flowed in his direction. He might have had his regrets about the immediate past but there was no sign that he was going to be any less aggressive in his pursuit of the band's income. As usual, he was suspicious and took 'precautions'.

Said Peter: "We thought that doing Knebworth rather than a full tour was the right decision. Absolutely. We didn't want to start all over again, so I said, 'Fuck doing a tour. We're the biggest band in the world, so we'd better get out there and show them we still are.' I said Knebworth was the right gig and I reckoned we could do two dates. I said to Bannister, 'This is the biggest band in the world and we can do two dates.' I was absolutely confident. We did have a bit of a row with Bannister over the attendance figures. But I had the arena photographed from a helicopter the first week and sent the pictures to NASA to be analysed. There were 210,000 people in there give or take two per cent, they told us. Well, we got paid in full. There was also some battle over VAT I recall. I think we had 180,000 the second week. We had the photograph of the aerial shot hanging in the office.

"We also had a few nice photos from the festival. We took some beforehand for publicity. Jimmy moaned about his hair because Richard Cole had driven him there in his Austin Healey with the top down. His hair was all in knots when he arrived for the photo shoot. Another bollocking for Richard. Bonzo also complained that the pictures captured his love handles and so they had to be airbrushed out. The sky was too dull and we had to overlay a sky scene from a shot from Texas to give it some colour!

We went through a lot of traumas just to get one picture of the band."

When the last show was over Robert Plant said guardedly to the audience, "It's been quite good." Peter Grant wasn't entirely happy with the shows either. "It was a bit rusty although we'd been to Copenhagen to get the sound sorted out. That was always one of my strategies to warm up in Europe, usually Scandinavia. Jimmy was up for hours rehearsing with the lighting guys to give them the exact order so he would project the bow outwards to make sure the laser effects were spot on. That really was a fantastic moment to watch from the side of the stage. And backstage during the day it was great seeing all the families come in. We had a special 'ligger's enclosure' marked out. We banned the magazine *Sounds* though, which was a typical move when the press got up our nose."

Knebworth House has been in the Lytton Cobbold family for several generations, and David and Chrissie Lytton Cobbold, the present owners, encountered Peter Grant over the two weekends. "He came up to the house after the second concert," wrote Chrissie in a book about the Knebworth concerts that was published in 1986. "An enormous man with long black hair, neither of us cared much for him."

Ms Lytton Cobbold also shed some light on the difficulties encountered by promoter Freddie Bannister. "After the August 4 concert the County Council and newspapers stated that the attendance had been anything up to 200,00 people," she wrote. "The licence was for only 100,000. Freddie said 93,000 had paid for tickets to come in. Peter Grant, whose band was paid on a commission basis, thought Freddie was cheating him. For the second concert he brought his own staff to count tickets and money.

"Freddie was worried but there wasn't much he could do about it. Peter Grant's 'heavies' took over our office, turfing our staff out. David was furious and ordered them out. They eventually left, taking the money with them. Peter Grant would not believe that Freddie hadn't pocketed the proceeds from the first concert."

The sands of time were running out for Led Zeppelin. Says Richard Cole: "They did the two weekends in Knebworth and they were the last concerts I ever did for them. That's where Peter asked for aerial shots of the audience. It wouldn't have made any difference how many people were there. They had paid us a million pounds in cash before the show. We split it up and put packets of £200,000 in the trunks of each car."

That, of course, was doing things Peter's way.

Within four days of its release Atlantic received an additional 900,000 orders for *In Through The Out Door*, the new Led Zeppelin album, and by the end of September it had shipped three million copies. All nine previous albums now returned to the *Billboard* charts during October. *In Through The Out Door* stayed at number one in the US charts for seven weeks and was in the top twenty for six months. It wasn't even a classic Zeppelin album, although songs like 'In The Evening', 'South Bound Saurez', 'Fool In The Rain' and 'Carouselambra' showed the musicians were opting for new ideas and not relying on the kind of music that had brought them so much success in the past. It was certainly unlike the early blues-rock albums that had made their name. An interesting feature was the use of different sleeve designs, each showing a different version of the same scene, a man sitting in a typical American bar. There were six different sleeves, each packaged inside a brown bag, It was all part of the oblique strategies employed by Grant and Page.

Said Grant: "Jimmy came up with that great idea of using a watercolour on the inner sleeve from one of his daughter Scarlet's books. Then Atlantic went and spoiled it by telling everyone. We wanted it to be a surprise. Still, whichever sleeve it had, it still sold a bucketful which pleased us greatly of course and seemed to bolster the US record business at the time."

Before attempting a return to America, where chart returns showed the vast mass of the record buying population desperately wanted them back, Grant decided to arrange a full-scale European tour. In April 1980 the band began rehearsing at the Rainbow Theatre in Finsbury Park, north London. It was then announced Zep would play 14 dates in Germany, Holland, Belgium and Switzerland.

As John Bonham celebrated his 31st birthday, rehearsals moved from the Rainbow to Shepperton studios, now owned by The Who. It was around this time that Jimmy Page bought the actor Michael Caine's former home in Windsor for around £900,000.

The 'Over Europe '80' tour began in Dortmund, Germany on June 17, and was followed by shows in Cologne, Brussels, Rotterdam, Bremen, Vienna and Nuremberg, where the show was halted after three numbers when John Bonham collapsed, reportedly from physical exhaustion. He recovered in time for the rest of the dates, which ended in Berlin on July 7. When they played in Munich there was a surprise guest appearance by Bad Company's drummer Simon Kirke who joined Bonzo on a version of 'Whole Lotta Love'. In Frankfurt, Atlantic Records executive Phil Carson played bass on the band's version of R&B standard 'Money'.

Said Grant: "The idea to tour Europe in 1980 with a stripped down stage set came from a discussion with Jimmy. We said, 'Let's forget the big lighting rigs and go back to basics.' Meanwhile, Robert kept insisting at the time that he wouldn't go back to America. At Knebworth he even sang the wrong words to 'Stairway'. Unforgivable really. He was in a difficult frame of mind. And then there was all that speech he made on stage. 'We're never going to Texas anymore . . . but we will go to Manchester' and all that. And as he's saying that, he's eyeing me out at the side of the stage.

"So we did the European tour, and we had this big meeting down at my house that went on all night. All the others said it was down to me to get Robert to agree to go back to the States. I mean we just had to carry on really. [America] was where a sizeable amount of the market was, simple as that. So purposely I played it down with Robert, and Bonzo would tell me he'd say to him, 'How come G hasn't said anything to me about America yet?' I never said a thing. But I have an outstanding memory of coming off the Europe tour, landing in the Falcon jet in England, walking across the tarmac and Robert coming up to me and saying, 'OK, I'll do it but only for four weeks.' So I said I'd give him a call in the next few days and we were able to set up the autumn tour. We were fully operational again."

One familiar face was missing from the European tour. Richard Cole had been replaced by Phil Carlo as tour manager. It was the first time Ricardo had missed a Zeppelin tour in twelve years, since the band first played in Denver, Colorado in 1968. It seems he had been sent away to sort out his drug problems. Explained Grant: "I'd paid for the doctor's visits and all that and he just wasn't getting better. He had a massive problem so I thought the only way to shake him up was to blow him out. I told him I wouldn't want him in Europe and he said, 'You can't do it without me,' but I said, 'Well, we've got to.' He was shattered and he spoke to Jimmy, but I had made the decision. The next we heard he was in Italy with some dreadful girl. But I can't take away what he did for us in the peak years, he was always there and always reliable. He was always employed by me. We needed him for America, so I thought this would shake him up. But it didn't seem to do much good."

Grant was fairly pleased with the way the band coped with the

European tour. "By and large it went very well. We had trouble with Bonzo in Nuremberg, but a funny thing occurred there as well. When he collapsed they wrapped him up in a red blanket in the ambulance. They strapped him in with this hand bell and he says, 'How do I look?' and I said, 'Like fucking Father Christmas!' He said, 'Don't make me laugh, it bloody hurts.' But he'd eaten 27 bananas that night so it was not surprising he was ill!"

Richard Cole now admits he wasn't in a fit state to have coped with the European dates. "I was so fucked up on heroin I was sent off to Italy to clean up and I ended up getting arrested over there." Unbeknown to him, Cole had arrived in Italy on the day of the notorious Bologna railway station bombing. The police were rounding up all the suspects they could find. Richard was arrested at the Excelsior Hotel in Rome and taken in for questioning. He has some fascinating theories as to quite why a rock'n'roll tour manager should be arrested on suspicion of terrorism.

Cole: "It was some bullshit thing set up by some ex-CIA guy who worked for Peter Grant. He was so paranoid he had the strangest people around him. It was a fit-up. But what they didn't gamble on was the fact that I knew people in Italy. I was fortunate enough to be in a cell with a couple of the Godfathers, or at least sons of Godfathers from The Mafia and I did them a couple of favours. I earned their respect and had some open-ended contracts, whenever I needed them, y'know what I mean?"

The circumstances of Richard Cole's trip to Italy are still somewhat mysterious but he is convinced that his old boss wanted him out of the way. It wasn't entirely to do with a health cure. "How was I set up? Well, it was a mixture of things. I had to go to Rome to meet someone, who turned out to be fictitious. I smelled a rat. I checked the hotel register where I was supposed to meet him the day before and his name wasn't on it and he didn't have a reservation. But I was so fucked up my wits weren't about me. The next thing was I got arrested on a terrorism charge." Richard was held in a local jail then transferred to Regina Coeli Prison. He later went to Rebibia, another prison near Rome where he was held for two months without charge. His incarceration meant he had to undergo enforced withdrawal from heroin addiction.

Back in London Peter Grant was arranging for Richard to be sent $500 a month while busily arranging the band's first North American tour since 1977. It could only go ahead once he'd got Robert's grudging consent. The plan was to play 19 dates, starting in Montreal on October 17.

Queues began to form at box offices as soon as tickets went on sale. Even if John Bonham had qualms about returning to the States and Robert Plant was uneasy about singing 'Stairway To Heaven', all these feelings had to be set aside to placate the hungry Zeppelin machine. The tour was arranged under the banner 'Led Zeppelin – The 1980s Part One'.

Said Grant: "I knew we couldn't cover everywhere in four weeks because Robert's schedule was going to be 'two days on, then one day off.' But I reckoned that once Robert got over there and got into the swing, he'd be okay. So it was a 'Part One' of what I hoped would be further visits. We had a meeting at Blake's Hotel in London to get it organised and set the first dates up. It was looking good."

It seems strange that Grant was quite so determined to get the band back to America, given all they had been through and the musicians' state of health. Was it just for the money? They already had an avalanche of income from record sales and publishing royalties. How many more cars, houses, farms and antiques could they buy? While there was talk of vast amounts of cash to be had from 'live' concerts, it seemed that in reality it didn't always flow so readily to the musicians.

According to John Bonham, when they played at the Earls Court concerts in 1975, he had received hundreds rather than thousands of pounds. It seemed almost a blind, compulsive act that led Peter Grant to risk pushing his charges, no longer young men but fast approaching middle age, into yet another maelstrom of rock'n'roll schedules, where they would be surrounded by all the old temptations. Cue yet another round of flights, concerts and media scrutiny. There was also the added fear of what might lay in store from any enemies they might have made on previous trips. The adrenalin would flow and they would walk the walk. But was it worth the candle?

In September the band began more rehearsals, this time at Jimmy Page's new home in Windsor. John Bonham felt depressed and uneasy about going on tour again and expressed the view privately that his drumming was no longer up to scratch. He'd rather stay at home and let someone else play than launch into yet another gruelling marathon around the States. On the day he was due to travel from the Midlands to Windsor, September 24, he began drinking vodkas in a local pub at lunchtime and then carried on drinking at Jimmy's house until midnight. In all he consumed something like 40 measures of vodka during a 12-hour session, both before and during the rehearsals. Eventually he flaked out and was put to bed by Jimmy's personal assistant, Rick Hobbs. He never woke again.

John Bonham died in his sleep and was found by John Paul Jones and tour manager Benje LeFevre the following morning. They had waited a few hours before going into the bedroom to see how he was. Like Jimi Hendrix before him, the drummer had choked on his own vomit while he slept. LeFevre immediately phoned Peter Grant at home in Sussex to tell him the news.

Says John Paul: "I think he had been drinking because there were some problems in his personal life. But he died because of an accident. He was lying down the wrong way, which could have happened to anybody who drank a lot. Benje LeFevre and I found him. We tried to wake him up . . . it was terrible. Then I had to break the news to Jimmy and Robert. We had all been in such a good mood beforehand. It made me feel very angry – at the waste of him."

The police were called but there were no suspicious circumstances and a post mortem was arranged. Tributes poured in from all over the world, many from drummers who idolised Bonham. Grant's cherished plan for an American tour was immediately abandoned and all the dates cancelled. An inquest was held on October 8 and a verdict of accidental death was returned.

The funeral took place at Rushock parish church near Bonham's farm in Worcestershire on October 10, attended by family, friends and fellow musicians. For a few days the music world held its breath, wondering whether the band would decide to carry on with another drummer, as The Who had done when they lost Keith Moon. Many top players put their names forward, some even telephoning Peter Grant to offer their services. All were politely refused. On November 7 the three remaining band members went to Jersey in the Channel Islands to discuss their future. On their return they held a meeting with Grant. Said Peter: "After John died the other three went off to Jersey to think things over. When they returned I hired a suite at the Savoy Hotel in London, making sure no one found out about the meeting. They told me that without Bonzo there was no desire on their part to carry on. It could never be the same again. I was relieved. That was exactly the way I felt."

After the meeting an anonymous statement was released on behalf of the band on December 4, 1980. It read: 'The loss of our dear friend and the deep sense of harmony felt by ourselves and our manager, have led us to decide that we could not continue as we were." In other words, the party was over. It was the end of the most powerful rock band of all time. This was Led Zeppelin's ultimate swan song.

Said John Paul Jones: "When Bonzo died, we had been rehearsing for the American tour with a lot of optimism. The band was in good form but then it just had to stop. The music needed those four particular people to make it work. We could have had another band with another drummer, but it wouldn't have been Zeppelin. That died with John."

Jimmy Page was so distraught he contemplated never playing the guitar again, especially when he found that his Gibson Les Paul had gone missing immediately after Bonham's death. "It seemed like an omen," he said. The guitar turned up later but he said, "If I even looked at a guitar, it would remind me of a dear friend I had just lost."

Robert Plant felt strangely vulnerable as Zeppelin came to an end. "It was like staggering away from a great explosion, with your eardrums ringing. I found myself standing on a street corner, clutching 12 years of my life with a lump in my throat and a tear in my eye and not knowing which way to go. The dream was over and everything had gone."

Peter Grant felt much the same way. He was devastated by the death of the wild and wilful drummer whom he had looked upon as another son. "It was such a tragedy," he said. "People forget what a family man Bonzo was. And the manner in which some people tried to distort Bonzo's death was disgraceful. They said dreadful things about him. One journalist wrote that John had died after taking a concoction of cocaine and heroin known as a speedball. Rubbish! What really caused the problem was that John got very nervous in rehearsal situations and he died just as we were rehearsing for the 30-date US tour. That would have been followed by another US tour in 1981. We had also just extended our contract with Atlantic Records. John tried to overcome his nerves by drinking vodka and taking a Valium. That's what caused his death. The news about John was on the radio in Philadelphia within three hours. We didn't know how. Helen told me Mitchell Fox who worked for us had been on the radio talking about John, which angered me. It was a terrible time. We were getting calls from drummers and Atlantic Records were baying for a 'live' album. People had to realise that for Led Zeppelin to make music, it needed all four of them. And now one was gone. We had to make a statement to end all the speculation. And then came the beginning of the period of blackness."

Peter Grant slumped into depression and apathy as Led Zeppelin vanished into the history books. Meanwhile, his former assistant was languishing in jail and wondering what was happening back in England. Richard Cole had to rely on friends to bring him news of the outside world.

"A lawyer came to see me and brought me a newspaper cutting which was in Italian. He explained to me: 'One of your guys has died.' I thought it was Jimmy, but it happened to be Bonham, which was devastating, because he was the last one I would have thought. He was so strong and robust. It's still a mystery how he died. He was supposed to have died from drinking vodka. But forty shots of vodka was nothing for him. It was a tragedy, but who knows what happened that day. I couldn't go to the funeral. I was still in the high security wing, with the guy who shot the Pope."

With John Bonham dead, the band broken up and gone into mourning, Peter – divorced and smitten by a string of disasters – needed someone anyone, to turn to. Even his old friend Richard Cole was now out of the picture. Explains Cole: "Peter and I were still very close and he treated me well. I had everything I wanted and on the road we lived like kings. But the whole thing with Peter and me kind of fell apart in 1979. I was living with a girl called Cindy Russell. She then moved in with Peter. Not that I cared but I never spoke to him again for years."

Peter Grant was about to enter what he would later refer to as his 'dark period'. It would take many years for him to recover sufficiently and emerge from his seclusion to face a changing world. By then Peter Grant was also a changed man.

12

WE'LL MEET AGAIN

"People climbed onto their tables and shouted and cheered. Elliot Rashman who managed Simply Red was shouting out, 'Congratulations Peter, none of us could have done it without you!' "

– Alan Callan

After the death of John Bonham and the demise of Led Zeppelin, Peter Grant went into hiding, disappearing from the world into a hermit like existence. Aside from his cherished son and daughter, he had lost everything that was important to him. The great enterprise that had been his life's work and struggle was lost forever in a sea of drugs and violence. He locked himself away in Horselunges Manor, his home since 1971, pulled up the drawbridge and became a recluse.

There was still some work to do and certain matters that required his attention. He was the executor of John Bonham's estate, and as well as sorting out Bonham's financial affairs he helped the family get over their loss. There was outstanding business with Swan Song and there was also the problem of what to do with Jimmy Page, Robert Plant and John Paul Jones. In the event, it seemed that after the Savoy Hotel meeting they all simply drifted apart. Robert Plant in particular made it clear that if he were to launch a solo career, he would seek new management. Jimmy Page, traumatised by recent events and wracked by ill health, didn't even want to play guitar again, let alone think about forming a new band. John Paul retreated to the countryside and concentrated on writing film music, although this wasn't necessarily by choice.

Said Jones: "When the band split I didn't see Peter very often. He was pretty much incommunicado. No one saw him, so I had to write to him and say, 'It's been great – perhaps we can work together again in the future.' In the meantime I had to have some sort of career, which I didn't.

So I took the opportunity to rest for a bit. After all, I had been working solidly since I was 16. I was due a rest. But then it was very hard to find anything to do after Led Zeppelin. I could have joined another band, but I didn't want to do that. People were saying, 'Let's form a new Asia, another supergroup.' I just didn't want to do that and so I wrote film music for a while and started producing."

In the midst of this rock'n'roll mid-life crisis, Mickie Most could see that Grant and his former Zep men were doomed to drift apart. "It was almost like a marriage in a strange kind of way. I think they fell out when Peter did his disappearing act and no one could get hold of him.

"He was once so available for the boys and then all of a sudden he wasn't taking any of their phone calls. Peter, being the manager, had four guys who wanted his attention 24 hours a day. If they had a problem at five o'clock in the morning, they'd phone Peter. They wouldn't say, 'No, don't wake him up. I'll talk to him tomorrow.' They would phone because they think, 'You are getting your percentage. You've gotta be there for *me*.' They can be very selfish. He was like a father figure to them."

Most and Grant retained their mutual respect and Mickie tried to keep in touch with his old pal, but it was an increasingly difficult task, made worse by Grant's increasing dependence on drugs. "Right back to the early days when he first started Led Zeppelin, I think even then he was being introduced to some bad habits," says Most. "People with bad habits sometimes turn into people that they're not. They never turn into nicer people. So it brought out a person who was – let's say – not the real Peter. It's like alcohol. People drink too much and they become nasty. I think Peter got increasingly involved in illegal substances and that's not a secret. You'd phone him and he'd be in the toilet. 'But he's been in the toilet for three days!' It just meant he didn't want to speak to anybody. He became quite secretive and very elusive, more like a hermit. He had minders looking after him in his big moated place near Eastbourne."

Most was impressed by Horselunges and, before Peter sealed himself off completely, he attended parties there. "He'd throw big parties with jousting on the lawn and people would dress up in Knights Of The Round Table outfits, with jesters, drinking mead and all that. He had some fun there."

One of Peter's great delights during happier times at Horselunges was to devise exciting family day treats. As well as medieval jousting tournaments on the lawn, there would be serving wenches and roast pigs on spits. However, one such special occasion became a spectacular event, for all the wrong reasons.

Phil Carson and Ahmet Ertegun were invited down to Peter's house on the occasion of Warren's 16th birthday. Carson had brought a birthday present with him and Ahmet brought a crossbow for Warren at a sports shop on the way down. They drove to Peter's and found him reclining on his sofa bed. He was feeling unwell, but got up to see Phil and Ahmet and was grateful they had brought presents for Warren.

"Very nice, but you won't spoil his big surprise, will you?" said Peter. "I've got a motorbike for him . . . it's a Harley Davidson. A helicopter is going to fly over the garden and lower the Harley on a length of rope, right? It's going to be a wonderful surprise." Warren came home and his dad took him out into the garden. "What a lovely day, let's go for a stroll in the garden. Oh look, a helicopter, I wonder what that's doing here?"

The helicopter hovered over the garden and the motorbike was lowered on a wire hawser. It got to about 200 feet when the hawser snapped and the bike came down and smashed to pieces. Says one eye-witness: "It was at this point that the helicopter pilot made his big mistake. He landed. He was met by an enraged water buffalo, in the shape of Peter Grant.

"He came stampeding towards this terrified helicopter pilot yelling, 'I'm going to fucking kill you!' The pilot tried to take off, but not before Peter got one leg on the landing skid and tipped the helicopter to one side. The rotor blades then sliced through and demolished about ten yards of garden fence. It was a pretty good birthday surprise!"

Such incidents were few and far between as Peter slid into his 'black period'. Mickie Most: "When he was in his low period and had separated from his wife Gloria, everything went pear shaped and he went into a deep depression. I used to drive down there on my motorbike quite regularly and try to cheer him up. I'd sit there for hours with him, but the divorce really upset him and he couldn't come to terms with it."

Mickie tried to provide the fun and companionship they had enjoyed when they were both fighting to make their way in the music business. "We had a funny kind of understanding. We both knew where we came from and we knew that we'd got where we were, more by luck than judgement. We didn't take ourselves too seriously. It was like,

'Remember when we used to do the wrestling and you lent me a fiver when I was skint?' It was all that kind of stuff. We had that kind of relationship . . . when I was the hottest record producer in the world and he managed the biggest band in the world. You have to keep your feet on the ground and Peter always did, until unfortunately it all got too much.

"Once he started to get into drugs, life became not such a pleasant trip for him. We were very close, but I never got involved in any illegal substances. I never took any drugs and it never interested me. But a lot of the people I was very close to did and all of a sudden, I wasn't close to them anymore. They think on different levels. Unless you are doing what they are doing, you're not happening and you get frozen out. I had so many close friends I used to hang out with and when they get into that kind of stuff you feel like a spare prick at a wedding. They don't want you around because you are too straight."

Most believes that Led Zeppelin were struggling to hold things together even before John Bonham died. "They had done everything there was to be done. You can't do any more than fill the biggest stadiums in the world and sell millions of records. Somebody said to me recently, 'Why don't you go into the studio and produce another number one record?' I don't want to sound unappreciative, but another gold record wouldn't make any difference to my life. The first one makes a helluva difference. After 238 gold records, who's counting? Who cares? And of course it takes far too long to make records these days. We used to make them in a morning. By ten to one, a hit would be made and you could make an album in a day. Now they take months . . . and when they are banging away on their computers, it gets really boring."

After a period of respectful silence, rumours began to circulate that some former Zeppelin men might form a band called Cinema with ex-members of Yes, another Seventies supergroup in the midst of an upheaval. Nothing came of these plans and it became clear that Robert and Jimmy would pursue separate solo careers, without the involvement of their former guru.

The big man was suddenly redundant. Grant frequently said he was 'disappointed and hurt' that Robert Plant didn't want him for a manager and regretted that Jimmy wouldn't get in touch or even speak to him after the break-up.

Malcolm McLaren, manager of The Sex Pistols, who at one time had plans to make a film of Grant's life, wrote later about what he saw as

Peter's modus operandi: "Grant needed the camaraderie of hard, dangerous men who gave him a sense of power. The harder they were, the
tougher he felt, and only then was his desire for control satisfied. It all fell
apart when Grant aped the lifestyle of Jimmy Page, who then ostracised his
biggest fan."

Once he'd gone into hibernation, it was difficult to get Peter to pick up
the phone. Alan Callan insists that Page did stay in touch and often phoned
his old mentor. When Jimmy started work again, providing the music for
Michael Winner's *Death Wish II* movie and producing *Coda*, the last ever
Led Zeppelin album, G was still making his presence felt.

Coda, an album of outtakes from throughout Led Zeppelin's career
and one superb live track recorded at a soundcheck at the Royal Albert
Hall, was to be the last Zeppelin release on Swan Song. Robert Plant's
1982 solo début, *Pictures At Eleven*, was also released on the label the same
year, although his next album *The Principle Of Moments* would be on
Atlantic.

The tenth and final Zeppelin album was a poignant farewell released
with a minimum of publicity. Although it scraped into the top ten, copies
of the LP were spotted in the bargain bins at high street record stores a few
weeks later. Said Peter: "The album was the result of an agreement we
struck with Ahmet. It was both to fulfil the long-term album contract and
it was also done as a separate deal. When I made that deal with Ahmet we
owed him an album or two, but the *Coda* deal was a separate thing. We
had a meeting with the three of them and Pat Bonham (John's widow), to
sort it all out.

"Jimmy said he'd hoped we had enough material to release as an album
and Ahmet was great and paid an advance, knowing that if it was
substandard and we couldn't find enough material for a decent set, then
the advance would be refunded. It was called the 'Omega contract'. We
met in Frankfurt, Germany and verbally agreed to renew our contract
within the next year. We shook hands on that one. We did many a deal
with Ahmet on trust and the paperwork would follow many months later.
Ahmet was the only one who has ever said to me that I mourned too long
over John. Maybe he was right."

Swan Song was finally wound up in 1983. Peter now had time on his
hands to speculate on what might have been. "If Led Zeppelin had carried
on into the Eighties, I'm sure we'd have gone into the mega stadium
circuit, playing five nights at Wembley Stadium. The pace would probably

have slowed down and I'm sure there would have been solo albums."★

Even if Robert Plant and Jimmy had wanted Grant to manage them, his physical state now meant he wasn't up to the task. The gruelling years on the road had taken their toll and he admitted as much. "By 1982 I just wasn't up to it. Mentally and everything. I'd just had enough. I did negotiate Robert's five album solo deal. Shook hands with him on that."

Says Richard Cole: "Peter got Robert a record deal and Phil Carson got Jimmy a deal with Geffen Records. When a friend of mine went to see Page & Plant in Philadelphia, the pair of them were arguing. Page was saying, 'I'm not playing with him anymore.' It was all very strange."

When Jimmy wrote and recorded soundtrack material for the latest *Death Wish* movie in 1981, Peter described the process as 'another nightmare'. This complaint seemed to hinge on the pressure the director put on both parties for the material to be delivered on time. Movie deadlines were rather more immovable than schedules in the laid-back world of Swan Song. Michael Winner rang Grant and asked if Jimmy could do the job, but the guitarist was on holiday on a narrow boat sailing up the Thames. It took Peter an age to contact him. Eventually word got through and it seemed an appealing idea for Page to write and record music for a thriller.

Peter: "Now the first *Death Wish* movie ended with Charles Bronson in Chicago at the airport. So when Jimmy rang me he said, 'Yeah, let's do it,' thinking it would be set in Chicago. 'I could do a blues album. That would be really great.' We had draft contracts and all that and eventually we saw the rushes of the new film and it was a bloody street gang scenario set in New York! We stalled a bit, but eventually came up with the goods. But Michael Winner still wasn't happy. He sent someone down to my house to get the contract signed. He was wasting his fucking time doing that. I just left him outside all night. The music got done in the end – in fact Jimmy always worked better with a deadline. I saw Winner later at the National Film Festival. He told me he kept a 'Unique Letters' file and still had one I had sent him. It was the one that informed him I'd filed *his* last letter in my 'Silly Letters' file!"

★ Grant later revealed that Robert Plant had discussed making a solo album in the mid-Seventies, at the height of Led Zeppelin's career. "Robert asked if I would support him if he wanted to do a solo album. I said, 'Of course,' and then went on to ask who he imagined would play guitar. 'Umm,' he said, 'I suppose I'd have to have Jimmy.' 'What about bass?' 'Well again,' says Robert. 'It would have to be Jonesy.' 'And drums?' 'Gotta be Bonzo I guess.' 'Why do you want to do a solo album Robert?' He never mentioned it again!"

Striking out on his own, Robert Plant found a new musical partner in guitarist Robbie Blunt. They recorded *Pictures At Eleven* together followed by *The Principal Of Moments* in 1983. That same year he began a UK solo tour with a band featuring Blunt and drummer Cozy Powell. It was a good-natured expedition and Jimmy Page turned up to jam on one of the dates.

After approaching such respected figures as Genesis manager Tony Smith and Dire Straits' Ed Bicknell, Plant finally reached agreement with Bill Curbishly, who'd been managing The Who since Kit Lambert and Chris Stamp bowed out in the mid-Seventies. It was clear Robert was trying to erase the past, or at least those painful memories of 1977, but Peter Grant continued to take an interest in his former protégé.

"I remember when we got the slick of his *Pictures At Eleven* sleeve, there was a problem with the lettering. I phoned Robert and told him and we put it right, but he made me laugh because he said, 'I didn't know you got so involved in all the cover designs and stuff,' which says something about all the battles we had with sleeves in the Zep days. It was Jimmy and me who did the sweating then. It was surprising for some people that none of them wanted to work together again. I think there was an agreement that if they did get back together, any solo deal would be declared null and void, but they never really had the need.

"Actually Robert and I did have a bit of a falling out and I said the best thing would be for him to manage himself. I heard him call me a 'heavy manager' on the radio once. He was always a wag, Robert. Tony Smith got involved with him for a while. But people have got to realise Robert always wanted to be the boss of the band anyway. He finally got his own way. Bill Curbishly did an excellent job in managing Robert. And Phil Carson. Yes, dear Phil. He was probably getting his own back for when they had him on stage in Japan playing bass on 'C'mon Everybody' and they played so fast he came off with his fingers bleeding. Phil was the man from Atlantic and sometimes took too much of the limelight. Phil went blabbing a bit too much. And I must say that Robert can still be a little bitter. He made a comment, when he was on the bed with Paula Yates on the *Big Breakfast Show* about Jimmy getting a better deal than him, which was a bit naughty. He can get like that though, but that's Robert, larger than life as I found out so many times."

The solo projects by the former Led Zeppelin failed to achieve anything like the success enjoyed by the mother band. Says Mickie Most: "The

ingredient that was missing was John Paul Jones. He was very sound musically and had his feet on the ground. If you listen to the bass and drum
parts on the Zeppelin albums they really held it all together. Jimmy Page is
a great player with tremendous imagination, but everybody wants to play
along with him and it all becomes kind of rickety tickety. That's why he
needed John Paul Jones and John Bonham to lay down a seriously heavy
rhythm, cemented to the floor rhythm. They gave Jimmy the freedom
to fly."

While Led Zeppelin drifted apart Peter Grant stayed locked up at
Horselunges. He retained the custody of his children after his divorce, and
this provided some stability, but his depression got worse; nobody could
get him on the phone, which partly explained Plant's urgent need to find
new management. Among those he'd approached was Ed Bicknell, the
manager of Dire Straits, with whom he held an exploratory meeting.
Bicknell: "I said, 'Does Peter Grant know you're coming to see me?' And
he said, 'Well, I've written to him.' He had written a year earlier and
Robert still hadn't had an answer. I told him I didn't get into dialogue
with artists who were represented by other people, especially not *him*. I
didn't want to be hung out of the window."*

It was sometime later that Ed Bicknell got to know Peter Grant. "I was
living in Eastbourne and I knew that he lived at Horselunges. It was funny,
because all the local minicab drivers would say, 'Peter Grant was in Asda
the other day.' He had this Range Rover with the number plate LZ 1 and
everyone knew where he was. So later, when I met him, I'd say, 'Did you
have a good trip to the supermarket the other day,' and he'd say, 'Ere, are
you following me?' The cabbies would tell me everywhere he'd been. In
fact the minicab drivers wouldn't go to his house because they thought
there were crocodiles in the moat. There was all this rubbish, which came
from his days with Jimmy Page, about how they did black magic at the
house. Peter always used to say to me, 'It was really useful sometimes,
especially when we went into a record company office. Sometimes I'd
take Jimmy into Atlantic in New York and everybody would hide in their
offices because they thought he was going to put a spell on them. He was
very good at intimidating them.'"

* When Bicknell told Peter Grant about this exchange later, Grant replied: "I wouldn't have let
you drop Ed. You have my assurance on that."

While Robert was carving out a new career, Jimmy Page was also casting about for musicians he could work with and get back into playing. He teamed up with Roy Harper in 1984 and played some dates virtually incognito, including one at the Cambridge Folk Festival in July. It was a stepping-stone to forming his own new band The Firm, but instead of Roy Harper on lead vocals, he liaised with Paul Rodgers. It was an uneasy match, although they were blessed with a fine rhythm section, including bass guitarist Tony Franklin and veteran drummer Chris Slade. Jimmy also employed Phil Carson as his manager for the project. In November 1984 The Firm went out on the road in Europe and attempted to recreate some of the magic of Zeppelin and Free; Jimmy even revived his old showcase number 'Dazed And Confused'. In April 1985 The Firm played at Madison Square Garden in New York and a month later they were at Wembley Arena, where they were warmly received. But without Robert, Bonzo and Jonesy, the song clearly was not the same. It wasn't even the same when the first Led Zeppelin reunion was held at the American Live Aid show on July 13, 1985. Page, Plant and Jones were reunited at the vast JFK Stadium, Philadelphia, with Phil Collins and Tony Thompson depping for Bonzo on two drum kits.

The crowd roared as the 'Zep' quintet arrived on stage and blinked in the spotlights. Although the performance was a mess – the drummers couldn't work together – there was still a suggestion of the old magic, even if it was largely the result of the occasion rather than the music they performed. Those on stage hated it, however. Said Robert Plant: "It was bloody awful. I was hoarse and Pagey was out of tune. Phil Collins wasn't even at the rehearsal, which was painfully evident." After 'Live Aid' secret rehearsals were held, supposedly in a village hall in Bath, Somerset, in January 1986 with Tony Thompson on drums. It was rumoured that Robert Plant walked out of the sessions after just a few days.

Meanwhile The Firm broke up two years after a final album called *The Firm Mean Business* which came out in 1986. Another attempt at a Led Zeppelin reunion occurred at the Atlantic Records 40th anniversary party at Madison Square Garden, New York, in May 1988. They played 'Whole Lotta Love' and 'Stairway To Heaven' and were greatly assisted by having Jason Bonham on drums. Jason had been taught by his father and knew every note of all the Zeppelin classics. Even so, for many former Zeppelin fans these two ramshackle reunion gigs, screened around the world and captured on video, were a source of embarrassment.

Says John Paul Jones: "I did the Atlantic Records anniversary reunion, although Robert insisted he had his own bass player. Although they were touting it as a Zeppelin reunion it was only going to be Page and Plant at the time. But I thought if it was going to be a Zeppelin reunion, I ought to be there. But it could never be Zeppelin because Bonzo wasn't there. I don't know what Peter thought of it because I never saw him much in the Eighties as I had moved down to Devon."

In fact their former manager was not best pleased. He watched these performances on TV at home groaning inwardly. If he'd had his old desk at 155 Oxford Street, he would probably have kicked it to pieces. Certainly, if he had been in charge, he would have been kicking ass and making sure the musicians were up to scratch. He would certainly have bawled them out for forgetting the arrangements. Or at least he would have bawled out whoever advised them to make these inappropriate appearances. After all, he had prevented them from playing Woodstock in 1969 on the grounds that it wouldn't have done them any favours. As it turned out the much-vaunted Woodstock was a shambolic mess of a festival, though it did help make a few reputations. If Grant had been in charge of the Live Aid appearance it is doubtful he would have allowed them to play unrehearsed with two unsuitable drummers. But as Live Aid in America was run by his old foe Bill Graham, it was probably just as well he didn't show up.

"It was fairly dreadful really, because they were obviously unrehearsed," he said afterwards. "But it was nowhere near as bad as the Atlantic Records 40th Birthday show!"

Richard Cole was also among those watching these turbulent events from afar. "When they did those reunion gigs in the Eighties, I thought the same as everyone else who ever worked for Led Zeppelin, that it was atrocious. We remembered a great band, as did anyone who was a part of the real Led Zeppelin. It was like, 'What the *fuck* are you doing?' Those four musicians were like the four pieces of a jigsaw puzzle. Two pieces don't work. You've only got half the picture. Even three pieces don't give you the whole picture!"

To make matters worse, Peter Grant was dismayed at not being asked to attend the Madison Square show. "Actually, I was really upset that I didn't get an official invitation for that show," he said. "I may not have gone but that wasn't the point. Phil Carson thought I wasn't healthy enough. I am sure Ahmet expected me to be there, not realising what happened. I did feel a bit left out to say the least. Then there was this thing about Robert not wanting to sing 'Stairway' again. At least Jason got his wish to play with them all. In the mid-Eighties both Jimmy and Robert played Zep songs. Let's face it, people wanted to hear them. I remember being there when Jimmy did a solo version of 'Stairway To Heaven' at the ARMS show at the Royal Albert Hall. Amazing. Freaked out [drummer] Simon Phillips a bit though!"

The September 1983 ARMS charity event was in aid of former Faces bass player Ronnie Lane, who was suffering from multiple sclerosis. It marked Page's first major public appearance since Knebworth and saw him playing with old mates Eric Clapton and Jeff Beck. Jimmy played 'Stairway' as an instrumental, backed by session drummer Phillips. The ARMS show became a tour of America and it was clear that there was still a huge yearning among fans to see Page again.

Said Jimmy: "The ARMS shows did me the world of good. It gave me so much confidence. I realised people did want to see me play again. After Led Zeppelin I felt really insecure. I was terrified. On the ARMS tour I realised the fans wanted me back. Led Zeppelin was magic for me. It was a privilege to play in that band."

Even if the world thought Grant was a spent force and not worth inviting to a Zeppelin reunion, he kept a keen eye on developments. He was never a man to be underestimated, even at his lowest ebb and he never missed a trick. But as his health got worse he knew that eventually he would have to do something about his drug and weight problems or go under. In the event he would eventually make the transition – unaided – after a typically superhuman effort. The old Peter Grant re-emerged to take charge. This time, he took control of himself and not some feckless musician.

The pop world had marched on since Led Zeppelin had fallen out of favour. They were reviled and dismissed at the end of their reign in what was perceived as a cleansing of the Augean stables – a Herculean task indeed. But a new generation of musicians spoke highly of them and were so clearly influenced by their work that a timely reappraisal resulted in the band and its music being recognised again by the critics. There was a spate of 'Zeppelin clones'; bands that took imitation to almost insulting lengths, like late Eighties rock act Kingdom Come.★

Grant: "Kingdom Come? The worst load of crap I ever heard. Not that I heard that much. It was hard for the ears to take."

233

The original John Bonham rhythm tracks were sampled and recycled and their riffs were plundered. Audiences were desperate for Zeppelin at any price and in whatever guise. While Plant held out against a permanent reunion, it was obvious just how great a contribution Zeppelin had made to rock music. It was also becoming clear how important their manager had been in helping to create the band and in restructuring the modern industry. Just as musicians were in awe of Zeppelin, so fellow managers and record company men began to look up to Peter Grant as their mentor and a true pioneering spirit.

The sins of the past were gradually forgiven, and as the Eighties gave way to the Nineties it became a time for reverence and paying tribute. Grant, normally so suspicious and hostile towards anyone that came bearing gifts and flattery, was charmed and delighted. For the first time in his life he began to feel humble. Without actually changing his values or his beliefs, he simply let go of the angst and the aggression and became a much happier man for it. With grandchildren to dote on and the challenge of improving his health apparently succeeding, he no longer had to fight the battles of his youth. Even so, there remained a twinkle in his eye and even the mere mention of his name was enough to cause panic and induce a chill of fear. "Hello, this is Peter Grant here," was a phone call that still made people sit up and take notice. As he began to make a slow return to public life after years of isolation, he was helped in part by the renewed friendship of an old acquaintance.

In the years since Ed Bicknell had first come to him as a young student booker in the late Sixties, the former drummer had become the manager of one of the most successful bands of the Eighties. Dire Strait's album sales matched those of Zeppelin, except that *Brothers In Arms* was on Compact Disc, while Zeppelin's output was from the age of 12-inch vinyl and was still waiting to be transferred to the 'new' format. Bicknell inhabited the new world of computers, hi-tech accountancy, business plans, lawyers and VAT receipts. Grant was the man with his foot in the door and a bag stuffed with cash. Yet both had a great sense of humour and got on like box office on fire. Grant was fascinated by the way the music business had changed in his absence and the methods the 'new boys' employed. Bicknell, who had a university degree and had become an expert on law, was in awe of a man who had started in the music business with nothing but his wits and strength of personality.

Bicknell sensed the latent fear and the hostility that remained in some

uarters of the music industry towards the man who had so dominated the
revious decade. He was still perceived as a violent bully by many who
ad never even met him. "There were a lot of myths about Peter Grant,"
ays Bicknell. "Yet the person I knew never bore any resemblance to the
erson I had read about. People would say to me, 'How can you become a
iend of *Peter Grant?*' But I just thought he was a fantastic bloke. I would
ay that by the time I met him, because of all his past problems, he had
ndergone a great change in personality. You have to put Peter in the
ontext of the times when he was operating.

"In his day artists were ripped off all the time and he was simply
etermined to do his best for them, using the methods he understood.
Nowadays the music business is very 'legit' but it is also very boring!"

Simon Napier-Bell, who last worked with Grant in the Sixties, was not
ntirely surprised to see his fall from grace and understood only too well
what had happened to the starry-eyed wannabes who had become
world-weary rock music veterans. "Peter was always getting into trouble,
articularly in the States. I guess it was due to a combination of the
osition he was in, the power he had, the money and the drugs. It all goes
o your head, whoever you are. But I never saw him in that light, because
never bumped into him in that situation. I always found him very funny.
did a TV chat show with him on British Satellite Broadcasting when it
vas first launched, with Ed Bicknell. Ed is one big ball of humour and he
nd Peter were the greatest friends in the world. We did a great show with
ne, Ed and Peter. Suggs of Madness fame was the interviewer. Peter made
s laugh the whole time. Towards the end of his life, when he had lost
veight and given up drugs, he had become very benign and had either
ompletely forgotten all the nasty things he'd done, or he hadn't really
one them at all!"

When Bicknell met the man who led Zeppelin, Grant was coming out
f his bout of hibernation and didn't quite know what to expect. Bicknell
vas fascinated by the eccentric lifestyle Peter was leading down at
Horselunges. "He had two roadies there, two brothers who went shop-
ing at Marks & Spencer and brought back mountains of sandwiches and
ifles for him." Spotted by a baffled supermarket manager loading up all
is comfort food, they claimed they were buying it for a children's home,
o they wouldn't have to reveal it was actually intended for an 18-stone
ermit.

Bicknell: "When he lived alone in the house . . . to put it bluntly he

completely went to pieces. When John Bonham died, not only was it lik
the loss of a friend, it meant that part of his life had come to an end."

A mutual friend visited Peter and reported back to Ed that Grant'
house was falling down around him. Zeppelin researcher Howard Myle
also went to Horselunges in 1989 and found that Peter had virtually aban
doned the house. "He was living in a flat above the garage because th
house was in a state of disrepair. The stairs were rotten and there was an ai
of neglect. He weighed 18 stone, he was suffering from diabetes and h
was living on water tablets."

Bicknell understood the reason for the neglect, as the house, which ha
once rung with laughter and been the scene of wild parties, fell into ruir
"He had got into what he called the 'Peruvian marching powder'. He ha
developed a very debilitating and serious drug habit with cocaine. He wa
not motivated and didn't go out. He had everything brought to hir
hence the sandwiches and trifle. Why did he take cocaine? Because he wa
totally depressed. He felt responsible for John Bonham's death in the sens
that he felt he should have been there and could have saved him. Swa
Song had gone belly up because he couldn't cope with it and his empir
had gone. He once had all these bands, a publishing company and a recor
label and all of a sudden he ended up trying to run an empire, whic
wasn't what he really wanted to do.

"Peter always said to me starting Swan Song was a mistake because ther
were only 24 hours in a day. 'You've gotta have a life,' he said. 'Artists ar
very demanding.' He did not encourage the phone call in the middle c
the night but he got them just the same. After 1980 he sank into what I ar
sure a doctor would call clinical depression. Doing cocaine made hir
paranoid and it got worse and worse. After John died he got all thes
drummers ringing up saying they had been offered the gig with Le
Zeppelin, which was a load of bollocks. When he and the other thre
decided, quite rightly, to knock it on the head, almost everything he ha
lived for had gone. Although he had worked with other artists like Ba
Company and Maggie Bell, he repeatedly said that Swan Song was th
worst thing he ever did. As any manager knows, when you have succes
with one thing, it creates an illusion in your mind that you have some sor
of magic touch, which is rubbish. What you had was a bit of luck!

"Managers credit themselves with having much more impact on thing
than they really do. If you are really successful, then you are on a rolle
coaster ride and your skill is hanging on. You get paid a large amount c

money mostly for doing the job, but the rest for putting up with the grief. Being a manager is probably the worst job, because you are the bridge between the art and the commerce and you're never going to get into a situation where you are keeping both sides happy. That's impossible."

Bicknell does not share the naïve belief that the rock business was the great artistic crusade so fondly portrayed in the days when earnestly emulating the blues was likened to pursuing the Holy Grail. "It was driven totally by greed and the greediest people were the artists. Unquestionably," he says. "They may not start out that way, but as soon as they acquire that lifestyle they have to keep it going. So you get pop stars living in big mansions with trout farms thinking, 'Fucking hell, I need some money to put a roof on that extension – better see if we can get the band going again.' Look at The Rolling Stones, who have turned what they do into an enormous money-making machine. Mick Jagger once said, 'Anybody who doesn't make the most money possible out of this business is a fool.'"

Ed Bicknell first encountered Peter Grant after an appearance on a Tyne Tees TV show called *Wired* which was made by the same production team responsible for the ground breaking pop show *The Tube*, hosted by the late Paula Yates and Jools Holland. The new show planned an item on rock managers and, as well as inviting Metallica manager Peter Mensch, they wanted to interview Ed Bicknell and Peter Grant. Ed was surprised to hear they had filmed Grant at Horselunges in late 1989, as he thought he was still a recluse.

"When it came to my spot on the show I made some complimentary remarks about Peter Grant in my interview. The show went out and I thought nothing more about it. Then in May 1990 I was playing drums with Mark Knopfler in our spin-off group The Notting Hillbillies. We had put out an album that to our great surprise sold two million copies. We did a 42-date tour of the UK and one of the shows was at the Congress Theatre in Eastbourne. The back door behind the stage opened and I saw this large figure shuffle in, accompanied by a man who looked like a second-hand car dealer who in fact turned out to be a second-hand car dealer in a sheepskin coat!

"These two men came in and sat on a flight case and I turned round and realised one of them was Peter Grant. He had changed in appearance by then. He was a lot older and had lost a lot of weight. The long hair, the turquoise rings and the caftan-like apparel had gone. I went over and was introduced and he said, 'Hello young man, I've come along to thank you for the really nice things you said about me on that TV show.' I invited him into the dressing room for a cup of tea."

The concert was being promoted by a friend of Bicknell's called Paul Crockford, who managed Level 42. Crockford was also a fan of the Zeppelin. "He [Crockford] came into the dressing room and an interesting thing happened which summed up Peter Grant in a way," continued Bicknell. "He was a bit young and nervous and recognised Peter, who I introduced as 'my manager'. Paul said, 'What do you mean manager?' I said, 'Well, I'm a musician now. I've gotta have a manager, so I've got Peter Grant!' Peter immediately picked up the joke and with a twinkle in his eye he said, 'I've come to count the tickets.' The blood drained from Paul's face and he said, 'You're not serious?' Peter said, 'Oh, I do hope we're not going to have a problem.' Crockford fled from the dressing room quaking in his boots. I said to Peter, 'That was brilliant the way you picked up on that.' And he said, 'Yes, I'm going to come backstage during the interval and count the dead wood.' Dead wood was an expression we used for the stub part of the ticket. When Peter checked out promoters in his day, there wasn't any computerised ticketing. You had to count all the ticket stubs and you could sit there for hours in the dressing room at 2 a.m. counting blocks of tickets.

"We got Peter a couple of seats and he watched the gig. He came back to the dressing room later. After everybody else left there was Crockford myself and a couple of roadies. We stayed up until 3 a.m. and Peter regaled us with anecdotes for four hours and we were heaving with laughter. He and I struck up this friendship and it transpired that by this time he had sold Horselunges and had moved into an apartment in Eastbourne. I had a house eight miles away in Polegate. We used to get together all the time and go to a Chinese restaurant called Mr Hau run by a man called Elvis Hau! He [Grant] came over the house as well and my girlfriend cooked us dinner. He was on a diet by then and working very hard at reducing his weight. But he stayed for dinner, tea and supper and by midnight my girlfriend Jenny whispered in my ear, 'There's nothing left!' And he'd eaten everything in the house."

And so began a friendship in which the old master took advice from the young contender. Bicknell and Dire Straits were making a killing from the introduction of the compact disc, the new user-friendly format that took over from black vinyl. He believed that the record industry pulled off the most successful feat in its history when the CD format was devised. As he puts it, "They managed to sell to people the same stuff twice and get more money for it the second time around!"

Peter Grant knew nothing of CDs. When a Led Zeppelin boxed set was planned for release in the early Nineties, Peter rang Bicknell and confessed that he had never had to deal with compact discs before. Bicknell: "He said, 'Ere Ed, what can you tell me about packaging deductions?' This is a device record companies have for clawing back money. On a CD it is 25 per cent, which is charged back to the act. Pete told me about a deal for his Led Zeppelin boxed set and asked me what I thought of the royalty rate. He was still acting on behalf of John Bonham's estate. I said that particular royalty rate was what a baby band starting now could expect to get on its first record. He said, 'Well that's what these cunts have agreed to.' He rang Ahmet Ertegun and the rate was lifted substantially. They were taking the piss. But record companies will do that because they can."

As Bicknell got to know Grant better he saw that the ogre of the music business was in reality a family man who had old-fashioned values and believed in providing stability and home comforts for his offspring. "One of the most remarkable things about Peter was that he brought up his kids as a single parent in a completely mad environment. Peter was very proud of Warren in particular, because he had become the head green keeper at the Royal Sussex Golf Course. Peter was also devoted to his grand-children, probably because he hadn't been around so much when his own children were very small."

Grant evidently decided to put an end to his isolation around 1990 and then started coming out of his shell. Says Bicknell: "He just literally decided one day that he was gonna kick the drugs. He had a bag of cocaine, about three pounds of the stuff in weight . . . something ridiculous. He locked himself in a bedroom with flagons of orange juice. He threw the bedroom key out of the window and stayed in the room for three or four days doing cold turkey. He never took another drug after that. Instead he took homeopathic medicine on a little dropper. He decided he was going to lose weight and get his health back together. He was going to be 16 stone by the time he was 60. So he would go for a walk up and down Eastbourne front nearly every day to exercise. In the meantime, he got the drugs and flushed the lot down the toilet. One of the guys looking after him said, 'Oh Peter, if only I'd known, I could have got you a refund!' He then sold the house to a friend called Anna."

Ed and Peter were both keen collectors of art deco glass and furniture. Bicknell was greatly impressed by Grant's huge collection of Tiffany lamps and William Morris glass. "He turned up at my house one day with a cardboard box full of straw. I thought it was half a dozen eggs and I nearly dropped it on the floor because it was so heavy. I opened it up and inside was an enormous chunk of decorative glass from the Maples furniture store in London. It had once been part of a frieze around the store and it had been dismantled when the store was knocked down. He had bought some of these sections of glass. He gave it to me and said, 'This is for you because you helped me live again.' I was quite touched by that. Not long after that he gave me a collection of framed rare cigarette cards. He was very generous in that way."

Peter sold Horselunges and moved into an apartment in Eastbourne where over a period of time he became a local dignitary. Even in retirement he seemed such a figure of authority that the local bench asked if he would like to become a magistrate. In effect he was being asked to mete out justice to the local villains.

Says Ed: "He thought that was wonderful! The irony of him of all people being asked to be a magistrate. He turned it down saying, 'It wouldn't look very good on my CV, would it?' I remember we were in a Chinese restaurant one night and he was chatting to a fellow at the next table. I said, 'Who's that?' And he said, 'Oh that's the Mayor of Eastbourne. He's my mate. 'Ere they're having a talent contest on the pier. Do you want to come and judge it with me?' So there we were, the managers of Led Zeppelin and Dire Straits, judging a talent contest on the end of the pier on the seafront. As I remember the bands were bloody awful!"

Thus, in the autumn of his years, did Peter Grant become a respectable, upstanding citizen of the Borough of Eastbourne. He was recognised as he drove around the town in any of his collection of unusual automobiles. He became a well-known figure, though certain myths persisted that no one could quite understand, or get to the bottom of. "When I moved down there, the local paper ran a headline that said 'Beverley Hills Comes To Polegate'," says Ed Bicknell. "I'm reading this and I'm thinking, this can't possibly be about me. The local rumours about Peter were that apart from keeping crocodiles in the moat, he was holding black magic orgies inside the Manor house, whereas in fact he didn't do any of those things. Once the drugs had been got rid of he started to live again, although he didn't want to get back into the business. He realised that his time had gone."

Peter maintained an interest in vintage American cars which he shared with an eccentric aristocrat called Lord John Gould, who helped Peter look after them and had access to the barn where they were garaged. One of the vehicles had belonged to Al Capone, and had a compartment fitted into the front passenger door which was designed to hold a Thompson machine gun. Gould hired the cars out for wedding receptions and Pete even dressed up as a chauffeur. "They once got paid £50 each and he said to John, 'I haven't been paid cash in years. Great!'" says Bicknell. "It's funny to think Peter Grant was driving around these young couples in a car that once belonged to Al Capone. And they didn't know who he was. During his last five years, Peter really enjoyed his life."

That same year – 1989 – Grant and Page renewed their friendship and went to see Frank Sinatra perform at The Royal Albert Hall, where they still owned a private box. Peter boasted it was the only place in the building where he could smoke cigarettes "and get away with it!" Further bridge building occurred in May, 1990, when Peter attended the wedding of Jason Bonham to Jan Charteris at St Mary's Church in Stone, Kidderminster. Peter joined in the wedding photographs outside the church with Jason, John Paul Jones and Robert. Although Jimmy was absent during the picture session, he later jammed with Robert, Jones and Jason at the reception.

As Peter's condition improved he began to venture further afield. In October 1992 Ed Bicknell took him out to Barcelona to see one of a string of Dire Strait's concerts. The band was playing to crowds of 15,000 in a vast auditorium for seven consecutive nights. "We sat him on the side of the stage on a flight case. The place was heaving and the punters were going mad. We had all the lights, bombs and dry ice and he said to me afterwards, 'That was so exciting.' He hadn't been in that position on stage for years and then we jumped into a limo to make a runner back to the hotel. It was like re-living the Led Zeppelin experience for him. My band was very nice to him and we went to a great restaurant in the old part of Barcelona with Mark Knopfler."

The friendship between the two men was enhanced by a mutual respect and understanding. Ed Bicknell was going through problems with his own band at the time, largely due to 'road fever'. Peter proved to be a man he could confide in. "That was partly because he was very discreet and partly because he could completely relate to what I was talking about. Also, he wasn't directly involved in the band business anymore. After meeting my band he said, 'I didn't realise what you were going on about. Now understand.' He was very helpful to me."

The two managers knew the importance of keeping up a 'front' - appearing all-wise and all-powerful. It was a relief to be able to discuss the problems they each knew only too well. Says Ed: "He was still in touch with Jimmy and would help him out, but he'd had a falling out with Robert over business matters. A lot of people had deserted him over the years. In our game you have genuine friends who will always be there for you. There are also a lot of people who are there, because of who you are and because you control a large economic asset. When you break up with a band it's interesting to see whose Christmas hamper list you get taken off! You go straight off the record company and publisher lists. After Zeppelin split there were quite a lot of Peter's friends who bailed out. That's why he enjoyed our friendship. I didn't have a motive. I liked him, loved him actually."

Peter and Ed would often go out to a local village restaurant near Eastbourne and reminisce about the old days until the last customers had gone and the waiters were hoovering around the tables. "He'd be telling me stories about Elvis Presley and Colonel Parker until one in the morning. It was amazing. He was actually advising them on the possibility of touring Britain just a few days before Elvis died."

Not all of Peter's former colleagues had forgotten him however. Some had simply moved on and lost touch, like his former PR Bill Harry: " knew he had been incapacitated for a few years and I tried to get information about him. I was very surprised when I heard he had got into drugs. never thought Peter of all people would get into drugs or anything like that. Why would he need to? He'd got his family and his successful career. When people began telling me that he couldn't move out of his bed and that he'd been on drugs, I thought it was very sad. I couldn't believe how much weight he had lost."

Peter himself admitted as much in one of the few interviews he gave later in life. "It's true I went through a drug period, particularly with cocaine. In the Seventies it was a coffee table drug. If you went to a movie executive's in Hollywood for dinner they wouldn't offer you After Eight mints with the coffee, they'd pass around a small bowl full of white powder with a straw."

Peter was proud that he'd managed to recover from the wasted years. He rang Mickie Most and told him: 'I've lost a load of weight. You wouldn't recognise me. I lost fifteen stone, because I had a heart attack.' "

Said Mickie: "Did you really? I never heard about that."

"No," said Peter. "I kept it quiet. It was a bit of a frightener."

The last time Peter Grant phoned Mickie Most he said, "I've just passed 60."

"I never thought you'd get to 60," replied his old friend.

"Nor did I!" replied Peter.

Others made more determined attempts to track him down. Since his incarceration in an Italian prison Richard Cole's situation had gone from bad to worse. He needed help and hoped his old boss might help him out. 'I remember, just before I got sober, in Christmas 1985, I was absolutely broke. I called him up and asked him if he'd lend me £500. He said he was skint and didn't have a penny. In a strange way it was a blessing because a week later I got sober. On the one hand I was pissed off. I would have thought he'd have at least five hundred quid hidden under the bed somewhere! But no – he wouldn't lend me anything – he was broke and didn't have any money. Then a pal of mine, Peter Nash, wanted to buy his house. So I brought him down to see Peter."

As 'executive producer' of so many Zeppelin albums it seemed extraordinary that Grant would suddenly plead poverty, but it was noticeable that his name seemed to disappear from the re-issued Zeppelin albums on CD. Maybe he had spent too much of his money on 'Peruvian marching powder' or he simply didn't want to encourage his former aide.

Cole was working for Patrick Meehan, manager of Black Sabbath at the time. "A friend of mine, Peter Nash, was interested in buying Peter Grant's house and he drove me down there in his Rolls-Royce. The watch that Elvis Presley gave me was in Peter's house and somehow that had got stolen. So I thought I'd never see my things again. But Warren was fishing in the moat and he came out with this bag and it had all my collection of photographs and slides in it! It was wonderful because they were the pictures I had taken over the previous 30 years since 1964."

The gifts, souvenirs and mementos that Grant and his men had collected over the years took on greater significance as slowly it dawned that an era had ended. Alan Callan remembers the delight that Peter took in being given gifts that seemed to celebrate his life and career. "We went to see The Everly Brothers at the Albert Hall and we went backstage afterwards and Don came over to see Peter. He said: 'Peter, I'd like to present you with a gift. And he gave him a walking stick. The top part was silver in the shape of a naked woman. Peter said, 'Every time I touch it I'll know Don Everly was there before me!' "

Phil Everly also paid tribute to the man who had been The Everly Brothers' tour manager back in the Sixties. At the same party he introduced Grant to other guests and said, "This man made everything possible. Without his efforts, musicians had no careers. He was the first to make sure the artists came first and that we got paid and paid properly."

As Grant lost weight and recovered from the demons that troubled him, he began to show his face more frequently at music business functions. ELO's drummer Bev Bevan saw Peter at the *Kerrang!* heavy metal magazine awards one year. "I saw Peter and couldn't believe how tiny he had become. He used to be such a massive man. He didn't look well at all and had shrunk so much and he had lost all his bombast. I had several takes before I believed it was him. We talked about Denny Laine because he had split up with his daughter and gone to live in America."

The subject of Denny Laine was something of a sore point with Peter as the former lead singer with The Moody Blues who later worked with Paul McCartney in Wings had fathered a child by Peter's daughter Helen, but the couple had later split up. When Laine's name came up in conversation Peter Grant glowered in much the same way as he once glowered at bootleggers. Ed Bicknell: "He came over to my house down in Eastbourne one Boxing Day, with Helen, Warren and all of their kids. Helen had broken up with Denny Laine, who was the father of Lucy, who was Peter's granddaughter, who he absolutely doted on. I said to Peter: 'What's it like having Denny Laine as a sort of son-in-law?' They weren't technically married. He looked at me and said, 'Waste of food.' That was the only thing he said.

"An hour later, he must have thought about him again because he suddenly said, 'What do you think Denny Laine is doing on New Year' Eve?' "

"I haven't the faintest idea," replied Bicknell.

"He's playing a gig in Latvia, with Rick Wakeman. Heh, heh, heh!"

"It was very cold in Latvia and Peter thought that was very funny," added Bicknell.

As well as turning up at lunches, Peter was also invited to take part in panel discussions, TV shows and conferences where he always proved an able and amusing speaker. Explained the newly slimmed down and active Grant: "I wanted to use all my experience and thought I had something to offer people. I did a TV programme called *Wired* and was asked why there were so few women in management. I didn't know, but there are a lot of bright ladies in business."

Indeed, Peter formed a partnership with co-manager Anna George to nurture Thomas McLaughlin, a ten-year-old guitarist and a singer song-writer called Tina Summer from Bournemouth whose songs and lyrics he liked. "But it was hard for me to get into managing another band," he admitted. "Thomas was an amazing player for his age. Ahmet came over to see him. Trouble is, he was one of those with a difficult father. You know, 'All I want for my boy is to hear him on Radio One, being a star!' I mentioned that to Brian May and he said that was the biggest mistake anyone could make!"

Peter's most memorable public appearance was at 'In The City', a significant industry seminar attended each year by top media and music industry figures. When the convention was held in Manchester in 1992, Peter's appearance at a debate on rock managers proved one of the most eagerly awaited events.

Recalled Peter: "I'd seen 'In The City' promoted in *Music Week* and I rang Elliot Rashman, Simply Red's manager, who was organising it and I'd also spoken to Ed Bicknell and they all wanted me to come, so I did. It was supposed to be a celebrity interview with the journalist Paul Morley. Someone tipped me off that he was going to do a number on me. I sorted him well and truly. He thought I was an old fart and he came unstuck. But it was great and I met so many people, and the good thing is so many new managers keep in touch. It's nice to share that knowledge."

Bicknell recalls how Peter dominated the event. "He rang one day and said, 'Oh Ed, I've been asked to go up to Manchester for a conference. What's a conference?' I explained how the music industry had become very businesslike. He said he would go, if I came with him. So we went to Manchester but his health wasn't too good. I remember just walking down the platform was quite a stretch for him. He'd already had one heart attack and was quite frail. The night before the conference got underway, a group of us went out to dinner and came back to the Holiday Inn and we sat in the bar."

It was a summit meeting of the kind that rarely happens in the music business. Gathered around the table were Gail Colson, who managed The Pretenders, Elliot Rashman, who managed Simply Red, Ed Bicknell, who managed Dire Straits, and, presiding over them all, Peter Grant, the legendary manager of Led Zeppelin. "We started talking about getting fucked by your act, which is something rarely mentioned in the management profession," recalls Bicknell. "Elliot said he could never imagine *his* artist would ever let him down. Peter said, 'Elliot, as sure as eggs is eggs, the day will come . . .' and he described what happened when a manager and his artist breaks up. Peter came across as a very gentle and wise person and he wouldn't slag people off. He was very discreet in that way. We were all very surprised.

"At the conference the next day Paul Morley★ had to interview him. Morley made an absolute tit of himself. He came on stage with a huge bodyguard and people began heckling. In the end I took over the questions myself."

Peter enjoyed himself so much he went again the next year. Recalled Grant: "I didn't do any interviews but I sat in on an interesting forum called 'Do we need lawyers?' which was quite fun. They said to me, 'Are you retired?' and I said, 'If something really special came along I'd think about it,' and within 30 seconds somebody's mobile phone went off and Paul Russell from Sony shouts out, 'There's an offer now, Peter!' and somebody else says, 'It must be Robert Plant,' and I said, 'Oh no, not a second time!'"

Grant was also invited to the Canadian National Music Week in Toronto in 1994 where he agreed to another Celebrity Interview and a young generation of Zeppelin fans hung on his every word. It proved to be his last major public appearance.

He had become such a celebrity that plans were made to make a movie of his life story. Behind the plan was another music industry maverick, former Sex Pistols manager, Malcolm McLaren. He planned to get financial backing from America for the project to be made by Glinwood Films and to be called *Hammer Of The Gods*. ("The hammer of *what*?" Peter would snort.) It would draw from the book of the same name by Stephen Davis and tell the story of "the south London heavy who became boss of rock'n'roll's most notorious supergroup." The film would have a screenplay by Barrie Keeffe, and the executive producers were Peter Grant and Terry Glinwood. The producers were John Goldstone and Malcolm McLaren.

Such a sensationalised picture might have worked in the rock years, but

★ Former *NME* writer and PR guru to Frankie Goes To Hollywood.

the world had moved on. The concept seemed less appealing in a scene dominated by rap and dance music. However the emergence of a new genre of British gangster movies seemed to provide the key. After all, Grant's bodyguard, John Bindon, had played gangster parts in movies. Why not portray Grant in the same light? McLaren may have had the idea, planted by Grant's appearance toting a Tommy gun in *The Song Remains The Same*. But if Peter was uneasy about his fictitious role then, he certainly wasn't convinced by the idea of reviving such an image in the Nineties. He had been at pains to shed his 'bad guy' image. A film along these lines wouldn't help with his rehabilitation.

Recalled Peter: "Malcolm McLaren came to me with an idea of doing a film based on my life story. We had a long chat with Barry Keeffe, who wrote *The Long Good Friday*. But nothing really came of it. Malcolm went to America to see a couple of film companies and they went, 'Oh, rock'n'roll. Forget it.' Then he rang me up and said, 'We're gonna do it.' The plan was to spend a few months writing the script and then to make the film for release in Christmas 1991."

Mickie Most recalls that Grant became heavily involved in the writing process. "One of the last times I heard from Peter was when he phoned me and said, 'I've sold the house, I'm living in Eastbourne in a flat and I've got living with me a guy who is writing a script for *The Peter Grant Story*. He's living with me so he can get the feel of my personality, all that kind of stuff. He's dying to meet you. Can he come up and spend a couple of hours talking with you, for his script?' The guy making the film was Malcolm McLaren but I spent two hours with the scriptwriter and when I heard the film wasn't going to be made, I could see why."

There were fears that the proposed film would damage rather than enhance Peter's reputation and depict him as 'a thuggish buffoon'. Some recalled with trepidation McLaren's previous film *The Great Rock'n'Roll Swindle*. Said one of Grant's friends: "There are fears McLaren will depict Peter as a gangster rather than a defender of the Zeppelin name."

Says Ed Bicknell: "Peter didn't like the script. When Peter was asked what he wanted left out of what appeared to be 'a chronicle of excess', he replied, 'My name.'"

When Grant and Bicknell went to Canada to visit the Canadian Music Week convention in Toronto in 1994, a researcher was assigned who spent the entire time questioning Peter. Ed: "He would sit in a room and regale this bloke with anecdotes. Of course the film never went anywhere but the stories were great. He told one story about bumping into Little Richard at a show in Florida. Richard was playing at a hotel and Zeppelin was in town. Said Peter: 'Let's go and see Little Richard, he'll be great.' As soon as Little Richard saw his old tour manager come into the room he stopped the band in mid-song and began calling out, 'Mr Peter, Mr Peter!' He then told the audience an unbelievably convoluted story about how Mr Peter had once rescued him by knocking out half a dozen policemen in Italy. It was on the same tour that Peter took Little Richard from Paris to Dusseldorf by taxi, because he was terrified of flying."

During the early Nineties the continuing fascination with the Led Zeppelin saga was fuelled by the release of specially prepared box sets with original material remastered by Jimmy Page. The first was a double CD set called *Remasters*, released on October 15, 1990, in the UK and Europe. This was a condensed version of the 54-track boxed set of six LPs or four CDs called simply *Led Zeppelin*, released in worldwide on October 29. This was followed by *Led Zeppelin Boxed Set 2* in 1993, a further two CD set. The CD sets were a big success and sold over a million units, despite their high price. The *Led Zeppelin* set came out at a time when vinyl LPs were finally being phased out, and so the box, with its distinctive picture of the shadow of a Zeppelin airship flying over a crop circle, was perceived as a fitting memorial.

At the same time Led Zeppelin bootleg CDs were flooding the market, some of them produced to a quality that matched the official product. It was extraordinary to think that despite all the years Peter had spent fighting bootleggers when he was managing them, Led Zeppelin became one of the most bootlegged rock bands in the world. Incredibly, one of the finest bootlegs of all time was a huge box of 19 Zeppelin CDs produced to the highest standard in Japan. These consisted of 'live' recordings of such superb quality that both Plant and Page bought copies themselves.

With all this activity, the clamour for a Zeppelin reunion increased but Peter Grant, relaxing in Eastbourne and unlikely to be consulted anyway, remained sceptical. "It would have been a vast earner and would have outsold anyone including The Stones, but would they have been any happier? I know Jimmy was always keen on the idea but Robert didn't want to do it. Let's face it, even if they had got the band together again it wouldn't have been the same and that Zeppelin mystique would have been gone forever."

Back in 1993, while Robert Plant was still pursuing his solo career and released his *Fate Of Nations* album, Jimmy Page had somewhat perversely linked up with Whitesnake singer David Coverdale for an album and tour. Then MTV brought Plant and Page together for an *Unplugged* show called *Unledded* which they recorded in London in 1995. Behind them were an Egyptian orchestra and classical musicians and as well as new material they played many old favourites. Soon the duo was united on a more permanent basis and, under the management of Bill Curbishley, they released the album *No Quarter* in 1994 and embarked on what many had thought was impossible, a complete world tour. This was in effect the Led Zeppelin reunion many had dreamed about, except that they did not invite John Paul Jones into the band, nor did they utilise the services of Jason Bonham. It was a good compromise however, as it meant Jimmy and Robert could work together again, produce some new music and not entirely ignore their past.

The pair began their US tour in Florida in February 1995, playing such numbers as 'Kashmir' and 'No Quarter' but studiously refraining from playing Robert's *bête noire* 'Stairway To Heaven'. On October 26 and 27 they made a homecoming to Madison Square Garden, New York, scene of many a past triumph. The tour continued around the world, visiting South America and Japan before returning to Europe in the summer for shows that included an appearance at the Glastonbury Festival on June 25. As the tour progressed they cut back on the Egyptian music and began to draw on some 32 Led Zeppelin classics. They played at London's Wembley Arena on July 25 and 26. The tour was hugely profitable, some alleging they had earned more than in the days of Zeppelin.

They had also done it all without their old guardian. Peter Grant came to see them at Wembley and he was made welcome and introduced to the public from the stage. Robert Plant paid a fulsome tribute and the cheers were loud and long. Peter was later seen holding court at the mixing desk after the show, surrounded by fans and signing autographs.

Peter's son Warren says that after his first flush of excitement at returning to public life, Peter began to cut back on his schedule. "In later years he stayed in touch with Jimmy and John Paul Jones, but less so with Robert. I think that when Robert did his solo thing, he was still under contract to Peter, but he went off on his own and dad was upset about that. But they buried the hatchet in the end and he went to see both Jimmy and Robert play. He liked doing those lectures for the music business and he was asked a lot to go to conventions, but he didn't want to get on planes and fly about. He thought about going back into business, but didn't really want to. He used to say, 'I've been there and got the T-shirt. Let someone else do it.' He just didn't want any more hassles. He just wanted to relax, although he did go over to Canada. He'd sooner go to a pub in Eastbourne and judge a talent contest!"

There was more praise for Peter when he was given a special award at the first International Manager's Forum dinner at London's Hilton Hotel on September 20, 1995. He and Alan Callan were both invited to the dinner. "We sat at the table with Ed Bicknell and some other managers. Suddenly they announced they wanted Peter Grant on stage. They were going to induct him into the Roll Of Honour.

"I'll never forget this. People climbed onto their tables and shouted and cheered. Elliot Rashman who managed Simply Red was shouting out 'Congratulations Peter, none of us could have done it without you!' Then Peter stood on the stage and said: 'I've been very lucky in my life. Probably never luckier than at this moment when all of you people are honouring me. But the truth is that luck comes from the great fortune of being able to work with great talent. It is the great talent that allowed me to be successful."

Grant also paid tribute to his many friends and among those he mentioned by name was Alan Callan, the man who had helped him run Swan Song. Said Callan: "That completely blew me away. I nearly fell off the chair. I talked to Ed Bicknell and we both agree that we think of Peter nearly every other day."

After Peter was inducted onto the British Music Roll Of Honour it was announced that future IMF Management Awards would be given in his name as the 'Peter Grant Award' to recognise 'Excellence In Management'. Says Ed Bicknell: "When Peter got the Manager's Forum Award two months before he died, Brian May let the cat out of the bag. Peter was very friendly with Brian, who he knew from Queen days. I had to do the presentation and it was supposed to be a secret. Unfortunately Brian said to him before the dinner, 'It's really great they are giving you this award,' and Peter said, 'What award? I didn't know I was getting an award?' "

Peter Grant died suddenly from a heart attack on November 21, 1995 aged 60. It happened while he was travelling home in his car. His son was by his side. Robert Plant and Jimmy Page were still in the throes of their reunion tour when they heard the news. Right up to the last days of his life Peter was still dealing with problems. Streams of faxes and phone calls came into his Eastbourne flat in Upper Carlisle Road from those who still perceived him as the man in charge of other people's lives and business affairs.

In the aftermath of Peter's death there were problems with his estate. Explains Warren. "There was no will. What happened was ironic. A couple of weeks before dad died he had fallen out with somebody he had put into his will. So he went to the solicitors and said, 'Cancel that. I want to rewrite it.' And he never got around to rewriting his will, so it went to probate. So while the estate came to Helen and myself, it took a time to value the income stream from the publishing royalties from Led Zeppelin. We had it valued and then the Inland Revenue said it was worth ten times that amount. We had a lot of people working on that and it cost us a fortune. In the end they met us half way. We get a percentage of the royalties and although it won't make us millionaires, it's quite nice to have an income and that keeps us going."

Peter Grant's funeral was held on a dark, cold morning on Monday, December 4, 1995. The service was at 10.30 a.m. at St Peter and St Paul's Church in Hellingly, the East Sussex village where Peter used to live. As the mourners gathered, the narrow lane leading to the small church was packed with long black limousines and standing in the churchyard were sombre looking security men. Alongside Warren and Helen were old friends and colleagues. Alan Callan was asked to give an address and he paid a fulsome tribute to Peter. "His greatness was that he was a man of many parts. He was as adept at the ominous glance as he was at the disarming remark. He could engage you in the greatest conspiratorial friendship and you would know that through thick and thin he would fight with you all the way, unless of course he thought you might appreciate the humour of a sudden change of plan. If you were his friend he would give you his all. His own success, that which he treasured most, was his family, Warren, Helen, Caroline, Amy, Lucy and Tiffany were his greatest joys. There was no role he enjoyed more than being a devoted father and doting grandfather. Wherever Peter is going now, I hope they've got their act together."

Added Lord John Gould: "He was proud of what he'd achieved in helping to revolutionise the music business. Some thought he had a reputation for being rude. Not really! He was just totally honest. With Peter there was no front, just an honest opinion."

Organising the star-studded funeral hadn't been an easy task. "In the week prior to the funeral I was getting all these phone calls," says Alan Callan. "I was called by Jeff Beck, Paul Rodgers and Simon Kirke, Jimmy and Robert. I was trying to help Warren about making sure the people he wanted to know could attend. I wanted to make sure others who couldn't attend would know about the arrangements, like Ahmet."

Among those who specially wanted to go was Peter's old pal Mickie Most but there was some confusion about his invitation. "I didn't go to the funeral. I asked for the details and I was told that the funeral was 'only family'. I was due to go the next day to America but I would have cancelled the trip and gone to the funeral. So when they said it was only family, I thought 'fair enough' and re-booked the flights and appointments for the American trip.

"Then I got a phone call from Peter's office, saying that Warren had phoned and said, 'Of course, you must come to the funeral.' So I said: 'I can't now, I've committed myself, because you told me yesterday I couldn't come.' Then they told me there would be a memorial service, to which I would be invited. Well that never took place so I thought it was very disorganised."

As the mourners filed out, the packed church was filled not with the sound of Led Zeppelin or any of the artists he had been associated with over the years. Instead Peter had chosen a sentimental record that harked back to the Second World War and his childhood. Even in the midst of sorrow the lilting theme raised a smile amongst those in the know. Said Alan Callan: "I thought it was so funny that he chose Vera Lynn singing 'We'll Meet Again' for his funeral music. I just loved the guy for that."

A wake was held at Worth Farm, Little Horsted that entailed a long drive through the winding roads of the Sussex countryside to a small low ceilinged barn, which housed Peter's collection of vintage cars. Most of the mourners seemed deep in thought and avoided speaking to each other, as they gathered around a buffet table set up in front of the famed 'Al Capone' car. Jimmy Page, Robert Plant, Phil Carson, Paul Rodgers, Simon Kirke, Boz Burrell and Denny Laine stared bleakly into space, as if contemplating their past lives and wondering where it had all gone and what would they do next. When Jimmy abruptly left the proceedings the door slammed loudly behind him, and a gust of cold wind blew through the barn. Only Jeff Beck seemed outgoing, relaxed and friendly. He enjoyed chatting to his old Yardbirds colleagues Chris Dreja and Jim McCarty, sharing their memories of G with Jason, Debbie and Zoe Bonham and Phil May of the Pretty Things.

The obituaries were fulsome. Robin Denselow, writing in *The Guardian*, said: "Peter Grant was the most colourful and influential manager in the history of rock. He may never have become a household name like Elvis Presley's manager Colonel Parker, or The Beatles' Brian Epstein, but within the industry itself the man who guided the career of Led Zeppelin was regarded with awe and admiration."

The band members issued official statements. Said Robert Plant: "Peter Grant changed the rules. He rewrote the rulebook. He did so much for us that in 1975 he had to turn around and say, 'Look, there's nothing else I can do. We've had performing pigs and high wire acts. We've had mud sharks and all that – there's no more I can do because you really now can go to Saturn.' I owe so much of my confidence to the way he calmed and nurtured and cajoled all of us to be what we were. He was larger than life. A giant who turned the game upside down. Fierce, uncompromising with great humour."

Jimmy Page confined himself to saying: "Peter was a tower of strength as a business partner and a friend. I will miss him and my heart goes out to his family."

Peter Grant had devoted his life to rock'n'roll and to those artists who now struggled for adequate words to thank him. When friends asked, 'Why?' his answer was simple. "I did it for the adventures."

Acknowledgements

My own experiences of spending time with Peter Grant and his clients, including The Yardbirds and Led Zeppelin, have informed this text throughout. As far as Zep was concerned, I was there at the beginning, during the good times. Perhaps I was fortunate not to be around during the bad times.

The book has benefited from an extensive and largely unpublished interview with Peter that was carried out by Dave Lewis for his Led Zep fanzine *Tight But Loose*. I am grateful to Dave for allowing me access to this valuable material.

I would like to thank the following for their help and co-operation in writing this book: Keith Altham, Maggie Bell, Bev Bevan, Simon Napier-Bell, Ed Bicknell, Alan Callan, Chris Charlesworth, Peter Clifton, Richard Cole, Chris Dreja, Warren Grant, Helen Grant, Bill Harry, Steve Joule, John Paul Jones, Dave Lewis, Mickie Most, Howard Mylett and Michael Watts.

8/03 (48392)